IN THE BEST INTERESTS OF THE CHILD

IN THE BEST INTERESTS OF THE CHILD

CULTURE, IDENTITY AND TRANSRACIAL ADOPTION

Edited by IVOR GABER and JANE ALDRIDGE

Free Association Books   London

Published in 1994 by
Free Association Books Ltd
Omnibus Business Centre
39–41 North Road
London N7 9DP

98 97 96 95 94
7 6 5 4 3 2 1

ISBN 1 85343 152 4

A CIP catalogue record for this book is available
from the British Library.

Produced for Free Association Books Ltd by
Chase Production Services, Chipping Norton.
Typeset by Archetype, Stow-on-the-Wold.
Printed in the EC.

CONTENTS

ACKNOWLEDGEMENTS

The editors and the publishers are grateful to the copyright holders for permission to reproduce the following material:

British Agencies for Adoption and Fostering for an extract from 'Practice Note 13, The placement needs of black children' and for 'Practice Note 26, Children and their heritage', reproduced in full. The British Association of Social Workers for 'Practice Guide for Social Workers on the Placement of Black Children in Care', reproduced in full. The Commission for Racial Equality for an extract from 'Adopting a better policy – adopting and fostering of ethnic minority children – the race dimension'. The National Foster Care Association for 'NFCA Policy Statement: 1, Cultural and racial identity', reproduced in full. *New Community* for permission to reproduce Chapter 5, 'Black Identity and Transracial Adoption', which was originally published in *New Community*.

NOTES ON CONTRIBUTORS

Jane Aldridge is a modern languages teacher and mother of three transracially adopted children. She is a founder member of Children First and is the organisation's National Co-ordinator. She is also a lay member of a local authority adoption panel.

Elizabeth Bartholet is Professor of Law at Harvard Law School, where she teaches Family Law, Adoption and Reproduction, and Employment Discrimination. She is the author of *Family Bonds: Adoption and the Politics of Parenting*, which summarises and pulls together the three studies on which her chapter in this book is based, and many articles on adoption and reproductive technology.

Gloria Betts grew up in Ireland, where she was transracially fostered. She now lives and works in London and is training to be a psychotherapist. She is a member of the steering committee of Children First.

Phil Cohen is Senior Research Fellow and Co-Director of the Centre for Adoption and Identity Studies at the University of East London. His current research interests include the cultures of racism in East London. He is also an adoptive parent.

Jennifer Craven-Griffiths is Principal Lecturer in Law at Nottingham Trent University, where she established an MA in Children and Equal Opportunities. She is the mother of six children, two of whom were transracial placements.

Ivor Gaber holds a Professorship in Broadcast Journalism at Goldsmiths' College, London and is a producer at the BBC. He was a founder member of Children First and has three transracially adopted children.

Paul Gilroy is Reader in Sociology at Goldsmiths' College, London. He is the author of a number of books about the politics of 'race' and culture including *There Ain't No Black in the Union Jack* and, most recently, *The Black Atlantic: Modernity and Double Consciousness*.

Susan Golombok is Professor of Psychology and Director of the Clinical and Health Psychology Research Centre at City University, London. She has recently completed a study of parent–child interaction and attachment in adoptive families.

Ann Phoenix is currently working in the Department of Human Sciences at Brunel University. Her most recent works include a study of the effects of racism in the lives of young people of mixed parentage (with Barbara Tizard) and *Shifting Identities: Shifting Racisms* (with Kum-Kum Bhamani).

Barry Richards is Principal Lecturer in Psychosocial Studies at the University of East London where he is also Co-Director of the Centre for Consumer and Advertising Studies, and sits on the steering group of the Centre for Adoption and Identity Studies.

Rita J. Simon, a sociologist, is University Professor of Law and Public Affairs at The American University in Washington, DC. She has published extensively in the field of transracial adoption, notably *Adoption, Race and Identity* (with Howard Altstein).

Barbara Tizard is Emeritus Professor of Psychology at the University of London and formerly Director of the Thomas Coram Research Unit. Her research is noted for the application of psychological theory and methodology to educational and child care policy issues.

FOREWORD

Paul Gilroy

This rich and provocative book is overdue and desperately needed. It expresses a laudable desire to come to terms with the racialised politics of adoption and fostering outside the atmosphere of moralism, confusion and fear that was generated around discussions of these important questions during the 1980s. The contributors speak from a variety of different positions, histories and concerns. If they are joined at all, it is not by the dream of creating a premature consensus, but by the common hope of facilitating an open, rigorous and above all honest discussion in an area where for so long this has been simply impossible; where research will always be provisional, inconclusive and contested; and where the moving anecdotal evidence that has been cited by all sides points readily to incommensurable conclusions.

The chapters that follow are valuable because they suggest a number of important conceptual adjustments, and point towards a more fruitful mode of analysis. They are premissed on the need for innovation and freshness. For example, they signal a departure from some of the hastily imported American approaches to understanding the racial politics of these issues. If there was a time when these approaches were illuminating it is over. They have passed their sell-by dates and should be recognised as inappropriate not least because they are tied to experiences of social and cultural segregation that have no equivalents in this country. They are redundant here because they project an understanding of 'racial' and national identities and of white supremacy that makes scant sense in circumstances where the minority ethnic populations are smaller, more differentiated and dispersed than they are in the USA.

Exhausting the distinctive jargon of American racial politics is, however, only one aspect of a general crisis around the concepts and language in which these matters have been thought. The bitterness, anger and other strong responses that adoption and fostering generate supplement and extend the core problems. They are worth exploring in themselves as a separate topic. However, it is by no means obvious why culture and colour-matched fostering and adoption should produce such an intensity of feeling. It is essential to appreciate that these tides of unwelcome sentiment cannot be somehow placed on hold while a different kind of conversation is allowed to take place. They constitute the unique context in which these issues are understood and argued over. The issues that prompt these conflicts are important, and yet the feelings they arouse seem somehow out of proportion when seen in relation to the more profound and more intractable problems of poverty, crime, drug misuse and social, economic and political marginalisation that arise in a racially-structured society.

Perhaps because they are intractable, these more obviously political problems stubbornly refuse to generate the same degree of passion and fervour. In seeking to comprehend why the symbolism of adoption and fostering would provide the decisive point around which uniquely vocal and powerful forces would cluster we have to enquire into the capacity of adoption and fostering issues to animate and arouse. This book offers a starting point for this long task. The constellation of potent signs – mother, family, infant – that appears in the discourse of adoption should be acknowledged immediately. But it is the image of the fractured black family which has acquired a special political charge in the language and practice of social work that supplies the key to comprehending this strange intensity. We must therefore be prepared to ask some harsh questions about precisely *who* these questions excite and also about the role of these conflicts – to some extent independent of the issues to which they refer – in expressing lines of antagonism that traverse and fracture the special professional cultures of social services departments and other social work agencies.

Initially, this will mean understanding both the combative stance of the black professional groupings that made colour- and culture-matched adoption a political issue and the context for their activities created by social work orthodoxies that were palpably racist in their portrayals of black family life. Though the misplaced taboo against washing dirty communal washing in public still operates, it is not indiscreet to admit that simply asserting the strength and durability of black households and kin structures was a disastrous response to pathological diagnoses of black social and cultural life. The ruthlessly 'positive' images that were summoned up as an antidote to pathology suggested both intellectual and political weakness and were dearly bought at the price of an aching silence on a whole range of key issues in childcare policy. The assumptions that gave rise to pathology in the first place were not answered but inverted, and then deployed to animate a pastoral image of black family life which would lead a gullible observer to conclude that merely possessing the approved phenotypical characteristics could also inoculate the community as a whole against abuse, stress and dysfunctionality. In a racist society the opposite conclusion is more likely to be true. Racism itself should be recognised as a factor in increasing household stresses and conflicts around money, status and power, gender and generation. Cultural sameness and common bodily characteristics do not, by themselves, promote good parenting. This is an area in which no guarantees are possible.

It is even more disturbing that what might be called the triumphalist presentation of black family life was part of a wider drift in black political thought towards an implosive obsession with identity as selfhood. This is a large topic that cannot be reconstructed in detail here. Suffice to say that this sorry state of affairs culminates in the black family's appearance as the only domain in which political agency can be observed to operate and the only object upon which that agency can be exercised. The dangers of this situation should be obvious. As far as social work is concerned, nothing critical could be said about the black family or the tidy forms of pure community that were apparently to be constructed from its simple agglomeration without courting accusations of betrayal. Once these odious views were enthroned as ortho-doxies, the suggestion of unprofessional conduct also came into play. It was and remains necessary to undermine the social work practices in which pathological ideas about black sociality have been reproduced for a long time as an indisputable piece of practical wisdom, but overthrowing those ideas substituted one form of ethno-dogma for another. In the long term, moving away from that dogma and developing a rigorous critique of the occultism it created will require a supple and sensitive theory of racialised culture and identity that can yield more insights than the commonsense alternatives currently on display. This book makes a contribution to that activity.

In pursuing these long-term goals we will confront a number of seemingly insuperable problems both conceptual and political. The first, but not the most fundamental, is the tragic anti-intellectualism that intrudes into these discussions. It transmits a non-negotiable belief that the questions we need to analyse are able to resist the ethical force of logical argument, clarity and other analytical procedures. This hostility is doggedly pre- and apolitical in the sense that it privileges the narcissistic impulses of those who wish to experience their own cultural or somatic characteristics reflected back upon them in the hall of mirrors that absolutist understandings of identity provide. It is perni-cious because it wants to substitute a form of therapeutic solidarity for the tricky negotiations involved in thinking politically about adoption and foster-ing. It is destructive because it operates by means of a number of highly contentious but usually unstated assumptions about 'race', ethnicity, culture, the family and other kin relationships, identity and individuality, selfhood and autonomy.

The essays that follow contribute much to clearing the thickets in which these pivotal concepts are entangled. Some suggest both implicitly and explicitly that we should not rush towards according 'race' and ethnicity an automatic privilege over other dimensions of social difference like gender, class, language and location in calculating the characteristics of any particular individual subject or group or in comprehending their association. Others hint that quantifying and assessing the racial or ethnic self is a more hazardous and evasive operation than professional commentators in general, and social workers in particular, like to admit. They will certainly ask you to consider whether the methods chosen to help organise enquiries into identity may be implicated in the results produced, especially where the chaos, instability and flux of social self-construction are ignored or obscured by a desire to figure the self in over-integrated and absolutely different forms. As you read on, you will encounter the suggestion that the models of self that routinely circulate in these discussions are crude and mechanistically configured. They do not illuminate the complex causal relationships between body, consciousness and behaviour that are presupposed by the idea of discrete and separable racial groups. I would add that no matter what the Children Act (1989) says we should be wary of reifying 'race' and ethnicity so that they appear as things rather than processes, and that a degree of scepticism is a valuable ally in approaching the firm disciplinary gestures emanating from forces that want to maximise the difference between racial and ethnic groups in order to repress the differences within those groups.

Conflicts around fostering and adoption have recently been misinterpreted as a clash between the totalitarian tribunes of 'political correctness' and its stalwart free-thinking opponents. This is not a useful way to proceed. It strengthens the hand of those who seek to undermine and repudiate the valuable critical voices inside social work and social policy. As purity-seekers from all backgrounds and cultures join hands and combine in the dismal dance of absolutism, it is important to remember that these political conflicts have taken shape in an area beyond the grasp of simplistic distinctions between the left and the right. I would suggest that at root they are not usually manifestations of political ideology at all, but of something anterior to it. They express contrasting approaches to comprehending culture, self, kinship, ethnicity, nation and 'race' that blur the lines between formally opposed views at opposite ends of the political spectrum. In this unstable space, even when radical rhetoric is employed, to be conservative is to be engaged in a politics of cultural conservation: that is to subscribe to a doggedly positive and always over-integrated sense of culture as the essential substance of racial, national and ethnic differences. In this view, 'race' *is* culture and identity rather than profane politics and complex history. The junction of those two foundational terms – 'race' and culture – indexes something so important and yet so fragile that it can be readily destroyed.

Whether the social and psychological processes we term culture and identity are really so insubstantial and frail cannot be debated here. The idea that priceless, essential identity is in perpetual danger from difference and that its precious purity is always at risk from the irrepressible power of hetero-culture is central to the invocation of victimage that has in turn been integral to these debates. Here the image of the deracinated black child adrift on the oceans of whiteness that Britain supposedly represents is served up as a synecdoche for the plight of black settlers. This tragic tableau raises further questions by asking us why people should rush to identify with that imaginary child severed from the nurturance that its racial nature demands, and consigned to non-being as it strives in vain to remove the accursed pigment from the surface of its body. White supremacy has often viewed its racial others as infants – half-conscious, not-yet-beings incapable of operating without the genial guidance of those benign rulers who are also in some profound sense parents. If it is accepted that modern racism invites the dominant partners in the binary pairing of black and white to identify with the punitive authority and violence of the great white father/husband, is it also legitimate to ask whether subaltern enthusiasms for the litany of minority victimage reflect the extent to which the dominated have internalised the deepest codes of their subordination? If so, the politics of fostering and adoption may prefigure the oedipal crisis of racial patrimony.

The essays below are valuable, lastly, because they put a precious dent in the casual confidence in the professionalism of social services that has appeared regularly to embarrass the discourse of the colour- and culture-matchers. The gap between the rhetoric of communal self-reliance and its instant translation into an emphatically statist strategy for sameness management yawns wide. The colour-coders will need to be more precise and detailed in their accounts of cultural transmission if they are to be persuasive.

Perhaps the assertion that cultures are absolutely different from each other has been treated too respectfully of late. Areas of incommensurability will invariably exist but it is not possible to know their locations in advance of expeditions to discover where they might be. These areas change. They move around. New conflicts emerge while old ones fade away. The popular contemporary claim that 'you can't understand my culture but I can understand yours sufficiently to know that the two of them are incompatible' must be exposed now for the deceitful manner in which it seeks to monopolise the process of cultural interpretation and to turn modern British culture into a one-way street that leads to a dead-end. There is no purity to be found. Cultures can, indeed must, differ from themselves. How substantively different are the contemporary cultures of this country from one another? Why has the symbolism of unsought and undesirable 'transracial' contact become the primary means to mark the immobile boundaries that the absolutists seek to place between groups?

INTRODUCTION

IVOR GABER and JANE ALDRIDGE

The issue of transracial placements has become a potent symbol in our society – it was given a central place in the British Government's 1993 White Paper – '*Adoption: The Future*'. It has assumed a significance out of all proportion to the actual numbers involved in such placements. It has become a symbol because some in the ethnic minority communities have seen it as exemplifying the exploitation and repression of the black members of our society by the white majority. In the extreme it is viewed as a form of exploitation which at its heart comes down to a form of genocide – black children are being 'stolen' from the black community to provide childless white couples with ready-made families. And from this position it is argued that these black children, once placed transracially, are subsequently 'lost' to the black community because they develop no sense of racial pride or identity. Others have argued that transracial adoption leaves black children adrift – unable to identify with either black or white communities and unable to cope with the racism that is inherent in our society. But unlike other areas of perceived racism, the issue of transracial placements was one which provided an opportunity where it was possible to effect immediate change.

In the hothouse atmosphere of the debates around this issue it was easy to castigate those who regarded transracial adoption as a viable option for some children as 'racists' – a characterisation that made further argument unnecessary. As a result many social workers and those who work alongside them have, over the past few years, swallowed their doubts on this subject and taken the line of least resistance. On the other side of the argument, those opposing transracial placements in recent times have been denounced for supposedly practising 'political correctness' at the expense of the children for whom they are supposed to be responsible. As a result what should have been a major public debate on a crucial issue in our society has become to a large extent a bitter polemic, with the children in the middle suffering. Suffering might seem a strong word but is not an exaggeration, as the research undertaken by Hilary Chambers into the children featured in the 'Be My Parent' project has demonstrated (see Appendix 6).

Furthermore, much of the argument has been conducted in terms that imply the debate is essentially about finding Afro-Caribbean families for Afro-Caribbean children, or perhaps on occasion finding Indian, Pakistani or Bangladeshi families for children from those backgrounds. But in fact adoption panels are frequently faced with trying to place children with far more mixed racial backgrounds, not to mention other emotional, mental or physical complications, for which the chances of finding even an approximate racial match are remote.

There is another major difficulty facing those who get entangled in this debate. For not only is it charged with emotion but it is singularly bereft of hard statistics. It is a matter of regret, if not condemnation, that neither the Department of Health nor local authority social services departments keep any reliable statistics about adoption, fostering and ethnic origin. Whether these figures are collected but not divulged, or more likely simply not collected, is not clear. What is clear is that without such information meaningful debate has been rendered nearly impossible. Local authorities frequently claim they have no trouble in placing children with ethnically matching families but no statistics are provided about how long such placements have taken, nor indeed about how accurate the ethnic match has or has not been.

But even without such hard statistical information – and Hilary Chambers' research is significant because of the dearth of other material in this area – this volume is an attempt to substitute light for heat, rationality for emotion, research for anecdote.

All books on controversial topics have an argument. Sometimes that argument is spelt out, sometimes it can be picked out from the contents of the book, and sometimes attempts are made to hide it altogether. The book and the pre-existing interest of the editors in the question of transracial placements grew out of an increasing concern about the fate of black children waiting, seemingly indefinitely, for new families; and also out of a concern with what the debate about transracial placements was doing to the wellbeing of existing transracial families. These concerns were discussed several years ago by a group of black and white adoptive parents, social workers and young adults who had been adopted or long-term fostered. The group, which included the editors of this book, called themselves 'Children First in Transracial Adoption and Fostering' and its launch statement and current position can be found in Appendix 2. In brief, the group believes that finding the right ethnic match for children is important, and that it is crucial that there are ethnic minority social workers involved in the seeking out of ethnic minority substitute families. Children First also believes that there comes a point when social workers have to weigh up the costs of prolonging a child's urgent need for a permanent new family against the benefits of finding an ethnic match.

If this book has one abiding theme it is that what is important is not what is felt about the issue of transracial placements, but what is known. It is introduced by one of the leading writers on race and ethnicity in Britain today, Paul Gilroy. He has made a significant contribution to the debate about the nature of black culture and identity, most importantly in *There Ain't no Black in the Union Jack* and most recently in *The Black Atlantic: Modernity and Double Consciousness*. Gilroy rejects simplistic notions of black identity which have dominated the debate about transracial placements. He argues that a much more subtle concept of self and identity is required that makes sense for the range of ethnic minority communities in Britain today.

Following this introduction Gloria Betts, a trained counsellor, provides a moving personal account of her own history as a child in a trans-racial placement. It is not a 'typical' story – there is no such thing – but its very atypicality gives it a particular resonance which reminds us that beyond the politicians' ideologies and the academics' theorising lie very real, often heartbreaking stories. Betts provides the particular perspective of someone who has both experienced the situation for herself and can view it with the detachment of a professional counsellor.

Ivor Gaber, one of the co-editors, then looks at the background to the debate – a brief history of black immigration and a description of the development of the practice of adoption. Gaber traces how the concerns about finding placements for black children began to grow in the late fifties and how the trend changed from one of creating mixed-race families to the present-day one of trying to maintain a policy of same-race placements only. The story comes up to date with an account of the controversies of recent times, the issuing of the Social Services Inspectorate's guidelines on transracial placements (see also Appendix 8), the Children Act of 1989 and the changes in adoption law currently under discussion.

This narrative account of the development of transracial adoption, and the debate that has surrounded it, is followed by sociologist Phil Cohen's alternative historical approach. In a stimulating contribution Cohen traces the metamorphosis of the issue as it has been played out through the debates that have surrounded the changing notions of culture and identity, and in particular how that notion has been defined through Britain's particular historical experience.

Developing the theme of identity, social psychologist Barry Richards argues with both coherence and insight that it is a mistake to see identity as a single concept. It is, according to Richards, important to distinguish between psychological and social identity, and in making judgements about people's individual identities we must be clear which aspect we are talking about. The debate about transracial adoption has confused these two issues with assertions about social identity being mistaken for conclusions about personal wellbeing.

These two perspectives on identity are followed by an authoritative essay by psychologists Barbara Tizard and Ann Phoenix. They focus on the concept of 'positive black identity', and systematically demonstrate the problematic nature of that concept. They carefully analyse all three components of the concept and demonstrate how all three conceal more than they reveal. And they go on to review the recent research in the field and conclude that there is no empirical evidence which could justify the existing bans on transracial placements.

A key concept in the debate surrounding transracial adoption has been that of 'attachment'. Developmental psychologist Susan Golombok, whose work in this field has received wide attention, looks at the questions: how do babies and children form attachments, and how traumatic is it for mother and child to be parted? Much of the thinking in this area stems from the work of John Bowlby but, as Golombok demonstrates, recent research has taken our understanding on still further. We know that breaking existing bonds is painful and difficult for babies and children, but is it irreparable? Are there circumstances in which it is justified?

One of the leading scholars in the field of family law – Jennifer Craven-Griffiths – then examines the legal arguments and precedents that have surrounded the debate around transracial placements that began in Britain in the 1980s. She looks at the 1989 Children Act and the prospects for further changes in the law on adoption. She concludes that despite the references to ethnic identity within the Children Act the key issue remains the welfare of the individual child, and not broad-brush policy statements.

We then turn our attention to the debate as it has been played out in the key battleground of the United States. Rita Simon, whose own work in this area has had a profound impact on both sides of the Atlantic, reports the findings of her longitudinal study of transracial adoptees, which has been in progress since 1971. The conclusions she and other American researchers have reached are clear – that transracial adoptions can be and are a satisfactory substitute when same-race placements are not available. It is noteworthy that Simon's longitudinal study is the only one in this area which has followed adoptees from infancy to adulthood.

Elizabeth Bartholet, a distinguished legal scholar, provides a second view from America with a fascinating essay which intertwines a scholarly analysis of the legal situation as it has developed in the United States with the personal insights that she has gained from her own experiences as a transracial adopter – an interesting counterpoint to 'Gloria's Story', which is written from the perspective of a transracially placed child.

The final chapter written by co-editor Jane Aldridge, offers an update of the current situation and some positive proposals for 'good practice'. At the heart of these proposals is the notion of time limits for finding matching placements. Without time limits there is no one able to say to the adoption worker, 'you have looked hard enough for a match, now let's go for the best available placement'. That might be our conclusion, but to assist readers in drawing their own, we offer in the Appendices a compendium of documents central to this debate and pulled together for the first time. These include guidelines on transracial placements from the Social Services Inspectorate, the British Agencies for Adoption and Fostering, the British Association of Social Workers, the Commission for Racial Equality, the Association of Black Social Workers and Allied Professionals, and the National Foster Care Association. We print the full details of Hilary Chambers' research based on the appearance of children in BAAF's 'Be My Parent'. We also include the original launch statement by Children First.

Having read the contributions in this volume and the documents in the Appendices we do not expect readers necessarily to agree with everything proposed, but we do hope that in the future the debate will be conducted on the basis of research and reason rather than pain and anger.

1 'GLORIA'S STORY'

GLORIA BETTS

In July I celebrated my 40th birthday. Now the Autumn has arrived and, in some strange way, I feel that about my life too. It is a time for gathering all that I am unto myself, separating the facts from fiction. The acceptance of all that has happened in my life has not been easy. During the past six years, I have made a long and difficult journey into the depths of my own personal history, psychology and spiritual beliefs.

I am black, and was born in England of a Sierra Leonean mother and father. When I was six months old, my mother took me to Ireland where I was fostered with a white couple, who already had two sons of their own. The events surrounding my birth and subsequent fostering have always been vague. My mother has been most reluctant to tell me the whole truth. This much I have pieced together over the years.

When my mother's husband came to Britain in the 1940s to become a barrister, my mother was left at home in Sierra Leone with my older brother. Next door to my mother lived a handsome bachelor. They had an affair, and when my mother left for England to continue her nursing training, she was pregnant. Her story is that she was rejected by her husband when he heard that she was carrying me. (A few years ago this version was denied by an old aunt of mine.) Many attempts were made to reconcile the married couple, but my mother was angry with her husband for leaving her so long on her own while he was studying. She suspected him of having affairs while he was in Britain. Seemingly, he was willing to accept that he had behaved irresponsibly, but my mother refused to have anything further to do with him. They were divorced. I recently learnt, unfortunately, that he is now dead; and so too is his sister, who could have thrown some further light on this sad event. I never did meet my father. In fact, he has remained the 'unknown' throughout my life. That very early period of my life was, no doubt, very painful for my mother, and we have not been able to discuss this heart to heart.

The presence of a small black baby in Ireland during the early 1950s was a rare sight, especially in the small town in which I grew up. To most of the local people I was someone they had only seen in photographs or heard of in stories told to them about Africa, where many of the Irish religious orders had missions where their nuns and priests were engaged in teaching and nursing in the local communities. It was quite an experience for the locals to have their own 'black baby'. (The term 'black baby' came from the missionary boxes in churches and shops to support the work in Africa. On the top of these boxes was a figure of a little 'black baby'. The head nodded when a coin was dropped into the box.) People would gather around me wanting to touch my skin and feel my hair. I was a great source of interest, specially when my foster mother took me out in the pram.

'Is she yours?', people would ask. At first my foster mother would go into a long, detailed explanation. Eventually she would say 'Yes, Gloria is my daughter,' and, turning to my foster father, would add 'and this is my husband'. Yes, indeed, I was their daughter and their two sons were my brothers. I grew up feeling very much a part of the family, I felt loved and cared for, and had a deep sense of being myself. In those early years my colour was not a problem. I had a wonderful time with my foster brothers and all their friends. Quite often, when I was a baby, they would help to bath me and would occasionally be allowed to give me my bottle. My foster father was a very quiet and easy-going man. He was a policeman and, as far as I can remember, never arrested anyone. In those days the policemen collected the local rates. He would seat me on the back of his bike, and everywhere we went I would be loaded down with presents: pots of jam, money, religious medals and all sorts of things. He was a very skilled gardener, and I acquired my love of nature from him. He gave me a little garden of my own, where I grew my first flowers – poppies – and then a bed full of multicoloured poppies. I loved working with him in the garden. It helped me to feel connected to the earth.

My foster mother was a very vivacious woman who loved to sing and dance, and she had style. She was kind, caring and did the best she could for me. In her marriage she was the stronger and more dominant partner. When I was five years old my own mother came to take me back to Sierra Leone with her. She had finished her training. Though I had seen her occasionally during those early years, I was wary of her and cried when she wanted to bath me. I was not told why I had to leave – at least I do not remember; not that such decisions are ever explained to a child. This separation caused me a great deal of pain and sorrow. My foster parents and the boys were heartbroken. This was done with my best interests at heart. My mother was a stranger to me, and I had no wish to go anywhere with her, especially back to Sierra Leone.

With this move a great light went out of my life. I knew nothing of the vast continent of Africa, except from some simple childhood stories. Life in Sierra Leone was not at all what I had expected. My foster family was gone, and I never knew if I would see them again. I lived in an all-female household, with my mother's old nanny and with her eldest sister. My brother was living with his father. Mother, the matron of a chest hospital, was out at work all day. She also had a new man in her life. I had to make enormous social and cultural adjustments. The weather was unbearable. I was lonely and homesick. Apart from caring for old Nanny, I have no fond memories of Sierra Leone. I was six-and-a-half when my mother decided to send me back to Ireland. I believe that Nanny had convinced her that this was in my best interests. I went home by cargo boat. An acquaintance of my mother's who was on her way to the UK took charge of me. The journey was great fun, and I spent most of my time with the captain. My foster parents were waiting for me in England. It was wonderful to see them, to be home again, to be with my family.

Life continued as before, with its usual ups and downs. I had started at a convent school, and made many friends. I was still the 'little black baby'! I cannot recall being taunted at school because of my colour, although I am sure it must have happened occasionally. At least, I never remember coming home in tears because of some unkind racist remark; Ireland was truly a Christian country. When my foster father retired, my foster mother decided to go out to work to supplement his pension. She went to sea for a number of years before she had to come home because my foster father contracted asthma. She then trained as a beautician so she could work at home. She loved being at sea and spent most of her time sailing down the west coast of Africa to Nigeria. It was she who made me feel good about being black, whereas my own mother gave me confusing signals. 'Remember you are black and remember what the white man did to us', she would say. Yet it was she who had sent me to live with white foster parents in a white country, where I had no contact with any of my own people. My mother's remarks were completely alien, as at that time I had had no experience of racial prejudice.

The first major problems occurred during my teens. People would ask me when would I be going home, back to my own country. Mother also wanted me to return and I found this would upset me terribly. She feared that once I was twenty-one, I would refuse to go back to Sierra Leone. Naturally, I was attracted to boys, had crushes, and fell in love, but the boys were all white. Nothing ever came of anything. I belonged to a large crowd of boys and girls, and spent a lot of time going around with 'the gang'. Yet there was never anyone special for me. Only in later years did I realise that being black was the problem. At that time none of the boys in that small town would have had the nerve to take out a black girl. For them, certainly, I was emotionally and sexually an unknown factor, but I was not aware of this. Nevertheless I had a lot of fun as a teenager. During the school holidays there were many parties, and summertime was great too. I would go to our local beach, which was only three miles away, and spend all day there, swimming and fooling around with my friends. Later we would go to Joe's Café on the hill to play the juke box and dance. In many ways I did not feel excluded, but school was another matter.

The nuns, bless their hearts, saw me as a future pioneer in Africa, and naturally as a nun, fervently converting the continent. As a child I had more freedom than most, and did not like the discipline of school life. Much has been written and said about so-called 'convent girls' and the damage to our lives through being educated by repressed women. I cannot say that this was my experience. Not all the nuns were repressed, and some were brilliant teachers and kindly souls. The religious training and dogma were heavy going at times, yet I never felt weighed down. In later years I came to appreciate the discipline, and the many bells throughout the day calling us to prayers and lessons. Eventually I did rebel against the Catholic Church and many of its teachings. But in time I rediscovered my own 'truths'. In time the nuns realised that I was not cut out for the missionary life.

At home, there were the usual family disagreements. I was a troublesome teenager, having more to deal with than most. My foster mother was having trouble with one of her sons, and had little time for me and my problems. We were all living under stress. When I needed my mother most, she was not there to help. Neither my mother nor my foster mother were good at expressing their feelings. My mother was, and still is, a very angry woman, and my foster mother simply felt uncomfortable with any display of deep emotions. My mother was a sexual woman and needed a man in her life, but my foster mother put my foster father out of the marital bed when I arrived. (I learnt from her many years later that she had intended to leave my foster father, her second husband, many years previously, when the boys were much younger. However, he discovered her plans, then accused her of taking money from him. During the ensuing argument, he kicked her. In fact my foster mother regretted having remarried so young. Her first husband had died of TB only a year after their marriage, and then two years later she had met and married my foster father.)

Eventually, when I was older, I left school and then home. I did not go back to Sierra Leone. Instead I travelled as an au pair in Germany and then France. I had to return when my mother decided to come to England. She hoped to mend our relationship and to some extent we made an uneasy truce, yet we still remained strangers. She remained in England for a number of years. I worked for some time as a mother's help, and then I took a cordon bleu cookery course, which enabled me to command a better salary. Little did I realise that all those years of working with so many families would lead me towards a deepening interest in psychology. I learnt so much about people, their relationships, the effect divorce can have on children and how disturbing it is for them to live with warring parents. A home is a testing place to see people at their best and their worst.

During the late 1970s I became interested in the esoteric aspect of religion. I began reading books on reincarnation, and our life purpose on earth. It was the beginning of a long and fascinating journey into the world of spirituality and psychology. In 1984 I wanted to change my career to become a therapist. I continued to work as a cook/housekeeper, but found a job that allowed me time to pursue my new career. I continued working while I retrained, and took some workshops in transpersonal psychology. These, coupled with my deepening interest in spirituality, led me to look at my own life from a different point of view.

Looking back on my early childhood, and realising the extent of its psychological impact, was a great shock and revelation. I started to question my mother in depth about that period of my life, and why she had decided to have me fostered. This led to a lot of trouble with her, as she did not want to go into this subject at all. It was extremely painful and distressing for me, but it became easier to understand my lack of love for her. It has also become clearer, over the years, that I was an unwanted child. My mother was in a highly charged emotional state during the months she was carrying me, and had apparently considered having an abortion. She felt alone and abandoned living in England during the late 1940s, having parted from her lover (my father) in Sierra Leone, and then having been rejected by her husband because she was carrying me. Undoubtedly it must have been difficult to relate to me, her baby, under those trying circumstances; these feelings of rejection started before I was even born. There was no period of bonding with my mother and six months later, following my birth, I was taken to live in a strange country, with people who were strangers. Fortunately, I grew to love them all, but I never again trusted anyone deeply.

My father died ten years ago. Only recently has my mother been able to tell me anything about him, even though I had asked her repeatedly over the years. Emotionally, the past six years have been a nightmare. I could never get my mother to tell me the whole truth, and I felt so betrayed by her as a woman. I knew nothing of what it meant to be feminine, to be in touch with my own sensuality. My foster mother did what she could, but she was incapable of preparing me for a role she did not fully understand herself. During my teens she would refer all my emotional problems to my mother, whose usual reply would be 'I don't want Gloria becoming involved with any white boys'. It was rather late in the day for that, and any way she need not have worried, for the boys themselves were too afraid. My mother did not want me to marry a white man and produce mixed-race children.

I spent some time in therapy, just trying to sort out who I was as a woman, and what were my needs. The difficulty was in trying to unravel my own feelings from those of my mother. It was not easy to be my own black woman and not play the role my mother or society demanded. It has taken me a long time to separate my mother's anger from my own. The saving grace has been my ability to get in touch with my capacity to love. I knew what it was to be in love, but not to love someone with the whole of my being. It was a very painful experience, and it did not work out. Yet I learnt that I was capable of loving and so I was eventually able to identify the sensual woman in me. My interest in spiritual disciplines and studies helped me enormously, and gave me a deeper insight into the meaning of life: the reasons for this present incarnation, my choice of parents, and the many lessons I had to learn. When I attended the first general meeting of Children First, my early childhood experiences became clearer. I had found a place where my painful experiences were going to be of value to others.

As to the whole issue of transracial fostering and adoption, I am still in favour, in spite of my earlier experiences. After all, it was forty years ago, and much has changed since then. Life as a whole is moving towards a more integrated and multiracial society. There will always be those pushing against the natural flow of life, and I do not believe that black children should languish in care when there are suitable and willing white families to adopt them. This is not an ideal world, and until that momentous ideal event occurs, we must get on with the process of living life as it is. I am only too aware of the problem between the black and white races in the world. I am aware of the cruelties perpetrated by the whites against us throughout history, yet we have got to keep growing, progressing, however difficult it is at times to turn the other cheek. Otherwise none of us will survive. No race in the world is without its faults. None of us is blameless. Let us not involve our children in the problems we adults have created. They must not become pawns in the racist issue. Whatever my problems, they would have been greater had I not had the experience of a family who loved me, irrespective of their racial identity. Love for me includes some of these qualities: wisdom and understanding, mercy and discrimination, truth and beauty. I had a black mother who had a negative attitude towards white people, and a white foster mother who had a positive one towards black people.

I know, too, that I have benefited by being brought up in Ireland. At a collective level the Irish have more in common with Africa than do the British. We have a common relationship with the earth and nature spirits. In Ireland, many years ago, there were sacred images of the black madonna. Sierra Leone had been a British colony for centuries, and Ireland had also been ruled by England. These patterns in the collective life do affect the individual, even if most of us are unaware of them.

Today I am certainly more at peace with myself. The past is in perspective, and the process of integration has begun. The present situation with my mother is sad. We had much in common and much we could have shared. We could have eased our mutual pain together. In December 1989 I became a transpersonal counsellor, and now I am training as a psychotherapist. I feel like a modern-day shaman, one who walks the boundaries between different worlds, cultures and spiritual disciplines.

Ultimately we are all one, whatever our colour, whatever our religious beliefs. We come from the one Source.

2 Transracial Placements in Britain: a History

IVOR GABER

The last 30 years have seen a variety of shifts in the social work policies and practices surrounding the adoption and fostering of children from ethnic minority groups. These variations cannot be ascribed to any one particular cause; they represent a nexus of changes in society, demographics, politics and social work theory and practice.

When children from ethnic minority backgrounds first started coming into care in the late 1950s their chances of finding permanent substitute families were not high, the children being seen as difficult, if not impossible, to place, purely on the grounds of their colour. Over the next two decades the situation, in terms of their finding permanent families, began to improve as more and more white families began to take on the responsibility of looking after children from a different ethnic background, and as more adults from ethnic minority groups came forward as prospective adoptive parents. But over the past decade the situation has again reversed with the cutback in transracial placements resulting in children from ethnic minority groups once again having to spend longer in care than their white counterparts while awaiting new families.

The first recorded incidence of black immigration to Britain came as early as 1555, when explorer John Lok returned from his second voyage to Guinea carrying with him a consignment of black slaves (Hiro, 1992), but it wasn't until the end of World War Two that large-scale black immigration really began. This resulted from the economic boom of the fifties, when there developed a growing shortage of unskilled labour. Britain's birth rate had declined dramatically as a result of two world wars within 20 years. Hence workers were needed to staff the public transport systems, run the National Health Service and keep the cotton mills turning.

So began the mass immigration from the West Indies and the Asian sub-continent, a migration which because of discrimination in the housing market and a tendency for newcomers to group together, was concentrated in inner-city areas occupied by the poorest and most disadvantaged sections of the host community. But no government preparations were made in anticipation of these new migrants. At no stage did the British people or Government demonstrate any real welcome to the newcomers. Indeed there is much evidence to the contrary – as far back as 1948 a Home Office working party was looking into ways of reducing the flow of black immigration.

Over the next 10 years more than 200,000 immigrants arrived – mainly from the Caribbean and the Indian sub-continent. They represented just 0.5 percent of the UK population but their impact was far greater because, firstly, they were concentrated in a few areas of a few major cities and secondly, they were black. In 1958 the first race riots in Notting Hill, London, broke out, and 4 years later the Conservative Government of the day passed the first of a series of immigration control acts.

By the mid-sixties the post-war economic boom began to tail off. There was increased resentment of the new immigrants by some sections of the white working class, who saw the immigrants as competing for jobs, houses and social services. In 1965 the Labour Government passed the first Immigration Act specifically designed to curb black immigration. At the same time the first Race Relations Act was passed; its aim was to tackle the symptoms of racial prejudice that were growing daily more obvious.

Until this point, advocates of racial integration had based their arguments and rhetoric on the notion of creating a pluralist society with shared core values. But as the evidence of racial prejudice in the host community persisted this seemed to become an unreachable, perhaps even undesirable, goal. The number of new arrivals was so great that the relative ease of integration that had been achieved with previous groups of immigrants was unlikely to be repeated; older liberal ideals of 'colour blindness' and assimilation gave way to newer notions of ethnic pride and multiculturalism. And one area that was to become a fulcrum of these conflicting ideas was in the fostering and adoption of children.

As it is now practised in Britain adoption is a relatively new phenomenon and is peculiar to Western society, where a child without his or her own parents is, because of the predominance of the ideal of the nuclear family, believed to be disadvantaged. Modern adoption grew out of two major pieces of legislation: the 1926 Adoption Act, England and Wales (1930 in Scotland), which outlawed the practice that up until then had enabled natural parents to reclaim their child when s/he reached a wage-earning age; and the 1950 Adoption Act which outlawed so-called 'third party' adoptions in which children could be placed for adoption without the intervention of a local authority or recognised adoption agency.

Following the passing of the 1926 Act the annual number of adoptions in England and Wales rose steadily from 3,000 a year in 1927 to a post-war peak of 21,000 in 1946. But as 'normal' family life resumed the number of adoptions declined and stabilised at around 13,000 a year in the fifties. In the sixties the numbers again began to rise, peaking at 25,000 in 1968. This rise was largely due to changes in the lifestyle and outlook of a new generation who were riding high on a new wave of optimism in Harold Macmillan's land of 'you've never had it so good'. Thus at the same time as married couples were wanting larger families, increasing the demand for adoption, the availability of children also increased as a result of the loosening of conventions of sexual morality, encapsulated in the notion of the 'permissive society'.

However, in the seventies the number of adoptions fell dramatically, down to 12,000 by mid-decade – half the figure for 1968. This decline continued into the eighties, when the average number of adoptions fell to around 7,000 a year. Even more strikingly the number of healthy white babies being adopted fell dramatically, down from around 14,000 a year in 1968 to around 1,400 in 1988. The reasons for the stark fall are not difficult to identify. Firstly, the changing social climate had made the concept of the one-parent family more socially acceptable, a change which had also been reflected in alterations to the social security system. In addition, the housing boom made it easier for single-parent families to find accommodation, even if it was on the thirtieth floor of an inner-city tower block. At the same time as it was becoming more acceptable for a single parent to raise a child, the actual number of unwanted pregnancies was declining because of the greater availability of more efficient methods of birth control. In addition, the introduction of the Abortion Law Reform Act in 1967 had led to a dramatic rise in the number of . legal abortions.

As a result there developed an inbalance in demand between the number of childless couples seeking to adopt and the ability of adoption agencies to find babies for adoption. This change coincided with the reorientation of adoption practice away from pre-war notions of finding babies for childless couples to one of seeking the best substitute families for children in need. This in turn resulted in adoption agencies starting to look for homes for babies and children who, until then, had been considered 'hard to place' – these included sibling groups, children with physical and mental handicaps, older children and the children of the recently arrived Commonwealth immigrants.

Moreover, the introduction of journals such as *Social Work Today*, *Community Care* and *New Society* began to open the eyes of the new social work professionals to a range of practices and possibilities that until then had not been seriously considered. These changes in adoption practice were hastened by the emerging role of local authorities into a field which, until the 1959 Children and Young Person's Act, had been dominated by the older, more conservative voluntary societies. But there were other changes afoot as well which related to the change of mood of the sixties. This entailed a growing mood of selflessness and altruism, of being aware of a wider world and wanting to participate actively in solving that world's problems. This mood led both social workers and prospective parents to take a more active role in creating permanent substitute homes for these 'hard-to-place' children.

Furthermore, changes in adoption practice came about, not only because the agencies found themselves able to find families for these 'hard-to-place' children, but also because of growing evidence of the ultimately unsatisfactory nature of long-term foster care: a study by Victor George (1970) showed that up to 50 percent of such placements broke down within the first year. In addition there was growing dissatisfaction with the continuing use of residential care for long-term placements. It was becoming increasingly clear that the stability they offered children was even less than that of a foster family. 'Children need permanency' became the cry of the sixties, and 'permanency' meant adoption.

Undoubtedly, part of the initial drive in favour of transracial adoption was underpinned by the liberal philosophy of assimilation – the concept of the integrated society as symbolised by the multicultural family. This philosophy was based on the notion that skin colour was irrelevant and that everyone was the same underneath – the melting pot theory of the decade of peace, love and flower power. It was a time when the persistence of white racism and the need for ethnic minority groups to sustain themselves through their own cultures was not fully recognised. Such philosophies were prevalent in social services departments and adoption agencies throughout the country. Transracial placements were seen as positive steps towards a more integrated society although, as far as is known, there were no officers from ethnic minority backgrounds in senior positions in social services departments or adoption agencies to validate these notions.

However, despite the new mood, it was, at the beginning of the decade at least, still far from easy to place children from ethnic minority backgrounds. A 1960 research project for the National Council for Civil Liberties found that only five agencies – the now defunct London County Council, agencies in Bristol and Edinburgh, the Church of England Children's Society and Dr Barnardo's – were willing even to attempt to place 'coloured' (as they were then known) children. The rest felt it was 'improper'. At the time it was not uncommon for judges to refuse to make transracial adoption orders on the grounds that it was 'miscegenation' (race mixing) which they could not condone.

In 1962 the Adoption Committee of International Social Service of Great Britain, the organisation which liaises on social services issues between countries, became concerned about the growing number of British children from ethnic minority groups who were remaining in care with no obvious prospect of being placed in a permanent family. As a result they established an Action Committee which recommended the establishment of the British Adoption Project, aimed at finding permanent homes for these children. The British Adoption Project was formally established in 1965 and run jointly with the Sociology Department of Bedford College of the University of London. It had two purposes: one was to provide an adoption service specifically for children in Great Britain who were of diverse racial origins and to offer a liaison between agencies to facilitate the adoption of such children; the second was to answer two questions – could adoptive homes be found for these children and, if they could, how would such placements work out?

From the outset the project recognised the importance of matching children to parents who shared their own racial and cultural origins. They established a fundamental principle that children should be placed whenever possible with adoptive parents of the same racial background as themselves; and, in fact, one in five of the 53 babies involved in the Project was so placed. Thus were the beginnings of officially recognised drives to place the growing number of children from the ethnic minorities who were coming into care into permanent substitute families. Statistics on the numbers of ethnic minority children involved in adoption have always been difficult to come by since for many years agencies kept no figures relating to the ethnic composition of their children, their adoptive families or even their staff. However, the British Adoption Project did succeed in ethnically monitoring one year's adoption statistics. They calculated that of the 13,122 adoption orders made in 1966, 445 of the children were from ethnic minority backgrounds and that agencies knew of a further 415 children whom they might have placed but for their ethnic background.

Following the establishment of the British Adoption Project, the Agnostics' Adoption Society, Dr Barnardo's and the Edinburgh-based Guild of Service along with local authority representatives from Birmingham, Oxford and Somerset formed the Adoption Resource Exchange. The Exchange, which was to be administered by the Adoption Committee of International Social Service, was specifically committed to finding permanent families for children from ethnic minority backgrounds. The members agreed that after they had registered and approved prospective adopters they would exchange information to ensure that children were placed as soon as possible, even if this meant using a family from a different part of the country.

The Home Office gave its official backing to transracial placements in 1970 in its *Guide to Adoption Practice* (Home Office Advisory Council on Child Care, 1970). The guidelines stated that children of mixed parentage should be considered equally for black or white placements and even suggested that the placement of black children in white families in areas where there were no other black families, contrary to current thinking, was in fact desirable. But the guidelines were silent on the question of the desirability of ethnic minority children having substitute families which reflected their own backgrounds and they made no mention of adoption agencies making special efforts to recruit such families.

Despite the beginning of this trend towards transracial placements, many would-be white adopters were still being told by adoption agencies that there were no babies available for adoption, when, in fact, what they really meant was that there were no healthy white babies available for adoption. Consequently, in 1971, a group of adoptive and would-be adoptive parents formed the Parent to Parent Information on Adoption Services (PPIAS) in order to provide information to prospective adopters as to which agencies had children waiting for permanent families: children from ethnic minority backgrounds as well as the whole range of children who, because of physical or mental disabilities, emotional problems or because they were members of large sibling groups, were classified as 'hard-to-place'.

A year later the Home Office Committee on Adoption noted what it took to be an encouraging trend in the growing number of ethnic minority children being placed for adoption. It observed that in the previous year the Adoption Resource Exchange had placed 74 such children and went on to observe, 'The Exchange is now finding homes for all babies referred to it, and has extended its services to include older coloured children but there are still reports from certain areas of parents who want their children adopted being told that there is little hope of placing a coloured child' (Home Office Departmental Committee on Adoption, 1972).

Until this point, although there had been an implicit understanding that finding parents for 'hard-to-place' children was important, there was less recognition of the urgency of the task. However, in 1973 this perspective changed with the publication of Jane Rowe and Lydia Lambert's milestone research into children in care – *Children Who Wait* – which showed quite starkly that children who spent six months or more in care only had a one in four chance of ever returning to their permanent homes. In other words it was vital that once children were received into care immediate plans were made either for the child's return to his or her birth family or for his or her early placement in a permanent substitute family.

Children Who Wait clearly demonstrated that the longer a child waited in the care system the less likely she or he was to return to some sort of family life. Rowe and Lambert also looked into the number of children from ethnic minority groups in care and found that they accounted for one in four of the total. Their seminal research did much to increase the pace and rate of transracial placements. Families, mainly white, were coming forward in increasing numbers and with the new emphasis on 'permanency', adoption agencies and social work departments now started proceedings to place children from ethnic minority groups far more quickly than had previously been the case. In this atmosphere some bad placements were made with agencies approving some adoptive parents who had not seriously thought through issues of ethnicity and identity and who were unresponsive, or even unconsciously hostile, to their children's ethnic needs.

But, at the same time as the trend towards transracial placements was developing, the ethnic minority groups, especially Afro-Caribbeans who by now had been settled in Britain for the best part of two decades, were beginning to make their voices heard. Discussions had been taking place for

some time within the Adoption Resource Exchange about the small number
of families from the Afro-Caribbean communities putting themselves forward
as prospective adoptive parents. By 1973, although it was less problematic
finding white adopters for the children, there was an increasing tendency for
Afro-Caribbean birth mothers to specify that they wanted their children to be
adopted by families of their own ethnic background.

However, such families were few and far between. This was because of a
lack of the knowledge in those communities that there were Afro-Caribbean
children in care needing adoption; because the majority of Afro-Caribbeans
had come to Britain in the late fifties and sixties and had not yet established
themselves as stable family groups capable of taking on an adopted child;
because to many families from the ethnic minority groups the necessarily
bureaucratic social work procedures that formed the backbone of the adoption selection process were off-putting; and finally, because there was a
genuine misunderstanding as to what 'adoption', British-style, actually entailed.

In Autumn 1973 staff at the Adoption Resource Exchange wrote a series of
articles about adoption and fostering for the newspaper *West Indian World*.
These were designed to stimulate interest in the Afro-Caribbean communities
about the needs of children in care. As a result, Trinidadian social worker
Ermyne Lee-Kin convened a series of meetings with some colleagues to
consider how best to react to the situation. Out of these discussions came the
Soul Kids Campaign. Soul Kids first of all set out to discover the size of the
problem. It found that of the 117 children on the books of the Adoption
Resource Exchange at the time (1974), 72 or two-thirds were from Caribbean
or Anglo/Caribbean backgrounds. Other figures they discovered were that in
Brent in 1975, of the 70 children under 12 for whom family placement was
required, 47 were black; of 404 children received into care by Tower Hamlets
in 1974 21 percent were from non-European origins; and 54 percent of
children under ten received into care in Wandsworth were from Caribbean
backgrounds.

As a result the Soul Kids Campaign was launched in July 1975. It was an
attempt to persuade West Indian families to put themselves forward as
would-be adopters. The campaign made use of posters, leaflets, advertisements, newspapers, magazines, radio and television broadcasts all targeted at
the Caribbean communities. In its one year of existence it dealt with a total of
153 inquiries, leading to 17 couples being approved for adoption and 11
children being placed. However, its impact on the wider adoption and
fostering scene was more significant, being seen by many as a watershed in
that it demonstrated that with resources, resourcefulness and the involvement
of black workers it was possible to persuade Caribbean families to come
forward and offer themselves as prospective adoptive parents.

If 1975 saw the entry of more black adopters onto the adoption stage the
same year also saw the children in care themselves move into the spotlight

when the National Children's Bureau organised the 'Who Cares?' conference, designed to give young people in care a voice. And among the voices raised on that platform were those of the ethnic minority children; some of whom, but not all, spoke up for ethnically matching substitute families. Out of Who Cares? grew the National Association of Young People in Care (NAYPIC) which in turn was to lead to the creation of Black and In Care (BIC), a group which later succeeded in making a significant impact on the practice of transracial placements.

Throughout the seventies, as the debate about transracial placements gathered momentum, wider changes were also taking place in black people's perceptions of where they stood in society in general and more specifically on the issue of transracial placements. Much of the impetus for these changes came from the United States. The sixties had been the era of civil rights – John Kennedy was in the White House and Martin Luther King was knocking on the door. It was an era of 'blacks and white uniting to fight'. However, as the optimism of the sixties faded, so too did the appeal of civil rights and assimilation – to be replaced by the politics of black self-identity and, for some, separatism, articulated by, amongst others, Stokeley Carmichael, George Jackson, Eldridge Cleaver and Malcolm X.

Their ideas were taken up by black American sociologists and social work theorists, some of whom began to see, in the growing trend of transracial adoption, another example of white America degrading and oppressing its ethnic minorities. The American experience is dealt with in more detail elsewhere (see Chapters 8 and 9). However, it is worth noting some of the more significant items which influenced policy and practice on this side of the Atlantic. In the States the practice of transracial placements had started earlier and assumed much greater numerical significance than was the case in Britain. It was in full flow in 1972 when the American National Association of Black Social Workers first expressed its vehement opposition to such placements. In the same year, in an article in the magazine *Social Work*, Leon Chestang said that only black families could give black children an environment 'with optimal opportunity for growth development and identification' (Chestang, 1972). And three years later social psychologist Amuzie Chimezie wrote that for the black child 'psychosurvival is paramount and can only be obtained in a black community . . . It would be cruel', he wrote, 'to strip the black child of his psychological armour against oppressive racism while he still needs this armour' (Chimezie, 1975).

A different position was taken by sociologist Joyce Ladner, whose book *Mixed Families* was quoted by both supporters and opponents of transracial placements in support of their arguments. Ladner argued that transracial adoption was neither the panacea to America's race problems, as some naive whites claimed, nor the genocidal threat to the black community that some of her radical black theorist counterparts claimed. Instead, she argued, transracial placements would never become large in number and the important point was not any potential future transracial adoptees but how the existing placements were making out. Overall she was optimistic, expressing her conclusion that 'there are many whites who are capable of rearing emotionally healthy black children' (Ladner, 1978, p. 289).

Ladner's optimism was supported by two empirical studies into the outcome of existing transracial placements. Arnold Silverman and William Feigelman, in a survey of 153 adoptive families, concluded that there was 'little support for arguments contending that the placement of black children in white homes will produce damaging psychological consequences'. And they went on to say that 'when a choice had to be made between transracial placement and continued foster or institutional care, transracial placement is clearly the option most conducive to the welfare of the child'. Rita Simon and Howard Altstein, in a series of three studies between 1977 and 1987, tracked a group of 218 children, all of whom had been transracially adopted before 1972, and concluded that, in the main, these placements could be characterised as successful (see Chapter 8).

However, from the American experience it was the arguments of Chimezie and Chestang, not the empirical evidence, that found the greatest resonance amongst black British social work theorists and practitioners. John Small, a London-based social worker, argued that transracial placements were not a response to the problem of the growing number of black children in care needing new families, but a response to the needs of childless white couples for whom white babies were no longer available. He claimed that in effect the black community had become a donor group for white society, servicing, as he saw it, whites as they had serviced them historically. Small went on to claim that statutory agencies were deliberately breaking up black families and taking children into care because they did not want to accept other traditions of rearing children (Small, 1982).

However, at this stage Small's views did not necessarily reflect those of the wider black community. In 1980 Christopher Bagley and Loretta Young found that in a sample of 100 black families 'the majority of ordinary black people do not oppose transracial placements'. In the same year John Small became the first Director of the New Black Families Unit, established by the Independent Adoption Society to locate substitute black families for the growing number of black and mixed parentage babies and young children who were in the care of the London Borough of Lambeth and awaiting permanent placement. Within 28 days of its foundation 40 families had come forward, and 2 years later the Unit had received a total of 108 enquiries. Between 1980 and 1982 the Unit approved 19 families for adoption and placed 6 children.

Small explained that it had been necessary to establish the Unit because predominantly white social workers were rejecting as unsuitable black families who did not come up to their eurocentric notions of 'ideal type'. 'The Unit', claimed Small, 'has brought a new approach to family finding in the sense that its assumptions are different from more orthodox agei recognises and values the experience and competence of black fam parents and child rearers and accepts the validity of different life style child care practices.' (Small, 1982). But Mary James, the Head of the Independent Adoption Society, remained committed to the need for transracial placements. Writing in *Adoption and Fostering* she said that transracial placements should continue 'since most people agree that it is best for a child to be brought up in a family' (1981, pp. 11–16).

In 1981, John Fitzgerald, Director of the Agency and Exchange Services of the British Agencies for Adoption and Fostering (BAAF), made the position of his organisation clear. Writing in *Adoption and Fostering*, he said: 'The first question to ask about black children waiting for a permanent substitute family is should the aim be to place the child with a family of the same racial origin? In my view the answer is emphatically yes'; although he was sufficiently realistic to recognise that 'the chasm between that statement and reality is very wide' (Fitzgerald, 1981).

1983 was the watershed year in the debate about transracial adoption. For what until then had been a relatively low-key debate exploded when Owen Gill and Barbara Jackson published the findings of their BAAF-sponsored follow-up research to the British Adoption Projection. They traced and interviewed 44 of the 51 families who had participated in the original project, 36 of whom were transracial adopters. They found that despite the fact that most of the children they studied 'saw themselves as "white" in all but skin colour . . . [There] was no general evidence, however, that the absence of racial pride or identity was, at this stage, associated with low self-esteem or behavioural disorder'. And, in what came to be seen as a controversial conclusion, the authors argued that 'on the basis of the evidence presented in this study we can find little support for the criticisms of transracial adoption which are based on the anticipated difficulties of the child' (1983, pp. 132–3). Nonetheless despite this finding the authors ended their book by arguing that their findings should not be used as an argument against the attempts to make same-race placements wherever possible: ' . . . there are strong arguments for saying that wherever possible black children needing a permanent substitute home should be placed in black rather than white families', they wrote, but went on to say: 'But, there are large numbers of black children in urgent and immediate need of the security and love of a family, and it is clear that at least in the short term, transracial adoption, whatever its disadvantages or its strengths, will continue to play a part in meeting that need' (1983, pp. 139–40).

At the launch of the Gill and Jackson study representatives of the newly formed Association of Black Social Workers and Allied Professionals (ABSWAP) attacked the two authors claiming the study had revealed that the children did not see themselves as black or show any real sign of having developed a sense of racial identity. Gill and Jackson themselves had described the children as being 'white in all but skin colour'. And yet the study had described the placements as broadly successful (1983, pp. 130-3). Among those who attacked Gill and Jackson's work was David Divine, a black social worker in the London borough of Hackney who went on to become Director of Social Services at Brent, London. And John Small, in the *International Journal of Social Psychiatry*, wrote that it failed 'to recognise the identity needs of black children in a racist society. If "these black children have been made white in all but skin colour . . . have no contact with the black community and their 'coping' mechanisms are based on denying racial background" we must surely question Gill and Jackson's conclusion that "they feel confident in using the term 'success' to describe the experiences of the majority of these families and children . . . " ' (Small, 1984).

In the same year the House of Commons Social Services Committee set up an inquiry into children in care and the Association of Black Social Workers, whose first President was John Small, took the opportunity of stating clearly where they stood on the issue of transracial placements. Their submission, including as it did 'Good practice guidelines for transracial placements', has subsequently played a major role in the ongoing debate – their evidence being perceived as authoritative and the guidelines as helpful. 'Necessity has given birth to the Association', they wrote. 'We believe that institutional and individual racism permeates all aspects of services offered to the black community by statutory and voluntary agencies alike.' And they went on to argue that: 'The practice of transracial placements as an alternative care structure for black children is perpetuating racist ideologies and so poses one of the most dangerous threats to the type of society to which we aspire' (ABSWAP, 1983). 'The black child has an inalienable right to be brought up in a family which is similar in racial and cultural origin', they added, and went on to argue that 'a black child is often better off in an institution which is located in the black community, staffed by black people and offers the black child relationships in the black community than being placed in a white racist family'.

However, after calling for an end to all transracial placements, ABSWAP, in recognising the reality of the situation, went on to outline a 'Good practice guide' for such placements (see Appendix 1). But in case there should have been any doubts about where ABSWAP stood on the issue the guidelines ended with the unambiguous statement: 'Transracial-placements pose the most dangerous threat to the harmonious society to which we aspire . . . It is in essence "internal colonialism" and a new form of slave trade but this time only black children are used. Measures should be taken to make this practice unnecessary thereby terminating this dangerous aspect of current child care policy.'

Further opposition to transracial placement came before the Commons Committee with the evidence of the Commission for Racial Equality. They claimed that 'black families have imposed on them "eurocentric" assumptions of "good parenting" and "proper" family life which are then used to justify separating parents from their children' (see ABSWAP, 1983).

By this stage the argument appeared to be all but over with *New Society* declaring 'Black families for black children has become the rallying cry. The British Agencies for Adoption and Fostering has been won over to the cause.' And the pages of *Adoption and Fostering* carried, on an almost regular basis, accounts of initiatives to recruit substitute families from the minority ethnic groups.

However, at the same time as the theoretical debate was raging, practical steps were being taken to address the more immediate needs of existing transracial families. Parent to Parent Information on Adoption Services made available to all transracial adopters an information and advice pack on parenting children of ethnic minority backgrounds. The materials were well received by both white adopters and black social workers. At the same time a new agency, Parents for Children, specifically oriented to finding homes for children who until then had been difficult to place, was established and it immediately set up a working party charged with the task of finding black parents for black children.

In July 1984 the death of a four-year-old London girl who died as a result of injuries inflicted on her by her father was to have a significant impact on the debate around the issue of transracial placements. Her name was Jasmine Beckford and Jasmine's birth parents were of Afro-Caribbean origin. She was in the care of the London Borough of Brent who, after she had been assaulted by her father when she was eighteen months old, placed her for long-term foster care with a Mr and Mrs Probert. Mrs Probert was white whilst her husband was half-English and half-Asian and they had two black adopted children. At some undetermined stage Brent decided that this placement contravened their policy of placing children only within their own ethnic group and Jasmine was returned to her natural family, only to be tragically killed some months later.

A Panel of Inquiry was established to look into the circumstances of Jasmine's death; they did not dwell on the transracial aspects of the case but they did say that they did not 'support those who wish to place a complete ban on transracial fostering. Such a policy is the antithesis of the flexible approach which we favour' (Beckford Inquiry, 1985). William Ackroyd, the solicitor for the Proberts, writing in the National Foster Care Association's review of the case *In Whose Trust?*, wrote: 'There was no evidence that the issue of racism was properly discussed with the foster parents . . . so that conclusions about their views were inferred by white people who themselves had no particular expertise in this area . . . The family was described as "white orientated" . . . For example an interest in the opera was apparently an indication that a family is "white orientated", disregarding such singers as Grace Bumbry or Jessye Norman.'

'The issues are complex', Ackroyd wrote, 'and there are no easy answers;

in all social work practice any dogmatic rule which is applied to all cases without careful thought is likely to prove dangerous or wrong . . . Thus a direction that black children are to be placed in black families is only operable if careful consideration is given to the culture, lifestyle and child-rearing skills of a particular black family in relation to a particular black child . . . Even the terminology raises difficulties and a simple categorisation of families into black and white is bound to lead to problems' (Ackroyd, 1985).

The issue of the efficacy of transracial fostering was further discussed that year when John Small told the annual meeting of the All London Fostering Group: 'I have no doubt that some white foster parents are racist and don't realise this until they bring a child into a family . . . irrespective of how good you are as a foster parent you cannot protect the child from a society that is basically racist . . . unless you recognise this you are doing a great deal of harm to the children you care for and for yourselves' (Smith, 1984).

However, the other side of the argument was also put to the fosterers when Ermyne Lee-Kin, the founder of the Soul Kids Campaign, told the meeting: 'A rigid response to the child of mixed-race parentage is not on. We need to look at the culture in which the child started . . . We have seen black children who have been brought up by white families and seem to have made the transitions fairly successfully' (Smith, 1984).

At the same time further research was being published that, it was argued, threw doubt on the wisdom of pursuing a same-race policy irrespective of the length of time children were having to wait for permanent placements. Jane Rowe found that of a sample of 37 black and mixed parentage children in long-term foster care 11 were seriously disturbed (quoted in Rowe *et al.*, 1989); whilst Christopher Bagley and Loretta Young had investigated a sample of 30 ethnic minority children who had been transracially adopted and concluded that the children had made excellent adjustments, had good relations with their parents, were racially aware and displayed low levels of black stereotyping (Bagley and Young, 1980).

But if the research was moving in one direction the politics were moving in another. For the debate about transracial adoption and fostering was not taking place in a political vacuum – changes were taking place, particularly in the Labour Party in London, which were having a significant impact on this aspect of social work practice. Traditionally the Labour left had taken little part in local government. It was, according to one of the central characters of London Labour politics at the time, Ken Livingstone, the preserve of 'right-wing white old men'. But in the late seventies and early eighties this began to change and the new Labour left began to take an active interest in local government. Firstly, because in this decade central government, both Labour and Conservative, had begun cutting back on local government expenditure, forcing the left to mobilise to defend local services. Secondly, the national battles the left was fighting in the Labour Party inevitably spilt over into the local arena, with constituency parties demanding a greater say in the choice of local councillors, the writing of local manifestos and the selection of council leaders. Thirdly, with the prospect of gaining power nationally looking increasingly unlikely, local government gave the new Labour activists a chance to put into practice their ideas about workers' control, decentralisation of decision-making, etc. Finally, left wingers found it relatively easy to get selected for council seats because Labour had suffered a series of electoral reversals at local level during the periods of Labour Government in the sixties and seventies which had resulted in a clear-out of many of the old incumbents. Their replacements were described by Patrick Seyd in *The Rise and Fall of the Labour Left* as a newer type of councillor 'with experience of working within community action groups, or working in such local government professions as planning and social work . . . likely to encourage a new style of politics which was more open to community involvement and less likely to encourage professional detachment in local government' (1987, p. 139).

Thus it was that by the early eighties it was no surprise to find in power in London, at the heads of social services committees and in senior positions in social services departments, people who shared a common outlook on the placement of black and mixed parentage children in substitute white families. Two such were Janet Boetang, who chaired Lambeth's Social Services Committee, and Patrick Kodikara, who not only chaired the Hackney committee but in 1984 became Director of Social Services for nearby Camden.

In Hackney, working alongside both John Small and David Divine, Kodikara's department was responsible for the clearest statement yet against transracial placements. It was presented in 1985 in the 'Draft manual for adoption and permanent parenting procedures' by Hackney Social Services Department. It stated unequivocally: 'a child in the care of the London Borough of Hackney *must* be placed in a family which reflects its own racial and ethnic background'. And within a year of taking up his post as Director of Social Services in Camden Kodikara succeeded in implementing a similar policy there. Their policy document said: ' . . . as from 1st October 1985 the Directorate will only place children in its care with families that match their racial and ethnic origins'.

By 1985 other authorities were following similar policies which, either explicitly or implicitly, committed them to ceasing to make any further transracial placements. These authorities included Bradford, Brent, Islington, Lambeth and Wandsworth. Perhaps Wandsworth was the most intriguing case because since 1978 it had been Conservative-controlled. In May 1985 the borough organised a study day on recruiting black families, and their adoption and fostering team told the gathering that they had begun recruiting black families back in 1976 and could now place most black children with the right black family.

However, despite the strategic role of particular councillors it is probably a mistake to see the role of the politicians as anything more than the enablers of a movement in social work practice which was already well under way.

There is no simplistic relationship between the ascendancy of a left Labour regime in a town hall and a subsequent shift in policy on child placement issues. Elected councillors' active powers to change the growing practice of banning transracial placements were limited and there were boroughs which did not fit the apparent pattern. In Wandsworth, for example, the Conservatives, even had they wanted to, were unable to change the pattern of childcare work in their borough; whilst in Brent as late as 1987 the black Labour leader of the council, Merle Amory, was saying in an interview: 'Obviously in a perfect world, we'd find enough black parents for black children who need homes. If not, I believe it's much better to let the children be brought up by white parents – with support from the community – rather than to be kept in care' (Amory, 1987). (Ironically this statement was made at the very time that her Social Services department were doing precisely the opposite.)

By now the argument about the importance of race as a consideration in placement decisions was acknowledged. The newly launched 'Black and In Care' group considered the issue at their launch conference in 1984 and they came out with three recommendations:

1. Young black people should have the choice whether they are to be fostered with black or white foster parents.
2. Black adults should be involved in the fostering and adoption process involving a black child.
3. White people fostering young people should be educated about black culture. (Black and In Care Steering Group, 1985)

However, it was the video they produced the following year that had the most profound reverberations on the fostering and adoption world. It was a powerful quasi-documentary which appeared to demonstrate the failure of transracial placements. A succession of sad and angry black youngsters told their unhappy stories – how they had been moved from placement to placement, how their ethnic identities had been ignored or even derided, and of their pain in trying to come to terms with their blackness. It was undoubtedly a forceful indictment of poor placements and lack of planning. What, however, it was argued at the time it failed to address was the issue of good transracial placements – where children had been taken in by ethnically aware substitute families who had been able to nourish and nurture their ethnicity and identity. To support this argument it was pointed out that the young people in the video were, for the most part, children who had grown up in foster placements or residential care, without being adopted.

In 1985 the debate moved on to the national stage with a full page article in *The Times* on 28 August by Ben Brown, a black social worker at Dr Barnardo's, who had himself been fostered by both black and white families. In the piece he argued that 'white people can be educated to deal with black issues . . . there's no doubt that children flourish in a family home and the issue of black or white is really secondary'. On the other side of the argument John

Small stated that ' . . . black children who cannot be found suitable homes would be better off in residential establishments inside their own community, so that they are not cut off from their roots' (*The Times*, 28 August 1985).

At this stage PPIAS, the organisation of adoptive parents, which now had both black and white members, entered the debate. National Co-ordinator Philly Morrall put a tentative toe into the troubled waters by supporting the drives for more black families but also cautioned her members that 'I have one continuing anxiety and this is that children, black and white, are being allowed to drift without the security of the right family, while policy makers, politicians and social workers sort out their consciences . . . until a policy can be implemented without detriment to the children *now* waiting, then none of us can sit back and feel comfortable' (PPIAS, 1985).

Around the same time, a group of PPIAS members who had completed a racism awareness training weekend together began meeting to discuss the issues. There was, they believed, anecdotal evidence of ethnic minority children languishing in care, as a result of the growing practice of not placing transracially. Indeed several local authorities were claiming that they now had no trouble in finding matching families for their children, but the indications from childcare workers on the ground were pointing in another direction. The PPIAS parents made links with a number of black and white social workers, black adults who had been transracially fostered or adopted, and other experts in the childcare field including MP Joan Lestor, who was to become Labour's first Spokeswoman on Children. In June 1986 the group launched itself into the debate as 'CHILDREN FIRST in Transracial Fostering and Adoption'.

The Children First launch statement (see Appendix 2) sought to tread a fine line in supporting the principle of same-race placements, encouraging local authorities to increase their recruitment efforts to achieve more staff and prospective adopters from the ethnic minorities, but also in putting emphasis on speedy decisions being made to place children permanently, and if this meant placing them transracially, then so be it. Their launch statement concluded: 'There are numerous examples of successful transracial placements which have produced happy, well-adjusted and racially aware people. We therefore are fundamentally opposed to any policy which either implicitly or explicitly results in the implementation of bans on transracial placement.' The launch was greeted with hostility by the main adoption umbrella organisation, British Agencies for Adoption and Fostering (BAAF). Their management committee declared that the group's launch statement was 'factually incorrect and provocative (as in fact no local authority has imposed a "blanket ban" on transracial placements), inflammatory in its language and provoking polarised views in this complex area of child care policy and social work practice'.

In more measured tones BAAF's official journal *Adoption and Fostering* said: 'The crucial complicating factor overlooked by the campaigners, is that circumstances today are different from what they were 10 years ago. Then not many of us were conscious of the needs of black children in care or the wishes

of the black community . . . Seen in this perspective the campaign is misguided. It could muddle the issues and polarise opinion concerning matters
on which there should be basic agreement' (1986, vol. 10, pp. 2–3). However,
the strongest response came from the Black and In Care Group. In a press
release they accused Children First of being 'racist, naive and arrogant . . . in
a society where racism is rife and dominant, and where white people are the
perpetuators of racism, it is essential for the black child to be placed in a black
family . . . "Black and In Care" feels that these so-called successful cases
(referred to by "Children First") are insignificant in comparison to the vast
majority of cases where transracial placement is disastrous.'

Whilst most of the social work press followed BAAF's lead, support did
come from *Social Services Insight*, the magazine of the directors of social
services, which editorialised that 'Transracial placements are a desirable
alternative provided the potential families are identified carefully, properly
prepared and well supported. . . . In the past the importance of this extra
back-up needed by families of mixed race may not have been fully recognised,
creating unnecessary problems' (*Social Services Insight*, 1986, pp. 2–3).

In 1986, a survey undertaken by the National Foster Care Association
revealed that of 95 agencies they surveyed 23 had specific policies favouring
same-race placements – and three, Brent and Hackney in London and Bradford, had rigid policies which virtually excluded transracial placements
altogether. In the following year BAAF issued its own set of practice notes on
'The placement needs of black children' (see Appendix 3). Unquestionably,
the main thrust of these guidelines was intended to increase the momentum
towards same-race placements, stating that: 'the placement of choice for a
black child is always a black family'. However, they did acknowledge the
continuing need for transracial placements at least for an interim period:
'Although in the immediate future some transracial placements may have to
be made it is essential to recognise that there will inevitably be "gaps" in what
they can offer a black child . . .'

The BAAF practice notes drew heavily on what had become the new
orthodoxies about racism, ethnicity and identity; but just at the time when
they were becoming acceptable to the largely white social work establishment
they were being challenged by various black intellectuals who rejected what
they saw as an over-simplification of highly complex issues. One of these
challenges came from Dr Paul Gilroy whose book *There Ain't No Black in the
Union Jack* proved to be highly influential within the field of social theory.
Commenting on John Small's evidence to the House of Commons Social
Services Committee on behalf of ABSWAP, Gilroy observed: 'The tone of
ABSWAP and Small's work suggests that anyone who concedes that a black
child may be better off in a white household than in a local authority home,
is advocating the kidnapping of young blacks and their compulsory rearing by
whites. Theirs is the voice of a black nationalism which . . . is sadly misplaced

in this country where the black population is too small, too diverse and too fragmented to be conceptualised as a single cohesive nation' (Gilroy, 1987a).

At the same time as these concerns were growing amongst some social theorists a movement in the opposite direction was taking place on the ground, as more and more local authorities moved away from making transracial placements. The London borough of Hammersmith and Fulham, for example, adopted guidelines in 1988 which stated that: 'A same-race placement is the starting point from which other issues about the child's needs are then considered.' And Liverpool committed itself to removing ethnic minority children from white foster homes. 'Under no circumstances', the 1988 policy said, 'should the black child be allowed to remain so placed (in a white home) by default, on a medium or longer-term basis.' These views were strongly endorsed by the British Association of Social Workers, who in 1988 published their guide on the placement needs of black children (see Appendix 4). They stated: 'In order for a black child to develop a positive black identity and the skills to enable him or her to combat the effects of racism (s)he must grow up in an environment where it is thoroughly understood exactly what the child will have to face and where the child is enabled to develop that positive identity and the necessary skills.' BASW went on to state that 'No child should be placed in a permanent transcultural family placement.'

All these policy initiatives were being formulated on the assumption that *all* the research into this issue pointed to the damaging effects of transracial placements. However, psychologist Barry Richards, writing in *Adoption and Fostering*, had an alternative interpretation: he described the trend towards bans on transracial placements as 'based on . . . the result of a surprising confluence between the professional ambitions of social work and the political ambitions of certain tendencies within black activism. Guilt is another important element, the guilt of comfortable and usually white social workers about the control they may exercise over the lives of poor and often black clients' (Richards, 1987). Perhaps the most significant criticism of the theories behind the bans came in the pages of *New Community*, the official journal of the Commission for Racial Equality (see Chapter 5, this volume). There Professor Barbara Tizard, Director of the Thomas Coram Research Unit, and Dr Ann Phoenix, a psychologist also based at the unit, undertook a thorough review of all the research that had been published on this issue. Their conclusions were unambiguous: 'One may or may not agree with the political objections to transracial adoption,' they wrote, 'and we would certainly agree that more black people should be encouraged and helped to come forward as adoptive and foster parents. But we would contend that the psychological objections to transracial adoption are not well-grounded in either empirical data or theory' (Tizard and Phoenix, 1989).

The debate about transracial placements heightened in 1989. First came the publication of the Government's new Children Bill. Clause 18 gave the first legislative recognition to the principle that 'due consideration should be given to the child's religious persuasion, racial origin and cultural background'. Speaking during the Committee Stage of the Bill, in reply to Joan Lestor MP, who had raised the question of local authorities' taking black foster children away from their white families purely on the grounds of race, the then Health Minister David Mellor said: 'There is a difference between "due consideration" and a fixed rule which, as demonstrated by the honourable Lady and the mishaps of some local authorities, can be damaging to both children and to society' (*Hansard*, 1989).

Children First presented Mr Mellor with what they believed to be convincing evidence on two central points. Firstly, they claimed that despite denials to the contrary they had evidence that the bans on transracial placements did in fact exist and, more seriously, that these bans were having the effect of increasing the length of time that ethnic minority children were having to wait in care before being placed with new families. The wheel had turned full circle, they argued, black children were once again 'hard-to-place' (see Appendix 6). Their evidence was based on research undertaken by Hilary Chambers, one of the founders of PPIAS and a supporter of Children First. She had been monitoring the pages of BAAF's photo-listings album 'Be My Parent' (see Chambers, 1989). This album was used by adoption agencies who, on payment of a fee, were able to advertise their 'hard-to-place' children – although because of the time and cost involved agencies did not usually refer children to 'Be My Parent' until they had exhausted their local resources.

Chambers began monitoring the pages of 'Be My Parent' in March 1987 (see Appendix 6). She tracked the progress of all the black and mixed parentage children who were being featured and focused particularly on the healthy black children under five years of age, as there were no corresponding white children in the album since they can quickly be found permanent families through an agency's local pool of waiting adopters. When she began the project, Chambers found that the number of black children under five years with no physical or mental disabilities seeking families through the pages of 'Be My Parent' was 18. Two years later that figure stood at 54, and taking into account older black children and those with handicaps the rise was equally alarming – up from 69 in 1987 to 129 two years later.

However, it was not simply a case of more black and mixed parentage children appearing in the pages of 'Be My Parent'; this could have simply reflected the agencies' greater use of this medium in order to place such children. What was crucial was the fact that the research showed that black children were having to wait longer for a permanent family than their white counterparts. In March 1987 4 healthy, black under-fives had been in the 'Be My Parent' book for 6 months or more. By June 1989 that figure was 55; and of these 17 had been waiting a year or more. In addition to sending the Minister the Chamber's findings Children First was also able to demonstrate to the Minister of Health that BAAF's claims that they themselves did not operate a ban on transracial placements merited close scrutiny.

Over the years Children First Co-ordinator Jane Aldridge had been receiving a stream of complaints from prospective white adopters, telling her that no matter how long a particular child had been waiting in the pages of 'Be My Parent' BAAF was refusing to pass on their interest in that child to the relevant local authority. Aldridge asked 'Be My Parent' editor Steve Hunt if this was in fact the case. He confirmed that this was so but was at the request of the agencies placing the children and not because of BAAF policy. However, Children First claimed that in fact BAAF was actually refusing to accept entries for 'Be My Parent' unless agencies specified that the child required at least one ethnically matching parent.

In August 1989 the issue of transracial placements came back into the headlines when a High Court Judge ruled in support of a decision by London Borough of Croydon to remove from a white fosterer the seventeen-month-old mixed parentage child she had been caring for since the age of six days and was seeking to adopt. What attracted most attention was the judge's support for Croydon's claim that the child's ethnic needs were a legitimate factor in the authority's decision – although, as he and the authority maintained, this was far from being the only factor involved. The actual circumstances of the case are secondary to the national attention it attracted. For although eventually the Appeal Court upheld the High Court's decision Minister of Health David Mellor decided that a ministerial inquiry into transracial placements would be appropriate.

He outlined his anxieties to the annual conference of the Directors of Social Services: 'I would urge you all to ask yourselves, in making decisions about the adoption and fostering of children from ethnic minorities, are you always acting in the best interests of the child?' He went on to observe that

> the department's guidelines are quite clear, that it will usually be in the best interests of a child to be placed with parents of the same ethnic origin. But this is just one of a number of points to be borne in mind. It must not become a rigid and dogmatic rule which resists common sense . . . Our considerations of these matters continue, and have extended to some voluntary agencies and umbrella organisations who seem reluctant to move away from an over-prescriptive and dogmatic approach. (BBC radio transcript, 22 September 1989)

And Mr Mellor left journalists attending the conference in no doubt that this last reference was to BAAF. Chris Hammond, BAAF's Director, was clearly concerned at this implied threat to her organisation. She said in a press release that she thought Mr Mellor had been 'misinformed' about BAAF's actual position. She strongly denied that BAAF operated any bans on transracial placements and went as far as to say that 'transracial placement may well continue to be the most appropriate option for some children'.

In January 1990 the Commission for Racial Equality published its guidelines (see Appendix 7). And whilst they stressed the need to find ethnic minority parents matching as closely as possible those of any prospective child, they did recognise that in some circumstances transracial placements would still be necessary. A month later the Government published the first fruits of its inquiry into the issue when it sent out a letter of guidance to directors of social services. Under the heading 'Issues of race and culture in the family placement of children' (see Appendix 8), the Chief Inspector of the Social Services Inspectorate stated the Government's position. Whilst emphasising the need for sensitive and efficient planning and recruitment that would result in suitable ethnically matching placements being available for children on reception into care, the guidelines state: ' . . . there may be circumstances in which placement with a family of different ethnic origin is the best choice for a particular child. In other cases such a placement may be the best available choice.'

On the vexed question of children being removed from successful foster placements simply because they were of a different ethnic origin from their foster parents, the guidelines were quite specific: 'Children should not be removed from placements which are otherwise satisfactory solely because the ethnic origin of the foster parents does not accord with the requirements of the general policies.' Finally, the guidelines called for the introduction of planning with time limits for each child in care. 'A child must not be left indefinitely in an interim placement,' the guidelines stated, 'or even worse, a succession of interim placements, while a permanent placement is sought. The plan for the child must include limits of time . . . within which progress towards objectives is reviewed and the plan revised where necessary.' So after a battle that raged for the best part of 10 years the Government had finally intervened with a clear statement of what it regarded as good practice – ethnic matching was to be encouraged but flexibility and the best interests of the individual children were to remain paramount. But the question remained as to how these guidelines would be implemented.

Meanwhile, stories about transracial adoption 'scandals' continued to surface in the national press. In 1990 the Labour council in Liverpool was in the spotlight when it decided to review the placement of a child in its care who had been living with a white foster family for a year. Both the foster family and the birth mother wanted the child to be adopted by the foster parents but the city council indicated to the birth mother that they were considering placing the child with a black or mixed-race family because, although the child looked white and had a white mother and father, they considered her mixed-race because she had had one black great-grandfather. However, after solicitors acting for the natural mother threatened the council with a judicial review the council allowed the child to stay with the foster family. A spokesperson for the council was quoted as saying: 'We have no policy as such on these matters but wherever possible we like to place children of mixed race with families of a similar background. At the end of the day we must take into account what is best for the child' (quoted in *The Times*, 17 March 1990).

Transracial adoption was clearly an issue that was not going to go away. The publication of the Chief Inspector's Guidelines in 1990 was not the Government's only intervention into the argument. For most of the previous year there had been detailed debate in Parliament about the new Children Act (which, in fact, did not become law until November 1991). The Act covered the whole area of the law as it affected children – this included children in care, child protection, residential care, childminding, fostering and adoption. Its main purpose, as far as adoption was concerned, was to tidy up the 1976 Adoption Act. It introduced 37 detailed amendments, perhaps the most significant being those that made it easier for adoptive children to trace their natural parents.

It did not directly address the issue of transracial adoption, but supporters and opponents alike were both able to point to parts of the proposed legislation as evidence of Government support for their position. Supporters were delighted that the Act's very opening section addressed the issue of the importance of acting quickly to provide permanent solutions for children in care. It said: 'In any proceedings in which any question with respect to the upbringing of a child arises, the court shall have regard to the general principle that any delay in determining the question is likely to prejudice the welfare of the child' (Children Act 1989, Part I Section 1 para. 2). And it went on to instruct the court to 'have regard in particular to . . . the likely effect on him (the child-in-care) of any change in his circumstances' (Children Act 1989, Part I Section 1 para. 3c).

However, opponents of transracial placements claimed that the section of the Act which instructed local authorities 'before making any decision with respect to a child whom they are looking after, or are proposing to look after . . . shall give due consideration . . . to the child's religious persuasion, racial origin and cultural and linguistic background' (Part III Section 2 para. 5c) represented legal backing for the notion of 'same-race placements'. But neither group could claim that the 1989 Children Act, nor the Chief Inspector's Guidelines, represented anything like a definitive Government statement on the issue of transracial placements. Yet those wheels were turning and in September 1990 the Government announced that since it was almost twenty years since the last review of adoption procedures, and because adoption practice and trends had changed so significantly – fewer babies being adopted but more children who were older and/or had special needs – they were undertaking a major review.

In fact the Government had begun considering how to reform the law relating to adoption as far back as July 1989 when it had set up an interdepartmental working group. A year later this group issued a series of consultation papers; these included a review of the research relating to adoption written by June Thorburn. In her paper Thorburn came to no firm conclusions, but in reviewing the literature about children from ethnic minority backgrounds noted: 'No large scale research studies support the fears of black social

workers about the dangers of trans-racial placements' (1990, p. 55). One of
the other consultation papers issued was on the subject of inter-country
adoption, an issue around which there was growing controversy, and which
had been one of the other factors which had spurred the Government to set
up the Review in the first place. Inter-country adoptions had been taking place
for some time but became a major issue following the collapse of Communism
in Eastern Europe and the discovery that in Romania (and to a lesser extent in
other countries of Eastern Europe) there were thousands of orphaned children
living in miserable circumstances, and apparently available for adoption by
families living in the West.

There was a rush of would-be adoptive parents to Romania, and in the chaos
which followed the downfall of former dictator Nicolae Ceaucescu it was not
difficult to obtain a child, sometimes more than one, and bring him or her back
to Britain without undergoing any of the normal procedures. One of the
problems that couples intent on adopting abroad had always encountered,
and which was intensified by the speed of events in Romania, was the
reluctance of local authorities in Britain to undertake home studies for such
couples and thus provide them with the clearance that most of the countries
where the children were coming from required. Local authorities gave many
reasons why such studies were problematic, most notably that central
government's cuts in their operating budgets did not equip them with
sufficient staff to enable them to undertake their basic statutory duties, let
alone additional work. However, it was also the case that many local authority
social services departments, following the lead of BAAF, were opposed to
inter-country adoptions on principle, partly because they represented another
form of transracial placements.

In October 1992, at the conclusion of the consultation process, the
Government published its initial response – a Green Paper entitled *Review of
Adoption Law* (Health Department, 1992). Noticeable by its absence was any
detailed reference to the issue of transracial placements. The Green Paper did
recognise the increasing emphasis, in adoption practice, on 'the importance
of a child's needs arising from racial and cultural background and the need to
seek adoptive families from ethnic minority groups', and it pointed out that
under the Children Act 1989 'services should meet each child's identified
needs and be appropriate to the child's race, culture, religion and language'
(paras 1.4, 1.5). The Green Paper went on to stress the need to recruit potential
adoptive parents from as wide a background as possible, to reflect the fact that
the children in need of adoption were also coming from as many different
backgrounds themselves and to this effect it recommended 'that agencies
should not be allowed to operate absolute rules governing people's eligibility
for consideration as adopters' (para. 26.4). In the public debate that followed
this was taken to be a reference to not excluding would-be adopters on the
basis of their age or sexuality. However, it also applied to those white

couples – an increasing number – who had already adopted a child from an ethnic minority background but were not being accepted as would-be adopters for a second child by some local authorities, on the grounds that they should never have been allowed to adopt a non-white child in the first place, and hence now constituted an 'unacceptable' mixed-race family.

The Green Paper also recommended, however, placing a new requirement on adoption agencies 'to give due consideration to such wishes and feelings of the child . . . as they are able to ascertain, and to the child's religious persuasion, racial origin and cultural and linguistic background' (para. 27.2, sub-section ii). So the argument remained finely balanced.

A Green Paper is a consultation document, and is usually followed by a White Paper which sets out the Government's legislative intentions. But between publication of the Green Paper in 1992 and the White Paper a year later, the issue of transracial adoption hit the headlines again in a way which many have subsequently been seen as having had a significant impact on the Government's thinking. In July 1993 Conservative-controlled Norfolk County Council found itself accused of practising what was characterised as the 'alien' American import of 'political correctness' – a particular target of the Conservative Government at the time, which was on the brink of launching its ill-fated 'back to basics' public and private morality campaign. 'Political correctness' was the phrase given to what some claimed was the over-zealous pursuit of notions of equality in word, thought and deed, in areas such as gender, ethnicity and disability by progressive-minded teachers, social workers and other professionals.

Norfolk became involved in the issue when the council's adoption panel told a mixed-race couple, Jim and Roma Lawrence, that they were 'too racially naive' to adopt a mixed-race child after they had said that they had 'not experienced any racism' since living in Norfolk. Mrs Lawrence was quoted as saying:

It is stupid to say I know nothing about race. I was born in Guyana and grew up in Brixton, which is a multiracial area. I did suffer a small amount of verbal abuse when I was at school, but I simply have not had any problems in the 12 years we have lived in Norfolk. The social workers seemed to think it was impossible for me not to be suffering some form of discrimination, so they have decided I am ignorant of the issue. (Quoted in *The Times*, 9 July 1993)

Geoff Gildersleeve, the council's Assistant Social Services Director, said in reply: 'Any coloured or mixed race child brought into a Norfolk family could stand out even more in the crowd because it is not a heavily multiracial county. We try to make sure parents are aware of the problems children will face' (Quoted in *The Times*, 9 July 1993).

The case attracted widespread attention. John Bowis, a minister at the Department of Health, called for a full report from Norfolk; and Health Secretary Virginia Bottomley accused some social workers of 'silliness'. She said she was 'completely fed up with political correctness overriding children's needs', and went on to say: 'We want to cut out the political correctness and put back the common sense; everyone involved in childcare must be reminded that the child comes first, not the ideology' (quoted in *The Times*, 13 July 1993). *The Times* devoted one of its famous 'thundering' editorials to the issue. 'The Lawrences' loss of the chance to adopt is a tragedy for them and for any child who might have had the benefit of all that they had to offer', it said on 10 July. 'The health minister, John Bowis, is right to demand a report on the affair. The government's expected White Paper on adoption must ensure that the real needs of adoptive children and the happiness of prospective parents are not subject to fashionable political prejudice', the paper demanded.

And *The Times* was not to be disappointed, for 4 months later the Government published its 'post-Norfolk' White Paper on adoption. It took observers by surprise. It was very brief but in launching it the Health Secretary, Virginia Bottomley, announced that she was not intending to follow it up immediately with any new Act. It was however, as far as the issue of transracial placements was concerned, unambiguous – which, given the Green Paper's almost total silence on the issue a year earlier, was particularly surprising. Any doubts that might have been created by some interpretations of the Chief Inspector's Guidelines or the Children Act were banished. According to the White Paper ethnicity was important and should be taken into account, *but* should never be the only consideration; which, according to some observers, had been the case in Norfolk.

An issue such as transracial adoption is in constant flux; its history has no 'end'. However, there are watersheds – defining moments – which leave no doubt as to what the current situation, in terms of policy if not practice, might be. The White Paper was one such moment and hence it is appropriate to end this particular history by quoting in full its relevant sections (4.31–4.34):

> The 1976 Act contains no reference to questions of ethnicity or culture though in recent years authorities and agencies have usually taken them into account. The Government believes it right to consider these factors alongside others in matching children and parents and will introduce a broad requirement to this effect in line with what is now in the Children Act.
>
> However, in some cases it is clear that those assessing parents may have given these factors an unjustifiably decisive influence and failed to make a balanced overall judgement of the parents' suitability. The Chief Social

Services Inspector has emphasised that ethnicity and culture are amongst the issues to be considered but they should not necessarily be more influential than any other.

There is no conclusive research which justifies isolating such questions from other matters needing assessment; or which supports the proposition that children adopted by people of a different ethnic group will necessarily encounter problems of identity or prejudice later in life.

On these, as in all other matters, any preferences expressed by the birth parents or ascertainable from the child should be given weight alongside others in an assessment that covers all his characteristics, circumstances and needs. In assessing prospective parents, what should weigh most heavily is the judgement made of their capacity to help and support the child through all the challenges he or she will face in life and not just any risk of difficulty attributable to ethnic background.

BIBLIOGRAPHY

Ackroyd, W. (1985) 'Beckford: a disappointing report which emphasises the isolation of foster parents', in Parker *et al.*, pp. 25-33.

Amory, M. (1987) 'Interview', in *Labour Party News*, Jan. /Feb.

ABSWAP (1983) 'Black Children in Care'. Association of Black Social Workers and Allied Professionals Evidence to the House of Commons Social Services Committee, London.

Bagley, C. and Young, L. (1980) 'The long-term adjustment and identity of a sample of inter-country adopted children', *International Social Work* 23(3): 16-22.

Beckford Inquiry (1985) *A Child in Trust: The Report of the Panel of Inquiry into the Circumstances Surrounding the Death of Jasmine Beckford*. London Borough of Brent.

Benet, M. (1976) *The Character of Adoption*. London: Jonathan Cape.

Black and In Care Steering Group (1985) *Black and In Care: Conference Report*. London: Children's Legal Centre.

British Agencies for Adoption and Fostering Management Committee (1986) 'BAAF Criticises Children First Campaign', *BAAF News*, July/Aug.

British Agencies for Adoption and Fostering (1987) *The Placement Needs of Black Children*. London: BAAF.

British Association of Social Workers (1988) *Practice Guide for Social Workers on the Placement of Black Children in Care*. Birmingham: BASW.

Brunton, L. and Welch, M. (1983) 'White agency, black community', *Adoption and Fostering* 7(2): 35-9.

Camden Social Services Department (1985) 'A review of the practice of the reception of children into care and their placement in foster and adoptive homes'. Unpublished.

Carmichael, S. (1968) 'Black power', in Cooper, D., ed. (1968) *The Dialectics of Liberation*. Harmondsworth: Penguin.

Carvel, J. (1984) *Citizen Ken*. London: Chatto & Windus.

Chambers, H. (1989) 'Cutting through the dogma', *Social Work Today*, 5 Oct.

Cheetham, J. (1972) *Social Work with Immigrants*. London: Routledge & Kegan Paul.

Chestang, L. (1972) 'The dilemma of biracial adoption', *Social Work* (USA), May.

Children First (1986) *Where We Stand: Launch Statement*. London: Children First in Transracial Fostering and Adoption.

Children First (1990) *Transracial Adoption: The Issues*. London: Children First in Transracial Fostering and Adoption.

Chimezie, A. (1975) 'Transracial adoption of black children', *Social Work* (USA), July.

Commission for Racial Equality (1989) *Racial Equality in Social Services Departments*. London: CRE.

Commission for Racial Equality (1990) *Adopting a Better Policy: Adoption and Fostering of Ethnic Minority Children*. London: CRE.

Dale, D. (1987) *Denying Homes to Black Children*. London: Social Affairs Unit.

Ellison, M. (1958) *The Adopted Child*. London: Victor Gollancz.

Feigelman, W. and Silverman, A. (1984) 'The long-term effects of transracial adoption', *Social Services Review* (USA), Dec.

Fitzgerald, J. (1981) 'Black parents for black children', *Adoption and Fostering* 5(10): 10–11.

Francis, P. (1987) 'A case of black and white: black children in care'. Leeds Polytechnic, CQSW dissertation.

George, V. (1970) *Foster Care Theory and Practice*. London: Routledge & Kegan Paul.

Gill, O. and Jackson, B. (1982) 'Transracial adoption in Britain', *Adoption and Fostering* 6(3): 30–5.

Gill, O. and Jackson, B. (1983) *Adoption and Race: Black, Asian and Mixed Race Children in White Families*. London: Batsford/British Agencies for Adoption and Fostering.

Gilroy, P. (1987a) *There Ain't No Black in the Union Jack*. London: Hutchinson.

Gilroy, P. (1987b) *Problems in Anti-Racist Strategy*. London: Runnymede Trust.

Gilroy, P. (1993) *The Black Atlantic: Modernity and Double Consciousness*. London: Verso.

Goring, S. (1988) *Issues Surrounding Same Race Fostering Policies*. BA dissertation.

Hammersmith and Fulham Social Services (1988) 'The placement of black children in care policy'. Unpublished.

Hansard (1989) *Parliamentary Debate: Children Bill [Lords] Standing Committee B 16 May 1989*. London: Her Majesty's Stationery Office.

Harris, K. (1985) *Transracial Adoption: A Bibliography*. London British Agencies for Adoption and Fostering.

Hayes, M. (1987) 'Placing black children', *Adoption and Fostering* 11(3): 14-16.

Hayes, M. (1989) 'When racial origin causes friction', *Social Work Today*, 21 Sept.

Health Department (1990) 'Issue of race and culture in the family placement of children'. London: Social Services Inspectorate. Unpublished.

Health Department (1992) *Review of Adoption Law: A Consultation Document* (Green Paper), London, October 1992.

Health Department (1993) *Adoption: The Future* (White Paper). Presented to Parliament, November 1993.

Hiro, D. (1992) *Black British, White British. A History of Race Relations in Britain*. London: Paladin.

Hodgkinson, L. (1985) 'The black and white of fostering', *The Times*, 28 Aug.

Home Office Advisory Council on Child Care (1970) *A Guide to Adoption Practice*. London: Her Majesty's Stationery Office.

Home Office Departmental Committee on Adoption (1972) *Report of the Departmental Committee on the Adoption of Children*. London: Her Majesty's Stationery Office.

Humberside Social Services Department (1987) 'Adoption policy on the placement of black and mixed parentage children'. Unpublished.

James, M. (1981) 'Finding the families', *Adoption and Fostering* 5(1): 11-16.

Kareh, D. (1970) *Adoption and the Coloured Child*. London: Epworth Press.

Ladner, J. (1978) *Mixed Families: Adopting across Racial Boundaries*. New York: Anchor Books/Doubleday.

Lansley, S., Goss, S. and Wolmar, C. (1989) *Councils in Conflict: The Rise and Fall of the Municipal Left*. London: Macmillan.

Laurance, J. (1983) 'Should white families adopt black children?', *New Society*, 30 June.

Laurance, J. (1984) 'Breaking the mould: profile of Patrick Kodikara', *New Society*, 1 Nov.

Layton-Henry, Z. (1984) *The Politics of Race in Britain*. London: George Allen & Unwin.

Liverpool City Social Services Department (1988) 'Anti-racism family placement policy'. Unpublished.

MacLachlan, R. (1987) 'Divine intervention: profile of David Divine', *Social Work Today*, 5 Feb.

Mullender, A. and Miller, D. (1985) 'The ebony group: black children in white foster homes', *Adoption and Fostering* 9(1).

Ouseley, H. (1984) 'Local authority race initiatives', in Boddy, M. and Fudge, C., eds *Local Socialism?* London: Macmillan.

Page, R. and Clark, G., eds (1977) *Who Cares? Young People in Care Speak Out*. London: National Children's Bureau.

Parker, R. *et al.* (1988) *In Whose Trust: The Jasmine Beckford Inquiry and its Lessons for Foster Care*. London: National Foster Care Association.

Pennie, P. and Williams, W. (1987) 'Black children need the richness of black family life', *Social Work Today*, 2 Feb.

Post-Adoption Centre (1990) *Preparing People to Adopt Babies and Young Children*. London: Post-Adoption Centre.

PPIAS (1985) 'Families for black children: where do we stand?', *PPIAS Newsletter* (Parent to Parent Information on Adoption Services). Autumn.

PPIAS (1988) *Information and Resources for Mixed Race Families*. (Parent to Parent Information on Adoption Services.)

PPIAS (1989) 'Families for black children and the transracial adoption debate: Where does PPIAS stand – again?', *PPIAS Newsletter* (Parent to Parent Information on Adoption Services). Autumn.

Prescod, C. (1987) 'The task for white professionals', *Adoption and Fostering* 11(3): 7–10.

Rajdev, S. (1987) *Mix and Match: The Issues of Transracial Adoption*. Leeds: Leeds Polytechnic Research Reports.

Ramdin, R. (1987) *The Making of the Black Working Class in Britain*. Aldershot: Wildwood House.

Raynor, L. (1986) 'Agency adoptions of non-white children in the United Kingdom: a quantitative study', *Race* 10(2): 153–62.

Raynor, L. (1970) *Adoption of Non-White Children*. London.

Raynor, L. (1980) *The Adopted Child Comes of Age*. London: George Allen & Unwin.

Reeves, F. (1983) *British Racial Discourse*. Cambridge: Cambridge University Press.

Richards, B. (1987) 'Family, race and identity', *Adoption and Fostering* 11(3): 14–16.

Rowe, J. and Lambert, L. (1973) *Children Who Wait*. London: Association of British Adoption Agencies.

Rowe, J., Hundleby, M. and Garnett, L. (1989) *Child Care Now: A Survey of Placement Patterns*. London: British Agencies for Adoption and Fostering.

Runnymede Trust and the Radical Statistics Group (1980) *Britain's Black Population*. London: Heinemann Educational.

Schroeder, H. and Lightfoot, D. (1983) 'Finding black families', *Adoption and Fostering* 7(1): 18–21.

Seyd, P. (1987) *The Rise and Fall of the Labour Left*. London: Macmillan Education.

Silverman, A. and Feigelman, W. (1977) 'Some factors affecting the adoption of minority children', *Social Casework* (USA), Nov.

Simon, R. and Altstein, H. (1977) *Transracial Adoption*. London: John Wiley.

Simon, R. and Alstein, H. (1981) *Transracial Adoption: A Follow-Up*. Lexington, MA: Lexington Books.

Simon, R. and Alstein, H. (1987) *Transracial Adoptees and their Families*. New York: Praeger

Sivanandan, A. (1986) *From Resistance to Rebellion*. London: Institute for Race Relations.

Small, J. (1982) 'New black families', *Adoption and Fostering* 6(3): 35-9.

Small, J. (1983) 'Black children in care: evidence to the House of Commons Select Committee on Social Services'. London: Association of Black Social Workers and Allied Professionals.

Small, J. (1984) 'The crisis in adoption', *International Journal of Psychiatry*, Spring, pp. 129-42.

Small, J. (1986) 'Transracial placements: conflicts and contradictions', in Ahmed, S., Cheetham, J. and Small, J. (1986) *Social Work and Black Children and their Families*. London: Batsford/British Agencies for Adoption and Fostering.

Smith, R. (1984) 'You have been brainwashed, John Small tells foster parents', *Foster Care*, Oct.

Social Services Insight (1986) 'Real children mean more than academic arguments', *Social Services Insight*, 12-19 July.

Soul Kids Steering Group (1977) *The Soul Kids Campaign*. London: Association of British Adoption Agencies.

Swanton, J. (1987) 'Transracial adoption: the politics behind the debate'. Birmingham Polytechnic, LlB dissertation.

Thorburn, J. (1990) *Inter-Departmental Review of Adoption Law. Background Paper no. 2: Review of Research Relating to Adoption*. London: Department of Health, Sept.

Tizard, B. (1977) *Adoption: A Second Chance*. London: Open Books.

Tizard, B. and Phoenix, A. (1989) 'Black identity and transracial adoption', *New Community*, Apr. London: Commission for Racial Equality.

Tonkin, B. (1987) 'A problem of identity: profile of Paul Gilroy', *Community Care*, 18 June.

Toynbee, P. (1986) 'Mix and match', *The Guardian*. June.

Wandsworth Social Services Department (1985) 'Conclusions from our experience: study day on recruiting black families'. Unpublished.

Weise, J. (1988) *Transracial Adoption*. Norwich: University of East Anglia/ *Social Work Today*.

White, H. (1985) *Black Children, White Adopters*. Norwich: University of East Anglia/*Social Work Today*.

Wilson, A. (1987) *Mixed Race Children*. London: George Allen & Unwin.

Zacune, C. (1988) 'Transracial adoption and social policy', University of Manchester, BA dissertation.

Zacune, C. (1989) 'Alternative families for black children and social practice'. University of Keele, CQSW dissertation.

3   Yesterday's Words, Tomorrow's World: from the Racialisation of Adoption to the Politics of Difference

PHIL COHEN

PROLOGUE: THE GENEALOGY OF DIFFERENCE

The following story is told about the great Yoruba Trickster God, Esu Elegba.

> There were once two friends who were thwarted in their friendship by Esu. They took vows of eternal friendship to one another, but neither took Esu into consideration. Esu took note of their actions and decided to do something to teach them a lesson. When the time was ripe, Esu decided to put their friendship to his own little test. One day the two friends were out in the fields tilling their land. One was hoeing on the right side and the other was clearing bushes on the left. Esu came by on a horse, riding between the two men.
>
> Later the two men took a break for lunch under the cool shade of the trees: said one man, 'Did you see the man with a white cap who greeted us while we were working? He was very pleasant, wasn't he?'
>
> 'Yes he was charming, but it was a man in a black cap I recall, not a white one.'
>
> 'It was a white cap. The man was riding a magnificent grey horse.'
>
> 'Then it must be the same man. I tell you his cap was dark, black.'
>
> 'You must be tired or blinded by the hot rays of the sun to take a white cap for a black one.'
>
> 'I tell you it was a black cap and I am not mistaken. I remember him distinctly.'
>
> The two friends fell to fighting. The neighbours came running but the fight was so intense that the neighbours could not stop it. In the midst of this uproar Esu returned looking very calm and pretending not to know what was going on.
>
> 'What is the cause of all the hullabaloo?', he demanded sternly.
>
> 'Two close friends are fighting', was the answer. 'They seem intent on killing each other and neither would stop or tell us the reason for the fight. Please do something before they destroy each other.'

Esu promptly stopped the fight. 'Why do you two lifelong friends make a public spectacle of yourselves in this manner?'

'A man rode through the farm, greeting us as he went by', said the first friend. 'He was wearing a black cap, but my friend tells me it was a white cap and that I must have been tired or blind or both.'

The second friend insisted that the man had been wearing a white cap. One of them must be mistaken, but it was not he.

'Both of you are right', said Esu.

'How can that be?'

'I am the man who paid the visit over which you now quarrel, and here is the cap that caused all the argument.' Esu put his hand in his pocket and brought out the special cap which he had made for his trick.

'As you can see one side is white and the other black. You each saw one side and therefore are right about what you saw. Are you not the two friends who made vows of friendship? When you vowed to be friends always, to be faithful and true to each other, did you reckon with Esu? Do you know that anyone who does not put Esu first in all things has only themselves to blame if things go wrong?'

And so it is said:

Esu do not undo me
Do not falsify the words of my mouth,
Do not misguide the movements of my feet
You who transform yesterday's words
Into tomorrow's new sayings
Do not undo me.

This story (see Gates, 1988) was irresistibly called to mind as I read through the statements of the main protagonists in the debate on transracial adoption. The intense and often bitter tenor of the argument had the feel, at times, of a family quarrel, or a dispute between close neighbours. It struck me that Esu's parable contains a lesson which we continually need to relearn and adapt to changing circumstances. It seems especially apposite to the 'black and white' terms in which the issue of race and adoptive identity has been posed in recent times. The story dramatises the fact that we fall into error (and conflict) when we claim to have a monopoloy of truth, or assume some absolute moral standpoint from which it can be pronounced. It is because they both think that the hat must *either* be white or black, that there is only one possible 'side' to what something can mean, that the two friends fall out.

What they forget is the principle of indeterminacy embodied by Esu. The trickster, who is often portrayed as having two mouths, is telling us that everything has *more* than two sides to it, but also that the truth is not guaranteed by adopting some superior 'third' position. Rather it consists in recognising that meanings are produced precisely through the interplay of oppositions, and hence are not fixed or unequivocal but always subject to negotiation and revision. Orthodoxies and fundamentalisms of every kind destroy the truth in the very moment they lay claim to possess it. The prayer to Esu begs him not to push this indeterminacy to the point where no one knows where they stand any more but also celebrates the creativity which this process releases, turning dogmatic clichés (yesterday's words) into a language which is capable of embracing the complexities of tomorrow's world.

The relevance of Esu's message, if it is not already apparent in the context which concerns us here, will, I hope, become so in the course of this chapter. I will try to show that the arguments which have been advanced to attack or defend transracial placements share very similar underlying models of adoption, 'race' and identity, even if they invest these terms with diametrically opposed values and meanings. By locating the genealogy of these models in a wider historical perspective, I will try to open up a rather different space of representation for these issues, and one which I hope will help to stimulate a more productive kind of debate.

Some Points of Departure

We could perhaps start by considering the issue of identity and difference. Those who have asserted that 'race' makes a whole world of difference to the making of identity and those who argue that it should be irrelevant have tended to assume that to have a satisfactory identity is to possess a unitary sense of self in which nothing vital is lacking. This 'positive self-image' is supposedly secured through a process of emotional bonding with parental figures; there are certain personal qualities or social characteristics of the parties involved which facilitate or inhibit this process taking place in the context of adoption. The argument then is about the conditions under which 'successful bonding', hence 'positive identities', can be achieved and how far physical and/or sociocultural similarities based on 'race' are salient to the outcome.

If we are to follow in Esu's footsteps we might want to depart from some of the assumptions which underlie this kind of argument. Is it really the case that identities can ever be complete or singular, or that they contain some internal essence which defines them for all time, for example as 'white' or 'black'? The African trickster directs us to a quite different model, one in which subjectivities are not unitary or fixed, but multiple and shifting. This standpoint has been advanced most strongly in the 'post-structuralist' tradition associated with the work of Foucault, Derrida and Lacan. Although these ideas today occupy an increasingly important place in the human sciences, they have not so far penetrated very far into the theoretical discourse of social work in Britain. This remains dominated by a peculiarly Anglo-Saxon mixture of naive empiricism and political rhetoric. What might be gained and lost by a shift in paradigm is beyond the scope of this book, although elsewhere it is a topic which is hotly debated. But there is, in any case, a tradition much closer to the adoption scene which is equally concerned to problematise issues of identity and difference within an account of how human beings come to be 'socialised'.

The object relations school of British psychoanalysis has long been concerned with the way children defend themselves against the painful recognition of their dependence on sources of external nurturance and knowledge,
or the threat of their loss, by constructing narcissistic self-images – images
which allow the child to maintain an ominipotent position, from which
everything is always and already known or possessed, and nothing is lacking.
This is not a purely infantile defence mechanism, something which is
outgrown in all but the most pathological cases. On the contrary, trace
elements of this structure can be found in many social ideologies and cultural
representations. It is there in myths of national or racial origin which
underwrite fantasies of fusion with the lost object by inventing a kind of
umbilical cord connecting people to their 'roots' via real or imagined relations
of kinship with idealised figures which represent an essential authenticity of
origins. All those who lack this privileged genealogical link are then regarded
as entirely worthless and alien beings.

Given the absolute centrality of lack and loss to children who have been
abandoned or rejected by their birth parent, it would hardly be surprising if
many of them developed a strong emotional attachment to personal myths of
origin which function as defence mechanisms in this way. In some cases such
children may imagine that there is a secret principle of consanguinity or
filiation linking them to their adoptive parents or, alternatively, fusing the two
sets of parents into a single composite figure. Or they may construct some
entirely make-believe community of belonging for themselves where they can
continue to 'rule OK', and from which one or other, or both sets of parents,
are excluded. The damaged narcissism of adoptees may therefore lead them
to seek out purified identities, identities from which all 'anxiety of influence'
(Bloom, 1973) has been purged, and which guarantee a sense of omnipotence
untouched by the presence of the 'other'. Racialised identities are one, but
only one, possible model for this process.

Whatever their cultural supports, life story-lines which construct such
'positive self-images' help the child deny the difference which is constitutive
of adoptive identities – the fact that the biological and sociological parents are
not one and the same, that there are usually important inequalities between
birth and adoptive parents, and that one family has been substituted or
exchanged for another through a specific external intervention by the State.
But even and especially, when all that is denied, the irreducible fact of
genealogical difference remains and creates the special conditions under
which issues of adoptive identity have to be negotiated and lived out.

It is not only children who may have a stake in 'fairy-tale' adoptions with
happy endings based on establishing some kind of elective affinity between
all the members of the adoption triangle. In the era of open adoption, social
workers too may be strongly motivated to entertain similar ideas. In an earlier
period story-lines which stressed an apparent symmetry of lacks – childless
parents and parentless children fulfilling each other's emotional needs – may

have worked to conceal an asymmetry in which the birth parents' loss was the adoptive parents' gain. More recently versions of the adoption story which either deny the salience of 'race' as a site of difference, or transform it into the guarantee of bonding between adoptive parent and child, may produce similar effects. In all these cases, the 'fairy-story' may support a collusive denial of genealogical difference.

I say 'may' because we still know very little about the way the official textbook models of adoption are actually communicated and lived out by the people most directly concerned. This is not just a matter of looking at how adoption policies are implemented by particular agencies or interpreted by individual social workers, or how far they are consciously acted upon by parents or children. It concerns the imagery and narratives through which patterns of identification are conveyed or resisted, the subtle structures of feeling and fantasy which are evoked, the strategies of disavowal which may be mobilised. One of the problems with much of the research which is invoked both for and against transracial adoption is that it often rests on rather crude, reductive measurements of attitude and outcome and ignores these 'other scenes' which govern the unofficial (and usually unauthorised) versions of the adoption story.

This leads us to a further set of considerations about how policy issues are contextualised within a particular reading of adoption history. Most authorised accounts tell a story of continuous progress, from the bad old days of the orphanage and foundling hospital to the 'age of enlightenment' represented by current practice. Such 'whig interpretations' repeat at the level of grand narrative the success stories told about individual cases in the idioms of child rescue with their familiar sequence of unhappy beginnings, the struggle to overcome them and the happy ending. Alternatively the narratives may be stories of continuous oppression and resistance, where the heroes are not the child savers but the victims of their misguided philanthropy, whose onward march to justice is inspired by the vision of an altogether different kind of better world. In both cases, however, it becomes rather difficult to account for the discontinuities and contradictions which inevitably comprise the history of both individual adoptees and the institution of adoption itself.

This reading of history has thrown a long shadow over the contemporary debate. The defenders of transracialism often argued for it as an extension of traditional enlightenment ideals which supposedly inform social policy; it was a way of making progress towards greater racial harmony, tolerance and understanding, inspired by universal values of human welfare and charity. Others, no less committed to the ideal of progress, were more embarrassed by what its opponents implied the practice might be continuous with, namely paternalistic racism. They tended to suggest that it was an emergency measure forced upon them by a specific set of circumstances beyond their control: the large number of childless white couples and black children in care, together with the dearth of black families interested in fostering or adopting them.

Demography and market forces are thus made to combine to make a history in which ideology has no place.

In contrast the 'anti' lobby has tended to operate with a conspiracy theory of adoption history in which the ideology of white supremacism is the main driving force. Transracialism is seen as not only continuous with the history of black oppression since the days of slavery, but with a whole range of other racist practices in contemporary white society designed to ensure that black people are kept in their subordinate place. From this vantage point, whatever the context or conjuncture, racism is always the 'same old story'. To end the practice of transracial placement was thus to make a decisive break with the past, to ensure that 'never again' would history repeat itself.

If we try and locate this debate in a rather different model of history, one which is as concerned to trace patterns of disjuncture in the way ideologies are reproduced as to detect patterns of difference in the way identities are made and remade, then we might want to question both these readings, and to suggest alternative points of historical departure for understanding the contemporary debate.

In what follows I have tried to develop three main propositions: Firstly, that the pragmatics of transracial adoption proceed neither from traditional humanistic ideals of welfare nor from tactical expediency. Their conditions of possibility lie in particular discourses of family and childhood, which do indeed articulate adoption practices to certain exclusionary definitions of 'race' and nation. Secondly, that these discourses are not, however, specific to the history of black oppression, nor are they necessarily continuous with other practices of racism experienced by black or white ethnic minorities in Britain today. They developed historically as a means of legitimating the adoption of children from the poorest sections of the white working class into the families of well-to-do middle-class professionals, or their transportation to the colonies. Transclass placements, which continue to be the norm, have always been articulated to discourses of 'race' and nation. It is only recently that black people in Britain have become their main focus. Thirdly, that the rhetorical terms in which transracial placements have been opposed in the 1980s, far from representing a break with the past, have actively reinstated many elements from earlier models of adoption supposedly superseded by more enlightened practices. This 'return of the repressed' may well serve to delegitimate same-race placements unless its special effect is recognised.

ADOPTION AS A CIVILISING MISSION

The adoption agencies which emerged at the high point of Victorian philanthropy were often inspired by evangelical Christianity. This was the case not only of Dr Barnardo's, but the ventures founded by Anne McPherson, William Quarrier and many others. As such, the language and strategies of these early child-savers were heavily influenced by the example of missionary societies which had played such an important role in rationalising the British colonisation of Africa and the Caribbean. But by the 1880s it was the 'dark continents' at home, the slums and rookeries of 'Darkest England' which were a cause for public concern. The social imperialists, in particular, argued that these conditions produced crime, immorality and the breakdown of family life on a scale which threatened the wellbeing of the nation and even the 'future of the imperial race'.

The position of children was seen to be symptomatic of these processes. Rising rates of illegitimacy and child abandonment were hailed as living proof of the degenerative effect of the urban/industrial environment. The theme of child-rescue became quickly associated with images drawn from the civilising mission to natives in the colonies. Destitute children were often referred to as 'street arabs'; they were portrayed as wild, unkempt, in a semi-savage state, as a result of their early privations. For purposes of fund-raising, the child-savers softened the incipient threat of the 'street arab' into the more vulnerable and appealing figure of the 'waif and stray'. The message was clear – with a mixture of Christian charity, quasi-parental discipline and hard work – some at least of these potential delinquents might have their young feet set on the straight and narrow path and grow up into honest citizens, who were some approximation of the godfearing Englishmen and women who had cared for them.

In principle the radicalism of the choice for family adoption, as opposed to continued placement in an orphanage, juvenile reformatory, workhouse or some other institution, lay in its practical stand against the more deterministic theories of child development, which during this period derived largely from the tenets of racial anthropology and psychology. The eugenicists, for example, continually stressed the connection between the health of the family and the nation, and the dangers of what they called 'nomadism' to both. Immigrants, unemployed or casual workers, and abandoned children growing up on the streets were all lumped together as members of the 'dangerous classes' because they were regarded as having no fixed abode, and thus no stake in either family or nation. Special measures were needed to restrict the 'natural promiscuity' of these groups and prevent their rampant reproduction from endangering the health of British racial stock. Juvenile reform institutions aimed to do this by providing a moral regime based on some approximation to the Protestant work ethic, designed to inculcate industrious habits, social deference and sexual restraint in equal measure. In practice children in these 'homes' were prepared for various kinds of unskilled manual labour and domestic service.

Against these views the early advocates of family adoption were often inspired by the belief that just as some colonial populations could be 'civilised' or 'Europeanised', so the children of immigrants and the labouring poor could overcome the deficiencies of their birth, provided they were 'caught' young enough and subjected to the right kind of corrective family influence. In principle (but not, as we will see, always in practice), family placement, regulated by careful agency selection, held the promise of social elevation undreamt of by all but the most aspirant sections of the working class. As sociologists would say today, it was designed to be a form of sponsored social mobility.

At this time the idea that individuals could 'change classes' challenged the still-prevalent model of a society divided into separate estates. Many members of the traditional governing élite still believed that social distinctions and inequalities were innate, and that, no matter what, 'breeding will out'. It is significant that opposition to the Adoption Act of 1926 came largely from members of the House of Lords who felt that by making the adopted child the legal heir of the adopted parents, the very foundations of aristocratic inheritance were being undermined. What price primogeniture as a means of keeping the estate together, or patrimony as a means of ensuring unbroken lines of descent when the eldest child might be adopted, and be of common, even degenerate, stock?

Family adoption was thus initially a strategy of class assimilation, predicated on the ideal type of the Victorian and Edwardian middle-class family, and modelled on forms of colonial paternalism. But it was a case of class mediated by religion. The criteria for selecting both babies and parents were largely denominational. Anglicans, Methodists, Catholics and Jews all sponsored their own adoption societies. As a result the family was seen and judged not as an isolated unit but as part of an imagined community associated with religious faith. This model served a number of purposes. Religious adherence provided a putative link between birth and adoptive parents in a way which might serve to conceal, neutralise or transcend possible discrepancies in social status. Religion was made into an internal guarantee that what was passively inherited from the family of origin might yet be put to good account and provide the foundations for transcending 'deficiencies of birth'. There was a frequent assumption that better-off members of the religious community should support their poorer brethren, and what better and more practical way than by volunteering to bring up their children?

Religious identification had a further and more hidden function in sealing the bond of silence placed over the fact of adoption itself. All that mattered was that the child was being brought up in the faith. Adoption was thus implicitly a strategy for enlarging the population of the faithful, while maintaining a principle of closed reproduction. This was of particular concern to religious and ethnic minorities. The Jewish and Catholic societies were largely formed out of a concern that children should not be 'lost' through adoption to other religious cultures. Although there was little opposition to outsiders marrying into the faith (as long as the children would be brought up Jews or Catholics), marrying out, like adopting out, was seen as an act of betrayal. Jewish and Catholic couples were therefore actively encouraged to adopt children of their own faith. Adoptive endogeny was the rule.

This may have been a defensive response to the evangelism of the protestant agencies, but it helped to disseminate the idea of adoption as a superior form of child rescue to a wider audience. En route it also helped to widen the social basis from which adoptive parents themselves might be recruited. For religious conviction might, in some cases, be regarded as more important than even marital or material status in considering the suitability of placements. Single professional women and respectable artisan families could thus be included within the fold, provided they could persuade the agencies that they too could offer a moral and social environment which approximated to some notional ideal of religious upbringing.

There were, however, contexts where religious matching served to strengthen the boundaries of class, rather than transcend or diffuse them. In many Irish Catholic and Jewish working-class districts, there were processes of customary or informal fostering and adoption which ensured that not only orphans or abandoned children, but children from large families who were temporarily 'too much' (or one too many) for their parents, were taken in and cared for either by close relatives, or by friends who lived in the neighbourhood. Only as a last resort, where these immediate networks failed or were simply not available, would an adoption society, charity or religious organisation be approached for help. This was most likely to happen in contexts where illegitimacy was regarded as a major stigma, depriving the mother of access to sources of support within family or community. Similar informal practices existed amongst the English working class. If the mother died, or could no longer cope, children were often 'farmed out' to neighbours or kin, on a temporary or permanent basis. Illegitimate children were often brought up by 'uncles' or 'aunts' who were in fact their birth parents.

As the term 'farming out' suggests, this practice derives from pre-industrial strategies for dealing with surplus or unwanted children. From at least the nineteenth century it was a common practice to 'put out' children, of both sexes, as apprentices or servants to other families, as soon as they reached an age when they could look after themselves. If the child was to learn a trade, a premium would be paid and a formal indenture agreement drawn up setting out the rights and obligations of both master and apprentice/servant. Otherwise the child's employer simply gave an informal undertaking to act *in loco parentis*. A somewhat similar contractual arrangement was made to apprentice orphans and foundlings 'on the parish' – whereby they would be 'put out' to local employers who undertook to feed and clothe them and provide them with 'training in good habits' in return for their labour. Needless to say the whole system was subject to abuse, largely due to its private, unregulated character. Stories of cruel treatment and harsh exploitation by brutal masters was a common thread linking the lives of orphans, foundlings, apprentices and servants in pre-industrial society.

If today this whole arrangement strikes us as odd, it must be remembered that in a patriarchal society, at a time when production was still centred in the family, the relationship of child to parent was in any case closely approximated to that of apprentice to master or servant to mistress. Some elements of that 'pre-industrial' model were conserved in the family ideologies of the industrial working classes, especially amongst artisans and the more 'respectable' manual workers. The apprenticeship model of child-rearing also became linked to new ideas of self-help and self-improvement which were becoming current amongst the labour aristocracy and lower middle classes in the late Victorian period. The two elements were combined in unofficial forms of fostering and adoption which were improvised to deal with illegitimate and unwanted children. The rationale for 'putting out' these children to other families was both to avoid the stigma attatched to their presence and to better their life chances elsewhere. It seems likely that this model was confined to the more privileged strata, who had access to the network of resources on which it depended. It was the more disadvantaged groups, single mothers, destitute families, who were forced to surrender their children to the early adoption agencies.

However, it would be wrong to suggest that the institution of legal adoption, through family placement supervised by statutory or voluntary bodies and inspired by religious/philanthropic concerns, marked a decisive break from long-established traditions of child indenture and farming out, or from strategies for policing the 'dangerous classes' based upon eugenic principles. Up until World War Two these different strands in public thinking were often intertwined in agencies' philosophies and practices.

The now notorious child migrant scheme which sent over 150,000 children to the colonies from the 1880s up to the 1950s is a good case in point. It was directly inspired, and largely organised, by religious philanthropy. Yet it was not just about reclaiming lost souls from a life of vice and crime on the streets of London or Liverpool. The evangelists of child migration also spoke in eugenic terms about the need to improve the racial stock by increasing the white population in the colonies. These two priorities were easily reconciled. For example, sending good English Protestant children to Canada was a means of buttressing the colony against French Catholic influence.

The scheme was based on a version of the customary 'farming out' system. Children were usually placed as 'apprentices' and domestic servants on farms in the rural interiors of Canada, Australia and South Africa. A glowing picture was painted of the healthy outdoor life these children would enjoy while they learnt a trade. The halo of betterment still surrounding customary fostering was adumbrated with social imperialist rhetoric about ensuring the future of the race in a Greater Britain overseas. Only in Rhodesia, where child migrants were placed in educational institutions designed for the white élite, were these ambitions realised. Elsewhere the scheme involved a particularly brutal form of indentured labour with punitive overtones. In the Australian outback and Canadian frontier-lands it seemed entirely natural to regard children as a source of labour power, and adoption as a form of poor relief. But the extent of sexual and physical abuse suffered by these children, especially in Australia, may not have been unconnected with the memories they evoked of the despised status of the first white settlers from which so many of their new 'parents' were descended.

An even crueller twist to the tale was added by the application of closed adoption procedures which severed all links with the birth parents. In many cases children were told that their parents were dead, when they were not; even if this did not happen, once children had been cajoled or bribed into 'volunteering' to go, they were in effect given a one-way ticket to orphanhood. Even though very few children were ever legally adopted by families in their new country, communication with relatives or friends back in England was discouraged and sometimes actively prevented. Maintaining such ties would, it was argued, prevent the young migrants from putting down roots and making a fresh start. In fact, the only point of continuity in their lives was the harshly authoritarian nature of the institutional regimes to which they were subject in both 'mother country' and colonies.

In retrospect what is significant about the child migrant scheme is that it combined elements of both legal and customary adoption in a way which ensured that the children had the worst of both worlds: apprentices who never grew up to be masters, migrants who found themselves in juvenile penal colonies rather than promised lands, adoptees who were made to lose one set of parents, but never gained another. Here we have a clear example of a case where discourses of race, nation and empire directly presided over injustices, systematically done to large numbers of white working-class children under the rubric of adoption as a civilising mission.

But this was not the result of the application of some single, all-embracing ideology, still less a 'genocidal conspiracy' to rob the proletariat of its youth. Rather, it was the outcome of a complex articulation of many different elements, some of which in different contexts and conjunctures held quite other implications. As we will see this story has reverberations for the debate on transracial adoption that are all too contemporary.

HIDDEN AGENDAS IN THE ADOPTION CONTRACT: FROM PHYSICAL MATCHING TO EMOTIONAL BONDING

The child migrant scheme highlights an important distinction between customary and legal adoption based on the nature of the contract involved. Whereas farming out, in its original form, depended on processes of negotiation carried out through informal social networks, and was, therefore, in principle if not always in practice, both traceable and revocable, legal adoption in its closed version involved a contract regulated by the State, which severed absolutely the links between the two families and kept the facts of its early life secret from the child by placing all documentation in a sealed record. The

1926 Act institutionalised a process of collusive denial at the heart of adoption proceedings. Adoptees were not only kept in ignorance about their birth parents but had no right to trace or contact them. Instead they were inducted into a fictional kinship system in which they were made to believe that their adoptive parents were the only ones they had.

It was not enough, however, to maintain the official secret of adoption by law. A more active and subjective principle of concealment was required if legal fiction was to be lived as autobiographical fact. For this adoption agencies mobilised a further way of classifying and selecting their baby and parent populations – physical features. The ideal was the perfect physical match – the baby or child should have the same colour hair and eyes, the same skin colouring and facial type, the same build and constitution as its adoptive parents. This was supposed to enable the adoptee to 'pass' as the natural child of its new parents. It was to provide a cover story and avoid questions being asked. This practice originated with commercial 'baby farming', in which infertile couples paid a premium to a private agency to supply them with a suitable offspring. But it was carried over into the matching criteria applied by public adoption societies.

Whether this practice could be described as racial matching is a moot point. It certainly may have involved the deployment of racial typologies; babies and parents may have been variously classified as Celtic, Anglo-Saxon, Semitic, for example, as an adjunct to religious/ethnic matching processes. In the case of babies of mixed parentage, the imputed possession of 'Jewish', 'Irish' or 'English' features may have been used to sort out the sheep from the goats.

We just do not know enough about the early history of adoption agencies or their practices to be able to say what weight was attributed to physical characteristics as opposed to moral or social criteria in making placements. It does seem unlikely, however, that the practice was fully racialised, simply because the racist assumption – that moral, mental and social characteristics can be inferred from physical ones – also implies that these characteristics are only transferable through blood relationship. The eugenic belief, for example, was that children of inferior stock would not only be morally defective, but introduce their congenital taint in hitherto healthy strains of the population through interbreeding. Physical matching assumed the opposite, that a 'make-believe' racial resemblance would create the social conditions for changing the direction of mental and moral development, and in this way 'constitutional deficiencies' might be largely overcome.

During and after World War Two the view that nurture could prevail over nature was given added impetus by new theories of child development. Attachment theory as elaborated by John Bowlby and his associates at the Tavistock Clinic in London became widely influential in the child welfare field. This work arose out of research into maternal deprivation during the war years, and more especially the experience of evacuees – the largest experiment in fostering ever undertaken. Perhaps as a result the issue of 'loss', while being made central to the account for the first time, was treated as contingent on particular, traumatic life-historical events rather than as a structural condition of human subjectivity as such.

Bowlby's model stressed both the plasticity of the early attachments as well as the permanence of their effects in later life. The human infant could become emotionally attached to a woman who was not its birth mother, provided that this happened early enough and in a favourable enough environment. Bowlby's views were important in rationalising a shift in policy, away from institutional care in children's homes and towards long-term fostering and adoption, even for older children and those with special needs.

In the 1960s Bowlby's ideas were also taken up in a more simplistic vein in a burgeoning literature of popular psychology, especially via primers for good parenting, produced by women's magazines. Data drawn from ethological studies of primate behaviour were used selectively and in combination with elements drawn from folk psychology to produce the notion of primary emotional bonding between mother and infant as being the key to the individual's future wellbeing in life. If that bonding process did not occur, or was interrupted, the child would fail to develop a satisfactory personality and all manner of social pathology would result.

The magical power of bonding was thus linked to a new mystique of motherhood and this in turn was connected to changing ideologies of the nation and family life. The movement to rebuild post-war Britain through the operation of a welfare state required a new strategy of 'correct' child development in which the citizen parent (and especially the mother) is educated into new responsibilities for ensuring the healthy mental and emotional development of the next generation. For example, it becomes the mother's job to encourage her child in constructive play, since this promotes cognitive and social skills, and prepares the child to do well at school. Healthy psychological adjustment to social norms is thus made a prerequisite of national reconstruction.

At the same time the post-war family was invested with a new, specifically therapeutic function. It could, and indeed had to, compensate for the emotional damage which had been caused by wartime separation and loss. New techniques of surveillance and new theoretical discourses in the human sciences were mobilised in order to open up the psychosocial interior of the family for inspection and reform since it was this which was regarded as decisive in determining the outcome of child development. The family was thus enclosed within itself; its culture was no longer placed within a wider social nexus, whether of class, ethnicity or religion. The family became its own imagined community. It lacked nothing – except a child – to complete itself. In this way the process of attachment or bonding was radically freed from the constraints of physical or cultural matching; or rather, it became defined as a process of psychological matching, or identification, which potentially transcended, or denied, the salience of cultural or physical difference.

The therapeutic family was at the centre of post-war change in adoption policy. The religious/philanthropic model was largely diplaced by new secular articles of faith. Foster carers and adoptive parents were scrutinised for their personality traits and incipient neuroses, rather than (or as well as) their religious beliefs or social standing. They were trained up in theories of child development which privileged their reparative rather than their civilising function. They became barefoot social workers and counsellors, rather than moral educators. The idioms of child-rescue thus took a new psychological turn and new figures appeared in the promotional literature addressed to prospective clients. It was no longer so much a question of reclaiming the wayward child who had been led astray, but of healing the traumatised child whose learning difficulties and delinquencies had been induced by early failure in the bonding process.

In this the foundling had made the transition from being a source of additional labour and an object of philanthropic endeavour, to become a focus of emotional investment in the family as a therapeutic enterprise. Adoptees became special in a new way. The stigma of illegitimacy was increasingly lifted from their shoulders by changing social and sexual mores, and the advent of the single-parent family. Instead they were made to carry another burden of representation, as a site for the projection of social hopes bound up with the post-war dream of a better, even classless society. Their 'specialness' was intimately connected to the themes of an emergent consumerism, the fact that they had been singled out and chosen by their new parents: *Yours by Choice*, as the title of a popular primer for adoptive parents so aptly put it (see Rowe, 1992).

Adoptees were also made distinctive by the special measures which were now taken to prepare them for placement. The dearth of babies and toddlers (consequent on the changes noted above) plus moves to limit and close down children's homes meant that for the first time significant numbers of older children were available and in demand. New forms of counselling and autobiographical work were developed to help them adjust successfully, and participate in adoption as a therapeutic enterprise. The commonalities of hardship and deprivation which hitherto linked the life stories of orphans and runaways, the abandoned and delinquent, gave way to a much more differentiated set of provisions, and thus experiences. What henceforth marked out adoptees from their erstwhile peers in adversity was a heightened self-consciousness about issues of origins and identity. As a consequence of all these shifts in emphasis, the calculation of invisible emotional assets or deficits now became much more central in selecting and matching children and parents, and these factors in turn regulated the supply and managed the demand for placements.

In principle the new model was more democratic than the old. It was continually stressed that working-class parents were as likely to have the desired psychological make-up for fostering and adoption as anyone else. In

Winnicott's phrase they were certainly 'good-enough parents' in providing a warm, emotionally sensitive environment, which would facilitate attachment or bonding. In practice, however, the model worked best for those who already spoke its language, indeed who had already internalised its norms in the process of their own upbringing – namely professional, white, middle-class couples.

This model was greatly popularised in the 1960s and 1970s through its links with the personal growth movement, which stressed the possibilities of overcoming early conditioning through a variety of 'liberation therapies'. These aimed to enable people to discover or retrieve their 'authentic selves', and experience a new oneness with their inner being and the external world. Personal politics, rather than charity, now began (and perhaps ended) at home, and the world could be remade through the adoption of new kinds of relationship which broke the stranglehold of the old bourgeois, patriarchal norms. This may also have provided a personal rationale for white middle-class couples adopting black children; once the family was reinvented as its own imagined community it seemed possible for everyone to build a harmonious multiracial society in their own back yard.

Adoption agencies, however, were not the places to be caught up in this fervour of social experimentation. The nuclear family, not the commune, remained their ideal for adoptive bonding! Hippies did not, on the whole, come into the category of 'good-enough parents'. Neither, for a long time, did single parents or gay couples. For although psychological factors had replaced philanthropic ones, they were still often linked in practice to the operation of traditional moralistic criteria. In particular the persistence of denominational adoption societies has ensured that religious criteria continue to be used alongside psychosocial ones. It is only very recently, and then as a response to demographic as much as ideological pressure, that some agencies have begun to open their doors to non-traditional family units.

The move to transracial adoption was not, therefore, undertaken in a spirit of commitment to multicultural parenting, or facilitating personal growth, although that may have retrospectively provided a rationale. But neither, of course, did it evolve in some ideology-free realm. Adoption agencies had their own grounds for rationalising the practice of transracial adoption. This arose from a conjuncture in the 1960s of the following elements: a model of child development which harmonised with the experience and values of their traditional base of recruitment; a model of bonding and matching which gave primacy to emotional rather than cultural or physical factors; and a model of the family which discriminated against non-European or non-nuclear forms.

The interaction of these factors meant that practices of advertisement and search, procedures of assessment and preparation, continued to be premissed on an ideal type of placement which indirectly discriminated against large numbers of potential foster/adoptive parents, including those from ethnic minorities. It helped to make the placement of black children with white families seem both normal and natural when a situation arose in which the supply of white babies dried up.

In breaking with the mandates of the civilising mission, the psychothera-peutic model opened up a new space in which issues of adoptive identity and genealogical difference could be officially represented rather than repressed. At the same time these issues were negotiated through the medium of feelings, at a level which seemed to be both classless and untouched by 'race'. Yet, in shifting from physical matching to emotional bonding, a hidden agenda was introduced into the adoption contract, inscribing it within an ideology of child-and-family centredness which was culturally and socially specific to the white, professional middle class, and which rendered other ways of bringing up children suspect. It was this class and colour blindness which set the stage for the subsequent racialisation of adoption.

IDENTITY POLITICS: FROM ROOTS TO 'RACE'

One of the larger ironies of recent adoption history is that the arrival of the new ethnic minorities as a major force on the scene coincided with the marginalisation of the old religious/philanthropic model which had served the Jewish and Irish communities so well in preventing children being adopted 'out'. Lacking their own agencies, the immediate resort of black and Asian communities was thus to fall back on their own practices of informal fostering and adoption. This did not, however, always or even often result in endo-genous placement. Many children of West African parentage, for example, were placed with well-to-do white couples on the grounds that this would secure for them certain educational and social advantages. (Farming out rationalised as social betterment yet again!) At the same time this practice incurred the concern of social service departments and adoption agencies on account of its unregulated nature. In any case, the sad fact was that informal adoption, whether transracial or not, could in no way cope with the numbers of black children in need of families during the 1960s and 1970s.

There was, however, another development in this period which was to offer black parents and social workers greater purchase within the British adoption scene, and the beginnings of a platform from which to attack the practice of transracial placement. From the early 1960s groups of adoptees began to campaign for access to their adoption records, for the right to know the full circumstances which had led to their adoption, for the means to trace and contact their birth parents, and for counselling services to help them to deal with the often traumatic effects of disclosure. This search to discover one's true origins, over and against the various cover stories or myths which had been constructed to conceal or deny them, inevitably implied a particular model of identity and its role in the formation of the individual personality.

It was a genealogical model, a model of identity as a birthright or inheri-tance. To inhabit such an identity was to possess an authentic sense of selfhood. To lack such an identity was to lack a core personality – to be deprived of a meaningful sense of roots. The family of origin had now to be included within the imagined community of kith and kin and the search for origins itself made an integral part of adoption as a therapeutic enterprise.

The campaign for the 'right to know' established a new form of identity politics in social work and paved the way for the shift to current policies of open adoption. It gave a new twist to notions of bonding – stressing not the plasticity of attachments, but the primordial nature of the link between birth mother and child, and the long-term effects of early and traumatic severance on both. When the campaign against transracial adoption began in earnest in the early 1980s, much of its rhetoric about black identity and the primary importance of roots resonated powerfully with the agenda and language of the earlier movement. If the adoption agencies capitulated so quickly to the demand to introduce or rather reinstate the policy of racial matching, it was not only out of fear of being accused of racism but because this accusation evoked a perhaps more deep-rooted sense of guilt about the historical injustice which had been done to generations of white working-class adoptees.

But now of course the stakes around the issue of adoptive identity had been decisively raised. It no longer had to do with tracing individual birth parents, but of finding one's roots within a collective ancestry. The assumption of a black identity was made to mean more than being proud of one's own immediate origins. It meant actively locating an individual life history within the collective memory of a 'race'. Only if identity was completely racialised, so that no part of it could escape racial determination, and only if family genealogy was defined in the same all-embracing racial terms, was it possible to draw an absolute dividing line between white and black. Equally this was a bodily identity, an identity which was co-extensive with the skin, and by definition you were black (or white) all over.

For those campaigning against transracial placements such watertight binary categories were felt to be essential. Otherwise exceptions to the same-race rule might multiply to the point where the rule would become unworkable. For example, children of mixed English and Afro-Caribbean parentage, or children who looked white but had some remote African ancestry, or who came from non-white ethnic minorities which saw themselves as neither English nor black, might all slip through the net of racial classification and end up being placed with white families. As we will see the kind of discourses and strategies which had to be used to justify such a rigid system of racial classification had to be applied inflexibly or not at all.

The deployment of the binary typology also inevitably made 'race' the primary principle of matching and bonding. This indirectly created the conditions for a new myth of origins based on physical resemblance. For the placement of 'black' children with 'black' families meant that now they too could pass as 'natural' and could be provided with cover stories so that no one would ask questions. Indeed one of the key arguments against transracial placement was that the very visibility of the difference between parent and child advertised the fact of adoption, would focus external hostility and internal conflict, and thus undermine the chances of success. Same-race placements simply did not suffer from this problem.

The project of assuming a black identity thus became linked to a principle of equivocation about the fact of the genealogical difference. Differences of class, religion, ethnicity or lifestyle between birth and adoptive parents might be denied, concealed or magically transcended by appealing to an imagined community of shared 'blackness'. The affirmation of pride in common roots might not only provide a framework of protection against racism; in some cases it might become enmeshed in a collusive denial of the more painful and contradictory aspects of reality underlying not just individual cases of adoption, but the wider situation of black and Asian communities in Britain. 'Might' is the operative word here, not just because other, more positive, outcomes are possible, but because research into the psychosocial interior of 'transracial' placements over time has never been carried out in sufficient detail or depth to enable such issues to be addressed with any empirical confidence. In any case the agenda of debate was set by other priorities than discovering what was actually happening in the hearts and minds of those most intimately involved.

FUNDAMENTALISMS: ABSWAP VERSUS THE NEW RIGHT

Throughout the 1980s the field of adoption policy was one of the front lines of confrontation over the meaning of 'race' in Britain. It became a 'great cause' around which a new generation of black social workers could rally and find their own professional voice. It was also the site of a great historical reckoning, where customary practices which had long characterised the British adoption scene were for the first time defined, and challenged as racist. But the issue had reverberations far beyond the tight-knit world of adoption.

In staking its claim, the campaign against transracial adoption spearheaded by the Association of Black Social Workers and Allied Professionals (ABSWAP) drew on elements from both new and old models of adoption and subsumed them within an anti-racist perspective whose rhetorics initially owed most to the language of black cultural nationalism and Pan-Africanism imported from the USA. This provided a useful formula for exploiting residual white liberal guilt in the social work establishment. Unfortunately the heady mix of militant Afrocentrism and municipal anti-racism (with the odd dash of Marxism) was readymade to put off more traditionalist elements amongst the ethnic minority communities, especially the Asian Muslim groups, some of whom were, in any case, developing alternative strategies based on their own version of religious philanthopy.

At the same time the ABSWAP rhetoric was calculated to provoke confrontation with Thatcherism and the New Right. In fact the emergence of left anti-racism was partly a response to the growth of what Martin Barker (1981) called the New Racism. This was no longer based on quasi-biological arguments about white racial supremacy, but instead stressed the issue of cultural difference and pathology, to restate the assimilationist case. This position was most publicly articulated in Mrs Thatcher's infamous 'swamping speech', in which she portrayed the threat to 'our traditional way of life' posed by 'alien cultures' and called for a return to the Victorian values which had made Britain 'Great'.

The new racism combined elements of romantic English nationalism and a philosophy of libertarian individualism, and produced a new version of the civilising mission. In terms of this framework the unwillingness or inability of 'some people' to identify with the Conservative Government's tunnel vision of Anglo-Saxon history and culture was read as a sign of their irredeemable 'otherness'. A line was drawn within and between ethnic minority populations in terms of those who had adapted to or espoused the national enterprise culture, and those who had not, because they implicitly still clung to a primitive belief in communalism or socialism. The aim was to promote the advancement of the more responsible and deserving elements, whilst isolating and containing those who were regarded as belonging to the new 'dangerous classes'.

New Right racism found a perfect stamping ground in the debate on transracial adoption, with ABSWAP providing their readymade sparring partners. The case for white families adopting black children was restated as a new form of civilising mission with the English middle class playing a heroic role in providing a reparative environment in which the emotional and cultural deprivations associated with the Afro-Caribbean family could be overcome. Both sides therefore drew on similar elements from the philanthropic and therapeutic models, but gave them radically opposed articulations. As a result 'pro' and 'anti' positions became highly polarised, continually feeding off and reinforcing rival political rhetoric, but underneath were riddled by many of the same internal contradictions.

If we briefly review the main terms and protagonists of the debate we can perhaps see how this works in practice. Take, for example, the issue of cultural genocide. For John Small, the founder of ABSWAP, transracial adoption is 'a form of internal colonialism, it is like the slave trade, except children are used' (1991). It was removing the black communities' most valuable asset – its children – and represented a fundamental attack on the physical and cultural integrity of the race. This view was a more or less literal translation of the arguments put forward by an African-American psychologist, Leonard Chestang, who had taken a leading role in the US debate (see Maximé, 1986). For Chestang the fear of cultural genocide is linked with increased racial pride and the anxiety that any dilution of identity will threaten the transcendant feeling of unity in struggle against the oppressor society.

This position was comprehensively attacked by David Dale (1987), a senior social worker who published a pamphlet under the auspices of the Social Affairs Unit, a think tank involved in launching the New Right counterattack against socialist welfare policies during the 1980s. For Dale, the Small/ Chestang statements were alarming evidence of a form of political extremism and cultural pathology which was threatening to overwhelm traditional values in social work, values which he also associated with the preservation of English family life. For him the issue was one of parental choice – were parents free to choose the kind of child they wished to adopt? This was, as we have seen, the case which was made for the uniqueness of adoption in the post-war period, but one which was now given a sharper and more ideological focus. Dale believed that the issue of race was secondary – the parents just happened to be white and the children black, but that in no way affected the general principle of choice.

At first sight then it seems as if the 'anti' and 'pro' positions differ radically in terms of their reading of race. Dale totally denies its relevance. His form of transracialism involves the dogmatic assertion that race is irrelevant to the making of both personal and social identities, whilst at the same time tacitly affirming the superiority of a dominant 'English way of life' in embodying universal human values. In contrast, for Chestang and Small, 'race' is the primary determinant of identity in a racist society; their version of anti-racism entails the 'permeation' model of racism – it is everywhere, and everywhere the same – coupled with an explicit affirmation of the moral superiority of black cultural values and lifestyle vis-à-vis their white counterparts.

I think it can be argued that both positions are equally concerned with the 'future of the race' – only they are talking about different 'races', in different ways. Both see the present state of race relations through the prism of the imperial past. For Small the adoption of black children by white families in 1980s Britain recalls the practice under slavery whereby the white master used to adopt some specially favoured children from the plantation and train them up as domestic servants or 'house niggers'. In many cases these were mixed-race children whom he had fathered through the exercise of *droit de seigneur* over 'his' female slaves. The analogy was useful in establishing 'guilt by association'; but is it really an appropriate comparison?

Dale sees history through decidedly more rose-tinted spectacles. His arguments evoke an element of *noblesse oblige*, associated now with the white, educated middle class who help those less fortunate than themselves to get a better start in life. For the New Right, arguments about parental choice are intimately connected with a historical view of private philanthropy and self-help as superior alternatives to the welfare state. It was precisely the capacity to help others which staked the original claim to moral and cultural superiority associated with the civilising mission in the age of imperialism. But is this really a relevant model to apply to adoption in a multicultural society?

For both sides contemporary race relations are perceived in terms of their similarities or correspondences with certain key historical processes or events. Through the grid of this racialised memory, the varieties of individual experience and events are reduced to a compulsive repetition of the same old imperial story. Where they differ, of course, is that Small and Chestang do not want the future of their 'race' to be a repetition of its past enslavement (even if the present is), while Dale, and those who think like him, are locked in a collective daydream about the restoration of a form of ethnic hegemony which belongs to the nineteenth century.

Both sides use arguments about cultural difference – the historical uniqueness of the black experience of oppression in one case, or of the 'inherent tolerance of the English way of family life' in the other, in order to support their claims to occupy the moral high ground from which to pursue particular strategies of social reproduction. Both champion the importance of 'kith and kin' as the privileged means of transmitting invented traditions of imagined community, based on race, ethnicity and nation. At the same time both utilise the new model of adoption to claim unique therapeutic powers for their preferred family forms which lack nothing and leave nothing to be desired. For Small only the black family can transmit adequate coping mechanisms to enable the black child to overcome the emotional damage caused by racism. The black family is a haven of hope in a heartless, racist world. For Dale, only the white, English middle-class family can provide the cultural resources to enable the black child to overcome the handicap of his or her racial origin – including, he suggests at one point, its low IQ, and make a successful adjustment to 'the English way of life'. His Anglo-Saxon family is an island of individual freedom and tolerance, amidst a sea of prejudice.

These rival idealisations of cultural self-sufficiency and superiority are complemented as always by strategies of denigration addressed to the other side. For Small transracial adoption involves a process of pathological bonding, whilst the motivations of white parents in wanting a black child are equally neurotic. For Dale, Caribbean patterns of kinship have failed to adjust to British conditions and family breakdown has caused a whole range of social pathologies leading to high numbers of black children and young people in prison, or care. ABSWAP activists in the early 1980s accused white parents who adopt black children of committing soul murder by loving them.

Perhaps the most striking convergence is in the implicit model of adoption as a process of cultural assimilation. The black adoptee is supposed to unlearn bad habits (derived in one case from white society, in the other from black) and model himself or herself on the good example set by his or her new parents (in resisting racism or promoting civilised standards). This is, to put it mildly, a rather disingenuous view of what is involved in the adoption process! We are dealing with two complementary versions of the same underlying fairy-tale. In one case the issue of genealogical difference is disavowed through the assertion of common racial roots binding birth and adoptive parents; in the other it is denied through an extreme form of colour blindness. In both cases, the child's body is pledged to a myth of origins in which there is little or no potential space for representing and working through the contradictory identifications which are inevitably present; nor, in this version of the adoption story, is there much room for each set of parents to acknowledge that the other has something which they lack.

A final point of convergence is the strategy of textual citation which is used to authorise the rival arguments. Because these arguments rest on *a priori* positions, which derive from ideological abstractions rather than concrete analysis, they have to find some way of justifying their claims by reference to empirical reality. Usually this is done by quoting individual cases which apparently support the line being taken. So we get atrocity stories about black children being turned into misfits as result of being cut off from their own community, or being treated as white by their adoptive families. And we are given equally sensational accounts of black children being driven to despair because they are forced to remain in residential care, or are removed from white foster homes by the brutally insensitive policies of same-race placement. It is not that such cases do not exist, and do not have important consequences for the individual concerned, but that the rhetorical use which is made of them loads them with a burden of proof which they cannot possible sustain.

The citation of research studies follows the reverse strategy. It is not now a question of too much being made of too little evidence, but of complex findings being selectively quoted out of context and boiled down to simple propositions which supposedly corroborate this or that fundamentalist position.

One reason for the apparent symmetry in positions is that both sides are using reductive monocausal explanations to account for complex, multi-determined phenomena, in order to avoid looking at painful realities close to home. What if, for example, it turns out that West African/Caribbean kinship systems transplanted to the British context do prove to be particularly vulnerable to the disorganising impact of racism: equally they may support compensatory forms of community cohesion, which are especially well equipped to produce a vibrant culture of resistance, albeit in ways which are likely to lead to its criminalisation? Evidently we need an account which can make as much sense of the bad news as the good.

Similarly, if white social workers turn out to be more likely to pathologise the Afro-Caribbean family (perhaps in some cases assimilating it to earlier negative stereotypes of the Irish family), whilst holding to a more positive image of Asian families as stable, close-knit, committed to self-help, etc. (possibly corresponding to the Jewish model), then we need a perspective which can distinguish clearly between empirical differences in these family forms and the ideological constructions which are placed upon them. The precise weight to be given to these various instances in explaining the disproportionate number of Afro-Caribbean children in care, and the reluc-tance of members of their community to foster or adopt them through official channels, is not fixed; it cannot be established in advance of detailed investigation into particular contexts and conjunctures. All that is certain is that the interaction of all these factors will have to be taken into account in the final analysis.

Both sides, it seems, can recognise one side of the story but not the other. ABSWAP members feel they have to deny or discredit any evidence which might show black families in a less than favourable light, because this might lend credence to the pathological model; and it is indeed true that people like Dale lose no opportunity to make capital out of any such evidence in order to justify their prejudice. At the same time Dale cannot afford to admit any element of justice in the anti-racist case and persistently denies that cultural racism (viz., stereotypical perceptions of ethnic minority client populations) are institutionalised within social work practice. If he were to do so the foundations of his own arguments might stand all too clearly exposed.

The reductive nature of the arguments deployed on both sides is well illustrated in their attitudes to religion. Both have great difficulty in accommodating denominational claims because they introduce an intervening variable which disturbs the rigid system of binary categories, although both, for different reasons, would like to be seen to be acknowledging the validity of these claims. The fact is that where religion does continue to play a major role in the making of adoptive identities it is likely to be ethnically or racially marked in a way which does not fit into simple white and black definitions.

Islam has provided Bangladeshi, Turkish and Pakistani communities in Britain with a distinctive politico-religious identity (especially since the fatwa, condemning to death the author Salman Rushdie, was pronounced in 1989) in a way which tends to dissociate them from the category black. Black is effectively reduced to its initial African roots-radical meaning. At the same time the reintroduction of religion destabilises – or at least considerably complicates – the category black as the arbiter of same-race placement. For example, there may be persuasive grounds for placing a Muslim child of, say, Turkish origin with a Muslim family even if they are white-English, rather than putting them with an Afro-Caribbean family who have no such affiliations, simply on the grounds that they are black. Ethnically sensitive adoption practice does not necessarily have to mean a ban on transracial placement. Indeed, as this example indicates, it can mean the reverse.

The play of differences continually threatens those who hold to purified notions of identity. But how is the problem to be dealt with? For the ABSWAP fundamentalists, black is first reduced to a biological category and then reconstructed as a 'political colour' so that it can be magically expanded to include a large number of honorary blacks, including white ethnic minorities like the Irish or Jews on the grounds that they have a long and honourable history of resisting racism. But for the reasons I have just indicated this kind of subsumption was increasingly recognised as a disguised form of Afro-Caribbean hegemony.

Transracialists like Dale appear at first sight to have less difficulty in dealing with difference. They are quick to marshal 'common sense' on their side and point to the nature of parental love as providing the magical ingredient of emotional bonding which transcends social and ethnic divisions. Yet the form which this love is supposed to take is highly normative; it entails the inculcation of self discipline, respect for authority and so on which, for Dale, are the embodiment of 'traditional family values' associated with 'Old England'. Here we can see just how far the therapeutic model of adoption has been converted (or perhaps perverted) by Thatcherite individualism. Yet this contains its own contradictions. For transracialism cuts both ways. This position is in principle committed to encouraging the possibility of white children being fostered and adopted by black parents provided, presumably, the latter have acquired the requisite 'English family values'. Although there seems no immediate 'danger' of this happening at present, the logic of assimilation would ultimately point towards a scenario with which some of Mr Dale's supporters might not feel too comfortable.

The presence of ABSWAP has helped to ensure that the majority of the new black middle class will reject all forms of assimilationism and practise adoptive endogeny whether or not they hold to a position of racial separatism. The problem for ABSWAP was how to articulate this kind of black perspective, whilst at the same time legitimating its case by drawing on sources of professional thinking with which white social workers might feel sufficiently comfortable, or at least familiar enough, to enable them to lend their support to the ABSWAP perspective.

'POSITIVES AND NEGATIVES'

The first problem was that the theories of psychosocial formation which most nearly permitted a rigorous determinism to be founded on 'race' themselves either rested on racist assumptions or reached conclusions which supported them, as in the work of Arthur Jensen and Hans Eysenck. It was necessary to look elsewhere. A gamut of quite disparate and often conflicting models from various traditions of Western psychology were ransacked for ideas which could be pressed into service. Jean Piaget and Melanie Klein, Abraham Maslow and Erik Erikson all found themselves recruited to the 'cause'.

But how was it possible to assimilate object relations theory, behaviourist accounts of social learning and functionalist models of cognitive development to the same story-line – to make them say the same thing about race and identity? Clearly only by reducing them all to the same lowest common denominator. They were all apparently about the formation of 'self-concepts' and could be used to specify the conditions under which 'negative' or 'positive' images might occur. Then you only had to affix the term 'black' or 'race' to the formula to generate a series of prescriptive statements about what should, or should not be done, to create 'positive black identities'. Such statements could then be fleshed out with some suitably cautionary tales about the identity confusion induced in black children by being placed with white families.

The subtext in all this was the search for a psychological correlate to the category black, to ground the construction of black as a unitary/unifying social category in an equally unitary/unifying model of the psyche. 'Positive identity' was whatever seemed to support the full presence of the black community to itself across space and time. By definition such an identity left nothing to be desired; it was constituted by a retrieval of lost origins, in which no trace of 'lack' remained. In this formula 'lack' was a purely negative concept; indeed it was the very definition of a negative self-concept – the subject has been made to feel he or she congenitally lacks certain desired attributes by virtue of internalising derogatory value judgements placed upon him or her by others.

In order to fix and essentialise black identity formation in these terms it was necessary to work with a model of human psychology which rigorously excluded, or rendered pathological, any 'decentring' of the self. Any model which made lack and the 'other' a positive constituent of the subject's desire was taboo. In other words it was necessary to reject the very theories which were emerging in the 1980s to make a critique of the individualistic, ego-centric bias of Western philosophy and psychology. Instead it was these 'Eurocentric' models which were used as the basis of 'Afrocentric' definitions of the uniqueness of black identity!

The problem was compounded whenever attempts were made to introduce a more dynamic mode of analysis. The risk in doing so is that this may also introduce the complexity of actual choices, the contradictory nature of lived positions, into the picture in a way which destroys the fragile, one-dimensional clarity of the argument. To guard against this possibility meant using a model of human socialisation based upon rigid developmental laws, governing the unfolding of different stages of the life cycle. Ideally the model should anchor the psychic to the social in an unequivocal way so that at any point the individual is always, and only, having to deal with psychic conflicts prescribed by the social structure. Erik Erikson's model is understandably popular for this purpose, although there are many other less refined versions of the same story-line on the market.

The model of 'psychological nigrescence' which was popularised by ABSWAP in the 1980s took this kind of thinking to its logical conclusion. The black child who is the 'victim' of transracial adoption is supposed to go through a series of levels or stages: an initial 'pre-encounter' position of alienation or identity confusion, where the subject remains colour-blind or refuses to recognise that they have been the victim of racism; an 'encounter stage' where the fact of racism is confronted at the level of direct experience; followed by an immersion/emersion stage, where the child embraces a black identity to the exclusion of everything else; through to a final position of internalisation/ commitment, where a new sense of racial pride has been installed at the core of the personality and the subject is now free to engage in political activity as a fully fledged member of the black community.

What is interesting about this model is the way it inscribes a teleological view of black history, as an onward and upwards march to freedom, and as a normative schema of psychological development. In other words, the individual is supposed to repeat or recapitulate the history of his or her 'race' in the course of growing up, moving from the earliest phase of enslavement by racism to a position of personal and political emancipation. The model does, of course, have a certain resonance, given the way racist discourses infantilise black people; but whether the struggle against racism follows the unilinear trajectory described here, and whether the individual life course repeats the historical process, is quite another matter. The precedent, if not the provenance, for this kind of recapitulation theory does in fact belong to the wilder shores of nineteenth-century racial psychology, where equations between the infant and the primitive were routine. Stanley Hall, for example, inspired by Social Darwinism, insisted that the Western life cycle involved the transition from stone-age baby to civilised man, even though not everyone (especially the working classes) made it through to the final stage of evolution (see Hall, 1904).

There were, however, alternative story-lines. Chestang's theory of the 'dual black personality', involving a constant interplay between the 'transcendant' and 'depreciated' character, offered a more dynamic version of racial determinism (see Maximé, 1986). In this account principles of hope and faith, linked to processes of psychological individuation, might be mobilised to acknowledge and overcome self-destructive processes set in motion by racism. These were 'opposites seeking unity', but they might also result in divided selves. So black people needed to learn ways of maintaining an equilibrium between the two sides of their personality, primarily through positive identifications with black culture and history. So here the category black is promoted into a therapeutic principle of integration, maintaining a sense of unity which might otherwise dissolve into pathological splits.

In all these models there is a certain idealisation about the way the positive pole of identification is imagined to function. For example, it assumes a particular tunnel vision of 'black history' focused on a pantheon of 'heroes and heroines' who will provide 'positive role models' as a means of overcoming damaged self-esteem. Other, more complex and possibly less heroic aspects of historical reality are likely to get airbrushed out of the picture. Then history becomes an instrument of collective narcissism, or a struggle between goodies and baddies.

These theories admit social processes into the psychological, only to fix them there as immobile determinisms. Equally they abstract from intrapsychic processes only what can be made to correspond in a simple one-to-one way with social structures. This makes the argument largely circular; for example, racist images are said to be internalised, when the individual behaves self-destructively in a way which inhibits the expression of racial pride. If the individual does not express a sense of pride in being black then this can only be a symptom of a neurotic or self-destructive defence mechanism. According to this logic the possibility that a member of an ethnic minority could behave self-destructively and yet not have internalised negative racist stereotypes does not exist. For the 'internal racist' is only ever a model or copy of the external one.

The theories chosen by ABSWAP to state their case were formally adequate for the purposes of making the hard-and-fast distinction between healthy (same-race) and pathological (mixed-race) bonding which was so crucial to establishing a new strategy of 'political correctness' in adoption. If the aim was to pursuade white social workers that the ideas with which they had grown up as part of their professional common sense did, after all, support the black perspective, then the strategy must be judged a great success. The question remains as to whether too high a price has been paid by abandoning the field to impoverished ideas which foreclose the terms of debate. The racialisation of adoption and the ensuing polarisation has meant that theories or research findings which pointed to a more sophisticated understanding of the issues tended to be sidelined.

It was especially ironic that none of the ABSWAP advocates could afford to follow in the footsteps of Frantz Fanon, the founder of black liberation psychology, in utilising elements of Lacanian psychoanalysis to interrogate the discourses of the 'other', or the 'sliding signifiers' at work in transcultural identification. Nor could they draw on that tradition of social psychology which demonstrates the historically constructed and culturally relative nature of psychosocial formations. Such models would have rendered permeable the very boundaries they wanted to fix, and made distinctions between levels of reality which they needed to conflate. Perhaps even sadder, in the light of their own 'roots-radicalism', was the initial failure to draw on models from indigenous African psychology which offered a similarly multidimensional reading of identity and difference.

Today, however, the same models and evidence are re-emerging in the space created by new debates around open adoption, dual heritage or multicultural parenthood, and inter-country adoption; they also have a new salience in reopening the debate on transracial adoption because they address moral dilemmas and social contradictions which have emerged within the practice of 'same-race' placements in a way that the more fundamentalist positions are unable to do. So let us in conclusion look at the emergent agenda.

TOWARDS A POLITICS OF DIFFERENCE

If there is a common thread to the histories we have briefly reviewed in this chapter it lies in the way successive generations of adopted children, white and black, have been made to carry a special burden of representation, as the vehicle of wider social ideals and conflicts to do with race. The ideologies and discourses which have made adoptees the object of these adult projections have further complicated and sometimes damaged their lives, over and above the inevitable difficulties created by their traumatic early months and years. In the ordinary course of events most children are only dimly aware of the wider forces which shape their lives, until they have grown up and it is too late to do more than trace their retroactive effect. But for better or worse, adopted children are in a position to recognise sooner, and with greater prescience than most, the role which particular policies of state play in the government of the most intimate registers of their identity.

The plea to 'put children first' cannot then mean building some kind of 'ideology-free zone' in which pure, disinterested decision-making takes place. This is a rationalist Utopia which has historically been fully complicit with a whole variety of knowledge/power games; it promises a state of enlightenment which belies the vested interests which are inevitably in play.

If we are to give greater priority to both the overt and hidden agendas which children bring with them into the adoption process we have to be more, not less, aware of the structural and unconscious processes which shape them; only on that basis can we work with children to create a space in which they can articulate their own questions.

These questions will be all the more awkward in so far as the answers do not fit neatly into the pigeon holes provided by what I have called the new 'political correctness' of adoption. Consider for example the big Ws: why couldn't my birth mother look after me, why did she give me up for adoption, and who or where is my birth father? Although these questions appear to be simple requests for information (and should be answered as such) they are always phrased through structures of feeling which go beyond that to a problem which is more easily expressed in the theatre of the body than in words: what marked me out for abandonment and how is it possible for me to reverse that fate?

The circumstantial evidence which is conveyed to the child will provide the raw material for a reconstruction of events organised into a myth of origins, which at some level allows the child to provide an answer to that more fundamental issue, in a way which provides principles of hope. This personal mythology can be as simple as a make-believe genealogy, or as elaborate as a fictional life story; it usually equips the child hero with an exalted or exotic parentage, associated with birth or adoptive family; a promise is made that one day the child will come into its rightful inheritance, and all the wrongs suffered as a result of its abandonment will be magically redressed and everyone will live happily ever after.

This fairy-story can undergo infinite variations on its basic theme. The child may be reunited with its birth parents, or return to wreak vengeance on them; black children may invent rich white uncles, white children find their 'roots' in some imaginary Caribbean paradise; poor parents can be transformed into millionaire film stars and conventional middle-class families made to inhabit a more excitingly Bohemian world. The point is that these fantasies do not stand in any simple relation to social reality; they cannot be legislated for or against by some kind of social engineering of the child's world.

And because these constructions are about fictional families centred on imagined relations to the 'other', not actual identifications, they cannot be used to measure or read off social attitudes. Black children in same-race placements are just as likely to need to invent imaginary white companions to support their heroic deeds, as those living with white foster parents. Conversely, it may well be that transracial adoptees are more likely to choose same-race figures as the co-natural support of their more adventurous auto-biographies, provided that the difference between their two sets of parents has neither been disavowed, or made into an unbridgeable divide. The fact that children can make up tall stories about themselves, featuring imaginary kinships with other races or classes is not necessarily a sign that they are suffering from 'identity confusion' or 'a failure to choose appropriate role models'; on the contrary it can indicate that their powers of imagination have not been damaged beyond repair.

Race provides one of a number of available image repertoires which children may use to explore, through fantasy, the vicissitudes of early adoptive identity. For adolescents the situation is complicated by internal and external pressures to produce purified identities purged of all trace of dependence on the m(other). Totalising ideologies which operate this kind of closure, by splitting the world into 'goodies' and 'baddies', and stressing a singular, exclusive and inherent source of 'authenticity', are understandably popular supports for the adolescent project. At this stage the issue of genealogical difference is anyway displaced from the family to the peer group. White working-class children adopted by middle-class couples find ways of reappropriating elements of that 'other scene' through involvement in the teenage worlds of street life, drug culture, heavy metal, raves or whatever else can be regarded as dangerously 'common'. Afro-Caribbean children who have been placed in white families may, in addition, become 'roots-radicals'.

But, and it is a big but, these experiments are only possible on condition that adoptive parents do not foreclose the issue of difference, either by repressive toleration or overzealous celebration. It is as destructive to force children to learn about their roots as it is to ignore the fact that they have another history and culture from which their adoptive parents are by definition excluded. Cosy tolerance, practised by the complacent, for whom difference makes no difference, is as undermining as the determined insistence on inculcating alternative ethnocentrisms. Differences will have to be made and negotiated through anger, pain, rejection and revolt, before they can create new alliances based upon more qualified and mature identifications. This is true for all adolescents but especially so in the case of adoptees, for whom difference is intimately connected with separation and loss.

Secondly, adolescents need access to appropriate youth cultures, in which the play of identity and difference is suffiently rich and varied to enable them to explore the elements of their dual heritage, and find their own individual niche. All adoptees by definition have a dual heritage; this fact may be more easily hidden under the rubrics of 'race and class' matching, than in situations where it is, from the outset, an undeniable fact of life. Subcultural styles may provide a medium in which the drive for purified identities is tempered by a playful bricolage of elements drawn from a diversity of sources – East and West, black and white, masculine and feminine, working class and middle class, where everyone is taking part in some game of adoptive identity.

This kind of situation is only found where these cultures already interface, in other words in multiethnic areas of large conurbations. It will not be found in the English countryside, in market towns, or the white middle-class suburbs, the so-called 'white highlands' areas. Moreover this kind of creative hybridity is a special feature of black and Asian youth cultures and flourishes in contexts where white ethnicities and popular racism are also strong on the ground. This *mise en scène* is not at present likely to be available to child immigrants brought to Britain through inter-country adoption; at best they may have access to only very small and highly localised refugee communities. Yet even under these circumstances ways may still be found of creating a symbolic space outside the family in which the child can explore its dual heritage. Diaspora is an *imagined* community, which does not necessarily require physical location in order to sustain a meaningful sense of membership, though it clearly helps.

In and against multiracialist Britain, hybrid ethnicities are increasingly becoming the cultural norm. Intermarriage and mixed-race relationships of every kind are producing a new generation in which purified notions of 'Englishness' or 'blackness' are a standing joke, especially amongst the young. Amongst many white working-class children this is producing its own inverse form of transracial adoption. Rap and Rude Talk become the dominant vernacular, a currency through which the local hegemony of Afro-Caribbean culture is negotiated by white and Asian youth, enabling them to entertain an imaginary kinship with this 'other race'. This situation is duplicated in many children's homes, where these children identify strongly with the style of resistance relayed by their Afro-Caribbean peers – seeing in it a form of self-empowerment directed against the world of 'them'. As a result many would prefer to be fostered or adopted by Afro-Caribbean parents, rather than by 'their own kind'; sometimes they get themselves adopted as a kind of mascot by the local black 'posse'. To be the only white member of a black gang is to become your own do-it-yourself ethnic minority; it is to embrace a difference which hides or cancels the fact that you are adopted. What looks from the outside like a personal anti-racist statement, turns out on closer inspection to be based on a form of splitting in which the idealised black is contrasted with the denigrated 'Paki' – a position which is often echoed by Afro-Caribbean youth themselves.

It is important, then, to be able to distinguish between various forms of adoptive identification; to want to have the good things associated with the other 'race', or class, without the concomitant disadvantages, is 'normal' in our kind of society. To seek to emulate the sound system or street strut of the black posse, without having to endure the racism, or to possess a BMW and yuppy lifestyle without the compulsive work ethic needed to pay for it is par for the life course in the post-Thatcherite era. To want to destroy these things because you realise you cannot have them is also an all-too-normal part of our contemporary culture of envy. But to want to *be* black when you are white, or vice versa, is an altogether more pathological enterprise. There is a world of difference between wanting to take the *place* of the 'other', and wanting to *be* the 'other'.

A similar distinction perhaps needs to be made in considering relationships to racism. There are two significant positions. The first is manic denial – racism simply does not exist, or only affects other people. The second is based on the permeation model in which racism becomes a global persecutory power, and the subject loses the ability to discriminate between people or practices which are racist and those which are not. In both cases racist discourses may become articulated through an 'internal saboteur'. This cruel and perverse figure is a symbolic representation of what Freud called the death instinct and is mobilised against what, or whoever, promises greater hope and vitality (viz., the adoptive family). The British psychoanalyst Fairbairn pointed out the element of dissimulation which is often involved in this process (see Fairbairn, 1952). The internal saboteur is a seductive bully, a psychic confidence trickster, who makes capital out of whatever vulnerabilities are exposed when important struggles for emotional growth are taking place. In the same way the internal racist sabotages actual struggles against discrimination by offering an omnipotent or omniscient standpoint from which they are judged to be irrelevant, either because of their necessarily limited nature, or because they are aimed at something which is supposed not to exist. Adoptive families, whether black or white, where the issue of genealogical difference is both racialised and disavowed, give this figure more than usual room for manoeuvre.

The 'internal saboteur' feeds off anxieties which are stirred up whenever the subject has to take a step into the unknown. In cases of adoption, where the child is deliberately kept in ignorance about significant factors affecting placement, anxiety is likely to be especially intense and get structured unconsciously through this figure. One of the ironies of the current situation is that whilst race continues to be a decisive factor in placement, it is no longer discussed as an issue. In the era of open adoption a veil of silence has been drawn over the whole question; in some agencies, social workers who may have reservations about the way current policies are being implemented are discouraged or afraid to voice their objections in case they are accused of being 'racists'. 'Political correctness rules OK', and gives the real reactionaries plenty of scope to make ideological mountains out of molehills. Although the children concerned may be unaware of what has been going on 'behind the scenes', at a deeper and more unconscious level they are undoubtedly affected by the climate of such regimes.

Against all this I have tried to show that there are arguments to be made both for and against transracial and inter-country adoption which are not beholden to fundamentalist positions, and which make dialogue more, rather than less, possible. I have tried to spell out some of the psychic and social conditions which may make for more, or less, successful outcomes and to indicate some of the problems and possibilities of different types of placement. Running through all this is the notion that we need a much greater understanding and sensitivity to the complexities of individual life histories so that decisions can be made on a case-by-case basis, rather than some general rule of thumb.

BIBLIOGRAPHY

The following were the main texts consulted in preparing the chapter:

PROLOGUE: THE GENEALOGY OF DIFFERENCE

Bloom, H. (1973) *The Anxiety of Influence: A Theory of Poetry*. New York: Oxford University Press.

Brinich, P. (1990) 'Adoptions from the inside out: a psychoanalytic perspective', in Brodzinsky and Schechter (1990).

Brodzinsky, P. and Schechter, M. (1990) *The Psychology of Adoption*. New York and Oxford: Oxford University Press.

Gates, H.L. (1988) *The Signifying Monkey*. Oxford: Oxford University Press.

Gill, O. and Jackson, B. (1983) *Adoption and Race*. London: Batsford/BAAF.

Kirk, D. (1985) *Adoptive Kinship*. Cleveland, OH: Wesleyan University Press.

ADOPTION AS A CIVILISING MISSION

Barret-Ducroq, F. (1987) *Love in the Time of Victoria*. Harmondsworth: Penguin.

Bean, P. and Melville, J. (1989) *The Lost Children of Empire*. London: Unwin Hyman.

Benet, M. (1976) *The Character of Adoption*. London: Cape.

Boswell, M. (1988) *The Kindness of Strangers*. Harmondsworth: Penguin.

Coveney, P. (1989) *Images of Childhood Bloomsbury*. London: Bloomsbury.

Donzelot, J. (1984) *Policing the Family*. London: Tavistock.

Lorimer, D. (1978) *Colour, Class and the Victorians*. Leicester: Leicester University Press.

McLeod, H. (1974) *Religion and Class in the Victorian City*. London: Croom Helm.

Pinchbeck, I. and Hewitt, M. (1969) *Children in English Society*, 2 vols. London: Routledge & Kegan Paul.

Stafford, G. (1993) *Where to Find Adoption Records*. London: BAAF.

Teichman, J. (1987) *The Meaning of Illegitimacy*. Manchester: Manchester University Press.

Zeliger, V. (1985) *Pricing the Priceless Child*. New York: Basic Books.

HIDDEN AGENDAS IN THE ADOPTION CONTRACT: FROM PHYSICAL MATCHING TO EMOTIONAL BONDING

Bowlby, J. (1975) *Attachment and Loss*, 3 vols. Harmondsworth: Penguin.

Fahlberg, V. (1988) *Fitting the Pieces Together*. London: BAAF.

Riley, D. (1983) *War in the Nursery*. London: Virago.

Rose, J. (1984) *The Case of Peter Pan*. London: Macmillan.

Rowe, J. (1992) *Yours By Choice*. London: Routledge.

Winnicott, D.W. (1990) *The Maturational Processes and the Facilitating Environment*. London: Karnac.

IDENTITY POLITICS: FROM ROOTS TO 'RACE'

Cheetham, J. (1982) *Social Work and Ethnicity*. London: Allen & Unwin.

Fisher, F. (1975) *The Search for Annie Fisher*. London: Cassell.

Haimes, E. and Timms, N. (1985) *Adoption, Identity and Social Policy*. Aldershot: Gower.

Kaye, J. (1991) *The Adoption Papers*. Newcastle: Bloodaxe.

Lifton, B. (1976) *Lost and Found – The Adoption Experience*. Harmondsworth: Penguin.

Tizard, B. and Phoenix, A. (1989) 'Black identity and transracial adoption', *New Community* 15(3).

FUNDAMENTALISMS: ABSWAP VERSUS THE NEW RIGHT

Adoption and Fostering (1987) Special issue on Black Identity, 11(3).

Barker, M. (1981) *The New Racism*. London: Junction Books.

Cheetham, J., ed. (1986) *Social Work with Black Children and their Families*. London: Batsford.

Cohen, P.A. (1991) 'It's racism what dunnit', in Rattansi and Donald, eds (1991).

Dale, D. (1987) *Denying Homes to Black Children*. London: Social Affairs Unit.

Dominelli, L. (1988) *Anti-Racist Social Work*. Basingstoke: Macmillan.

Maximé, J. (1986) 'Some psychological models of black self-concept', in Cheetham, ed. (1986).

Rhodes, P. (1993) 'Racial matching in fostering and adoption', *New Community* 18(2).

Small, J. (1991) 'Ethnic and racial identity in adoption', *Adoption and Fostering* 15(4).

Weise, J. (1987) *Transracial Adoption – A Black Perspective*. Norwich: Social Work Monograph.

Zaal, F. (1991) 'Transracial child placements in South Africa', *Journal of South African Studies* 18(1).

'POSITIVES AND NEGATIVES'

Erikson, E. (1968) *Identity and Crisis*. London: Faber.

Fanon, F. (1986) *Black Skins, White Masks*. London: Pluto.

Gilman, S. (1985) *Difference and Pathology*. Ithaca: Cornell University Press.

Hall, G.S. (1904) *Adolescence: Its Psychology and Its Relationship* . . . , 2 vols. New York: Appleton & Co.

Richards, B. (1987) 'Family, race and identity', *Adoption and Fostering* 11(3).

TOWARDS A POLITICS OF DIFFERENCE

Fairbairn, W.R.D. (1952) *Psychoanalytic Studies of the Personality*. London: Tavistock.

Hall, S. (1991) 'New and old ethnicities', in Rattansi and Donald, eds (1991).

Hebdige, D. (1987) *Cut 'n' Mix*. London: Comedia.

Tizard, B. and Phoenix, A. (1993) *Black, White or Mixed Race*. London: Routledge.

Rattansi, A. and Donald, J., eds (1991) *Race, Culture, Difference*. London: Sage.

Sollors, W., ed. (1987) *The Invention of Ethnicity*. Oxford: Oxford University Press.

Wilson, A. (1987) *Mixed Race Children*. London: Batsford.

Wieder, H. (1977) 'The family romance fantasies of adopted children', *Psychoanalytic Quarterly* 46.

4 WHAT IS IDENTITY?

BARRY RICHARDS

INTRODUCTION

> ... children need to develop a positive identity, including a positive racial identity. (BAAF, 1987)

> The issue of identity is paramount for the black child. Identity supersedes 'bonding'. Bonding without a sense of racial identity is 'pathological bonding' and is against the best interest of the black child. (ABSWAP, 1983)

The literature on transracial adoption, which for almost a decade has been very heavily weighted in opposition to it, is peppered with statements of this sort. They are the bedrock of the arguments against transracial placements. These arguments run broadly as follows: everyone needs a 'positive identity'; a key component of identity is 'racial identity'; racial identity (and the 'survival skills' based on it) can be acquired only from carers of the same race as the child. Nowhere in these self-confident assertions is there any attempt to define or reflect upon the meaning of the term 'identity'. Nor can we find any evidence produced to support the assertions, even when they are positing new concepts such as 'pathological bonding'.

All participants in the debate, whether for or against, will of course bring their own assumptions and preconceptions to what they say. However, in the interests of both a rational exchange of views, and the children whose lives we are discussing, we should all attempt to think about the terms we use, to know what justification there might be for our usage, and what confusions around it might be possible. In this chapter the term 'identity' will be considered with this aim in mind.

OFFICIAL IDENTITY AND SUBJECTIVE IDENTITY

Identity has become a key word of our times. It has acquired a range of meanings which reach deeply into our social experience, in at least two directions. Firstly, it stands for various ways in which, in modern society, we are all individually registered and identified by bureaucracies. The identity card, the identity parade and the identification number are examples of this. Each individual is registered in various unique ways by the authorities – by fingerprint, driving licence number or whatever. These registrations make up our administrative 'identities'. We are often suspicious of this bureaucratic-legal apprehension of our individuality, and anxious about having this sort of identity.

Secondly, it expresses something very different from these bureaucratic descriptions. It has become a word which people use to refer to some of the most prized aspects of their being, to something felt to be intimately connected with the vitality and meaningfulness of life. Without 'identity' in this sense, we fear ourselves to be lost, or empty, unable to live life to the full, perhaps even unable to live it at all.

It is this second, positive sense with which we are primarily concerned here, the sense in which 'identity' conveys something essential to the individual, something full of personal meaning. This sort of identity is often counterposed to one's official 'identity', in which there is usually no trace of one's lived experience. The face is contrasted with the number, the feeling person with the file card, the complex biography with the computerised record.

However, it is worth pausing for a moment to reflect on why the same word carries both types of meaning. Vocabulary is often a source of clues to hidden or unnoticed aspects of everyday life, and here, in the use of one word to do two jobs, there is perhaps a clue that these two apparently divergent phenomena, the official and subjective meanings of identity, may be connected.

The basic linkage is in the historical connection between the two; both bureaucratic identity and experiential identity are aspects of modern society. They each rest upon 'individuals' and their 'individuality' being accepted as basic elements of the social world, but this has not always been so. As Raymond Williams (1983) has argued, these categories as we now use them are of relatively recent origin, their emergence being traceable in the early modern period, particularly the eighteenth century.

Furthermore, in some contexts it can be difficult to disentangle the two kinds of identity, since there are some forms of group identity which seem to combine the two. Nationalist identity, for example, which is also linked to the emergence of industrial modernity (see Gellner, 1987), draws upon both the official (passport) kind and the subjective, passionate kind. Yet as will be shown it is crucial to maintain distinctions between different kinds of identity and the different processes through which they develop, even when they may be combined in some complex social phemonena.

THE HISTORY OF IDENTITY

Official identities have existed in some form and been widely recognised for a long time, and have been based since perhaps the late seventeenth century on extensive statistics about their populations which governments have gathered. The idea of an experienced, *authentic* identity has more recently come to prominence on our cultural scene. A lot of research would be necessary to establish just when, where and how this notion found its way into everyday thought, but it seems likely that it is only since the Second World War that the notion of identity has enjoyed the currency it now has.

It was in large part an import into the wider culture from the language of psychology. Writers in a tradition of social psychology known as symbolic interactionism (and one of its derivatives, role theory) have made considerable use of it, through often with a stress on identity as the product of a person's role designations in society rather than as an inner reserve of authenticity (see, for example, Stryker, 1987). The latter, more humanistic and more influential understanding of identity is derived primarily from the psychoanalytic tradition. The work of the psychoanalytic psychologist Erik Erikson was particularly important in popularising the concept amongst social scientists, social workers and others (initially with his book *Childhood and Society*, first published in 1950, and then later in *Identity, Youth and Crisis* (1968)).

Erikson saw the development of identity as central to mental health: in his view the foundations of it are laid in infancy and early childhood, and the period of most acute struggle for it is adolescence, although it is never finally secured and adults of any age may experience 'identity crisis'. In the 1950s the idea that we all have a need for identity became part of the thinking of market researchers and advertisers, especially in the United States where there was a widespread reaction against 'conformism' (see, for example, Dichter, 1960, Chapter 11).

By the early 1960s the concept of 'identity', although vague, was firmly established in much academic and professional thinking. Then in the cultural and political changes of the sixties it was taken up on a still wider scale, becoming part of the vocabularies of many diverse groups and causes, including feminists, black militants, gays, campaigners for the reform of prisons and mental hospitals, and the 'growth' movement. Through this diffusion it became, as it is today, a part of popular everyday language.

THE PARADOX OF SUBJECTIVE IDENTITY

Identity contains a tension within itself. This is to be found in the way that it embodies both difference and sameness.

To have an 'identity' is to feel distinctive, and to be able to relate to others as different from oneself. Any meaningful relationship one has with another must include an appreciation of the other's *difference* from oneself. To have a strong identity is to feel secure in one's own distinctive qualities, and to face the world in knowing possession of these.

Yet, at the same time, there is in our understanding of identity a strong component of *sameness*. Identity rests on a commonality with others, on a sharing of experience or attribute. Our identities depend on us identifying with something larger than ourselves, whether it be nation, religion, gender, class, region, language or something else (and any individual's identity will include a synthesis of a number of such identifications). In this respect, to have an identity is to be able to relate to some others on the basis of one's sameness to them; it is to belong, to a be part of.

It is largely because of the way in which 'identity' expresses both sides of this tension that it has become such a prominent theme in our culture. The tension or contradiction between individuality and collectivity, between independence and belonging, is a very deep one in contemporary society, and not surprisingly any idea or image which seems to hold together both sides of the contradiction is likely to be invested with much significance and hope. The term 'identity' has become a powerful symbol of hope; it is, we feel, with a secure identity that a person or a people can look forward to the future, able to face challenges and to hand on a good future to their children. And, conversely, the image of a lost or damaged identity is part of a language of despair, a despair that the tensions of life will not be contained, that conflicts cannot be resolved or repaired.

IDENTITY AS A CIVIL RIGHT

Much more could be said about the diverse dimensions of meaning contained in the word 'identity', and about its chequered social history. This diversity brings home the difficulty of being clear about what, on any particular occasion, it might mean, both to the users of the word and to those hearing it. Given its complicated range of meanings, it is inevitable that the word will be used in a number of different ways, not all of which will be consistent with each other. There are abundant possibilities for blurring and confusion. One of the first signs that something is wrong with arguments against transracial adoption is their failure to define this key word. It is assumed that we all know what it means.

These assumptions are possible largely because 'identity' connotes certain values which are very familiar to us in the dominant traditions of the modern West. It is, in part, simply a contemporary expression of the philosophy of liberal individualism, in which the rights of the individual are of prime importance. In fact, 'identity' does more than simply express this tradition; it extends it, so that individuals are now regarded as having rights not only to basic degrees of freedom, political participation and material provision, but also to a certain kind of cultural experience – to a sense of belonging, or of confirmation by one's surroundings, or of continuity with previous generations, or whatever.

' . . . or whatever': this returns us to the problem of *defining* identity. But, before we look more closely at that problem, the point to note here is that for many people 'identity' has become a civil right. That this has happened is a testimony to the flexibility and resilience of liberal capitalism; many of the radical, apparently subversive demands of the sixties have become incorporated into its broad tradition of democratic politics. The sphere of what are regarded as basic human rights has expanded from the political and material to include phenomena of a cultural and psychological kind, and in principle this is probably a good thing; the problem comes in being clear about what it means in practice.

PERSONAL IDENTITY AND SOCIAL IDENTITY

In order to be clear about what is meant, it is essential to keep in mind another distinction, one widely recognised amongst writers on the subject (see, for example, the essays by Harré and Hitch in Breakwell, ed., 1983). This is between two components of subjective or experienced identity, namely between 'personal' and 'social' identities. Social identity is what an individual possesses by virtue of membership of certain social groups: you are a black working-class woman, or a heterosexual Jewish doctor, or a male Geordie teenager. As these examples suggest, there are some kinds of social classification which are usually seen as being more important than others in defining social identity.

The social divisions of race, class and occupation, gender, sexuality, religion, nation or region, and age are the dominant forms of social classification, although of course people vary enormously in how they tend to classify others, in what group memberships they see as important. We also differ widely in what group memberships we feel are important to ourselves; for some Welsh people, to be Welsh is the paramount fact of their social identity, whilst for others their 'Welshness' is marginal to their sense of who they are. On the whole, though, whether we are talking about the social identity we ascribe to others, or feel to be our own, it is likely that these major social categories, including and often especially race, will loom large in our minds.

However, one's 'identity' is more than a sum total of the various identifications one has with particular social groups; these do not define the individual. We have to consider what distinguishes one person from another, even when they share membership of all the major social categories, and perhaps many minor ones as well. This is why the concept of 'personal identity' is necessary. It is harder to define, but is something to do with the way in which we are formed through our relationships with other *individuals* rather than through our relationships of belonging or not belonging to social groups. (In their chapter in this volume, Tizard and Phoenix are discussing something similar in their distinction between 'self-esteem' and 'racial identity' – see below, chapter five.)

Personal identity refers to the particular qualities, weaknesses and resources that are unique to the individual as a result of the unique relationships within which that individual grew up. Even within the same family different children will have different experiences. The parents' relationship, and their own states of mind, may well be different at different stages of their lives, which means that children arriving at different times will have different experiences. The family circumstances may change, significantly affecting the emotional climate in the family; and, above all, even against a background of constancy, parents will relate to their various children in different ways. This will be partly due to the parents' responding to some differences in the children which seem to have been there from the start ('Anne was always much more mischievous than Mary'; 'John used to cry all the time, while James is no trouble'). It will also derive in part from the parents' own needs and expectations about family life, which will in turn rest largely upon their own earlier experiences of their families of origin, of who takes after whom, of the places taken by girls and boys, elder and younger siblings and so on.

Through a very complex process involving the transmission of feelings and roles from one generation to another, together weaving the constitutional endowment of the children and the circumstances of the family, the personal identities of the children will be established. They will be carried forward by them into their relationships with others in later life, and into their general sense of being in the world. This personal identity cannot be reduced to, nor subsumed under, social identity, and it is a major confusion in much of the debate about transracial adoption that the term 'identity' is used as if it included personal identity, when the phenomena under discussion are aspects of social identity.

Crucial though it is to maintain the distinction, it is also important not to see it as an absolute. Personal identity *is* ultimately 'social'. The material and cultural contexts of family life will shape and limit the kinds of experiences which are possible or likely in that family. The accumulated social experience of generations – be it of poverty or privilege, oppression or opportunity – will be fundamental to what any parent brings to a relationship with a child, as it is an integral part of what kind of person that parent is.

Some psychological theories tend to talk of personal identity as if it were something that springs purely from *within* the person, in contrast to all external, social influences. This would imply some biological or transcendental source of identity, which is not the view taken here. Rather, personal identity can be seen as the product, in a particular individual, of all the social forces – many of them reaching far back into history – which have acted, directly or indirectly, upon the people with whom that individual has grown up.

For example, looked at this way, the experience of slavery and its aftermath will be found somewhere in the personal identities of all West Indian and American blacks. But, in any one person, that massive historical experience will have been mediated through the lives of many generations and individuals. It will have been combined with and modified by many other experiences, the patterns of combination and modification varying endlessly between families and individuals. Hence the *particularity* of experience, which is what defines us as individuals, and which is what the term personal as opposed to social identity, conveys. It is the condensation of a chunk of human history into one life-world, the unique impression formed by a host of forces as they converge upon a personality in the process of formation.

Perhaps it would be more accurate, and less misleading, to speak of 'psychological' and 'sociological' identities, instead of 'personal' and 'social' ones. This would make it clear that we have a personal identity which is not something outside of society and the social (in a broad and deep sense including history), but which is something different from the sociological description of the individual as belonging to certain social groups in the here-and-now – class, ethnic group, religion and so on. It is a psychological inner reality which has an existence apart from these ongoing group memberships in the external world.

The critics of transracial adoption have argued that transracially adopted persons are likely to have identity problems. By this they mean problems in the sphere of social identity, in that their ethnic group memberships may not be clearly established and recognised. There can be no doubt that being the only non-white person in a white family is a problematic situation for a child to be in, although, as will be argued shortly, this problem is one that can be, and frequently is, resolved in ways that may enrich both child and parents. Being the only non-white person in a white neighbourhood or town, at school, in shops, at play and so on is also a problematic situation, and is less easily resolved except by moving to another area. No sound defence of transracial adoption would ignore this, and the presence of some ethnic diversity in the child's everyday experience is a highly desirable condition for a transracial placement.

Yet even assuming this to be present, it is clear that the self-experience of a transracially adopted child is necessarily going to be, in some respects, unusual, and may require some careful and sensitive management by the parents if it is not to be a source of distress and difficulty for the child. An easy conclusion to draw, in the abstract, would be that it is best to avoid the whole possibility of any problem by not making transracial placements. In fact, that is a wrong conclusion, for three reasons.

Firstly, as is argued forcefully elsewhere in this book, the ban on such placements has condemned many non-white children to many more years of care than they would otherwise have faced, and in some cases has deprived the child of the chance of any adequate experience of family life.

Secondly, in the experience of racially mixed families (both those formed by adoption and by other means) there are valuable lessons to be learnt, and gains to be made, for the project of creating a basically harmonious multiracial society.

Thirdly, the available evidence suggests quite strongly that transracially adopted children do not necessarily suffer from serious 'identity problems', and indeed that in most cases they are basically as healthy psychologically as control groups.

I will not be reviewing this empirical evidence here (Tizard and Phoenix discuss some of it in their chapter); my concern is to consider instead the *conceptual* bases of the debate. Crucial though the empirical evidence is for rational analysis, it has played little part in policy formation in recent years. Even before the opposition to transracial placements became the orthodoxy, it was known from research that they were not necessarily damaging to children (see, for example, Bagley and Young, 1982). Further reports during the 1980s have strengthened this conclusion (for example, Gill and Jackson, 1983), but either these have been ignored or their findings have been traduced. So the argument has not been about the evidence, though it should have been. To set matters right, we need both to consider the evidence and also to untangle the conceptual confusions.

The argument against transracial placements has been that transracially adopted children are likely to have some particular problems in the area of social identity. However, it is *personal* identity which provides the main basis for a sense of emotional security, and given a stable and sound personal identity – the formation of which is basically unrelated to the ethnicity of parents and children – the problems of social identity can usually be adequately dealt with. Indeed some creative responses to problems of social identity, and thereby some valuable contributions to the overall process of social change, may be made by people who are secure in their personal identity or have, to put it differently, a basis of emotional strength from which they can work.

THE EMOTIONAL ROOTS OF PERSONAL IDENTITY

To consider more closely how personal identity is developed, and its relationship to social identity, we must return to the tradition of thinking from which, via Erikson, the concept of psychological identity arose, namely psychoanalysis. A major criticism of Erikson's work has been that he blurred the distinction between these two kinds of identity. In psychoanalytic thinking, whatever the ultimate connections might be between the two, there is a focus on the specificity of the personal and on those dimensions of emotional life which are profoundly internal. The interactions between inner states and external circumstances are studied, but the elements in this interaction are not collapsed into each other, as tends to happen in Erikson's writing.

Although the term 'identity' itself is not frequently found in most psychoanalytic writing, other terms such as 'ego' and 'self' are, and their meanings are often very close to the sense in which 'personal identity' is being used here. So within psychoanalysis the central task of emotional development can certainly be thought of as the formation of an identity, and anything likely to impede or disrupt that process will be seen to have damaging effects upon the individual, probably throughout life.

The bases of identity are laid, for better or worse, in the child's earliest relationships, primarily in the quality and stability of care given to it by those responsible for its early nurture. The baby and child has, in its parent figures (whether they are biological or adoptive parents or someone else), human material from which to construct an identity for itself, and with that material we all must work. There is in psychoanalysis a rich language of concepts – identification, internalisation, introjection and others – to describe how early images of others are taken in by the developing psyche, and how they constitute the raw material for the long and complicated process of identity formation.

This process turns on the paradoxical nature of identity that was observed earlier; it is constituted by both sameness and difference. This applies both to social identity – if you are Catholic you experience this both in your sameness to other Catholics and in your difference from people of other denominations and religions – and to personal identity. In other words we must be both like, and different from, our parents.

This crucial point is not recognised only by psychoanalytic psychology. Psychologists of many persuasions all understand individual development as premissed upon the work of separation and differentiation from parents, at the same time as there is some powerful modelling and identification going on. Different theories will understand the modelling differently: for behavioural psychology, the child learns to copy or imitate the overt behaviour of the parents. For psychoanalysis, it is more a matter of patterns of feeling being subtly transmitted, and of unconscious identifications building up and interacting with each other in the inner world of the child.

In whatever language it is described, the overall process is seen to be one requiring both identification with and differentiation from parent figures, in a complex dialectic of union and separateness. Race is not irrelevant to this process; if there is an obvious physical difference between parents and child such as skin colour, that will inevitably become involved in the child's struggle to establish who he or she is. This may happen in a quite mild and benign way, but it may not. Emotional development necessarily involves the child, and especially the adolescent, in periods of feeling distant and estranged from its parents, and of feeling hostile towards them – it seems that without some element of alienation and aggression, of hatred even, then the full state of separation and of psychological autonomy may not be achieved. If the difference of colour comes to symbolise for the child these feelings of loneliness and anger, such that they become closely linked to its experience of not being white, there is likely to be trouble in store.

However, there is no reason for this to happen unless the parents also have some feeling, probably unconsciously, that the child's colour does set it apart from them. This points to the need for careful screening of prospective adoptive parents for any traces of the kind of racist or 'subracist' anxiety which would be the basis for such a feeling. This is nothing unusual; there is a need for careful assessment in all cases, transracial or not. The problem here is whether the social services and adoption agencies have both the resources and the expertise to make such assessments. It may also happen if the child's experience prior to its adoption had been such that its colour had come to be the focus of negative feelings about itself and/or others, for example, an experience of abandonment or abuse by a black parent, or of a relationship with a parent who had very negative feelings about being black.

An important qualification of the argument for transracial adoption is that it may not be appropriate for a whole range of older children whose identities, personal and social, are already formed to a considerable degree. (And, partly for the sake of these children, the argument for black social workers and for the recruitment of more black adoptive families is irrefutable – I have covered this issue elsewhere; see Richards, 1987.) By the same token, however, this stresses the need for the earliest possible placement of a baby that is available for adoption. Months spent in a fruitless search for a racially matched family may limit the infant's chance to experience, through the early months of intimate nurture, that its body *belongs* with those of its parents.

In any family, adoptive or otherwise, multiracial or otherwise, the basic issue is the emotional quality of care, and the kind of experience which the baby and child will have of those caring for it. Will the child experience its parent figures as, overall, people who are good, loving and reliable? If so, it will be able to establish an internal sense of itself as good, lovable and stable. It will internalise its parents' caring qualities, and be able both to feel itself cared for throughout life, and to care for others. There will be enough good feeling in the parent–child relationship for the pains of conflict and separation to be weathered and contained.

This is a matter of the emotional resources of the parents, not of their physical characteristics. Personal identity rests on the nurturant and moral capacities of early care-givers, not on their colour. If it is established to an adequate degree, the individual will be able to make some creative response to problems in the realm of social identity. It has been pointed out that the emphasis in some social psychology and sociological theory on social identity as a simple reflection of group memberships does not do justice to the ways in which resourceful people act upon their social environments. Group memberships are not all experiential straitjackets in which individuals are helplessly trapped; rather they provide cultural materials which may be worked upon to a greater or lesser degree. Kitwood (1983) has shown that the idea that many young British Asians experience 'identity confusion' by virtue of their position 'between two cultures' is a stereotype which does not necessarily match the reality. The experience of the youth themselves may take a variety of forms, including a sense of confident movement between different cultural influences. Those youths he studied had stable and viable core identities which were based on their experience of solid family relationships.

The critics of transracial adoption argue that a social identity determined in a simple fashion by the structural position of being 'black' in a white family will of necessity be problematic, and will undercut the prospects for a positive personal identity. On the contrary, such understanding as we currently possess of the determinants of individuality and of mental health suggests that a strong personal identity, a sense of self grounded in good-enough early care, can lead to a vigorous and competent response to contradictions or tensions in the domain of social identity.

'Love is not enough', of course; it never is. There must also be material security, equality of opportunity, and the rights of citizenship. White parents adopting non-white children may be able to provide the first of these, but not the last two. Nor of course can black parents. But all parents can provide a basis for self-respect and the capacity for self-assertion based on a sense of social justice.

Moreover, there are not many people in today's world who can proclaim themselves to be without serious problems of social identity: the recomposition of the class structure, the erosion of some aspects of gender roles, the increasing mobility of labour and many other trends all contribute to the modern feeling that 'all that is solid melts into air' (or to the fragmented universe of 'postmodernity', as it is currently fashionable to call it). Perhaps one reason why the debate about transracial adoption has commanded so much interest in recent years is because it expresses, in the stereotype of the disinherited adoptee, a pervasive contemporary experience. We should not only beware of creating such stereotypes in our imaginations; we should even more beware of imposing, in practice, a spurious solution to *everyone's* problem on those people who we imagine are suffering it alone.

REFERENCES

ABSWAP (1983) 'Black children in care'. London: Association of Black Social Workers and Allied Professionals (extract reproduced as Appendix 1, this volume).

BAAF (1987) 'Practice Note 13: The placement needs of black children'. London: British Agencies for Adoption and Fostering (extract reproduced as Appendix 3, this volume).

Bagley, C. and Young, L. (1982) 'Policy dilemmas and the adoption of black children', in Cheetham, ed. (1982), pp. 83–97.

Breakwell, G., ed. (1983) *Threatened Identities*. Chichester: Wiley.

Cheetham, J., ed. (1982) *Social Work and Ethnicity*. London: Allen & Unwin.

Dichter, E. (1960) *The Strategy of Desire*. New York: Boardman.

Erikson, E. (1950) *Childhood and Society*. Harmondsworth: Penguin, 1965.

Erikson, E. (1968) *Identity, Youth and Crisis*. London: Faber and Faber.

Gellner, E. (1987) *Culture, Identity and Politics*. Cambridge: Cambridge University Press.

Gill, O. and Jackson, B. (1983) *Adoption and Race: Black, Asian and Mixed Race Children in White Families*. London: Batsford/BAAF.

Harré, R. (1983) 'Identity projects', in Breakwell, ed. (1983), pp. 31–51.

Kitwood, T. (1983) 'Self-conception among young British-Asian Muslims: confutation of a stereotype', in Breakwell, ed. (1983), pp. 129–47.

Richards, B. (1987) 'Family, race and identity', *Adoption and Fostering* 11(3): 10–13.

Stryker, S. (1987) 'Identity theory: developments and extensions', in Yardley and Honess, eds (1987), pp. 89–103.

Williams, R. (1983) *Keywords*. London: Fontana, 2nd edn.

Yardley, K. and Honess, T., eds (1987) *Self and Identity: Psychosocial Perspectives*. Chichester: Wiley.

5   BLACK IDENTITY AND TRANSRACIAL ADOPTION

BARBARA TIZARD and ANN PHOENIX

Since the mid-1970s in the USA, and more recently in Britain, influential groups of social workers have opposed the adoption and fostering of black children into white families. (These writers have almost always used the term 'black' to include Asian children, and also children of mixed parentage.) In 1983 the Association of Black Social Workers and Allied Professionals presented evidence to a House of Commons Select Committee in support of the claim that black children should be placed exclusively with black families. Both political and psychological arguments have been used in support of this claim; in this article we propose to discuss only the latter.

The main arguments are as follows:

1. That black children living in white families fail to develop a positive black identity. Instead, they suffer identity confusion and develop a negative self-concept, believing or wishing that they were white.
2. That unless they are very carefully trained, white families cannot provide black children with the skills and 'survival techniques' they need for coping with racist practices in society.
3. That the children will grow up unable to relate to black people and at the same time will experience rejection by white society.

These arguments have seemed compelling to many, especially when supported by disturbing clinical and personal anecdotes. They also get some support from the handful of British and USA research studies that have been carried out in this area (cf. Bagley and Young, 1979; Costin and Wattenburg, 1979; Gill and Jackson, 1983; Simon and Altstein, 1977, 1981). These have shown that the majority of transracially adopted children do indeed have little contact with their own racial group, since the adoptive families tend to live in predominantly white, middle-class areas. And whilst most studies report above average general adjustment and educational achievement in transracially adopted children, there is evidence that a sizeable proportion of the younger children 'misidentify' themselves as white, and show a preference for whiteness. For example, using the doll test, Bagley and Young (1979) found that half of their British sample of young mixed-race adopted children, almost all of whom had one white and one African or Afro-Caribbean parent, said that they resembled the white doll, and rather more said that they preferred the white doll. It is, of course, possible that a number of these children did in fact look more white than black.

A longitudinal study of transracially adopted children by Simon and Altstein (1977, 1981, 1987) in the United States found that at the most recent interview, when the young people were sixteen to twenty years old, 11 percent (all of mixed race) said that they would prefer to be white. Ten percent of the parents perceived their transracially adopted children as white. All these children were, in fact, of mixed race. The young people themselves were not asked this question. The great majority of families lived in all-white neighbourhoods. There was no difference between the self-esteem of the transracially adopted children and that of their white siblings, either adopted or born into the same families, and all groups seemed equally well integrated into their families.

In another American study, 30 transracially adopted children were compared with 30 black children adopted into black families (McRoy and Zurcher, 1983). On average, both groups of children were fourteen years old. They did not differ in the strength of their attachment to their parents and siblings, or in their self-esteem. However, they did differ in their racial self-perceptions. Whilst the inracially adopted children typically described themselves as black, only a third of the transracially adopted children did so, the rest describing themselves as either mixed, human, American, or, in three cases, white. However, only 27 percent of the transracial adoptees had two black birth parents, compared to 83 percent of the inracial adoptees. The authors noted that transracial adoptees who were living in racially integrated communities and attending racially integrated schools were those most likely to describe themselves as black.

Gill and Jackson (1983), in a British study of transracially adopted thirteen-to fifteen-year-olds, many with one or two Asian biological parents, found that most described themselves as 'brown' or 'coloured', rather than black. Few agreed with the statement that they 'felt proud of being black'. The majority of the children felt that their lives were very different from those of Asian and West Indian children in this country, and it was clear that they did not feel close to these groups. Nonetheless their self-esteem, as assessed by an inventory, appeared to be high. Few said that they 'would prefer to be white', or showed evidence of conflict or confusion about their origins. Their relationships with their white peers seemed to be at least average. The extent to which they had experienced racism, and whether their parents had helped them to cope with it, was unclear. But, as Small points out in discussing the study, 'They cannot always live in the protective arms of the family' (1986, p. 82). It is possible that at a later stage the difficulties he predicts, in terms of the children's inability to relate to their own race or to cope with racism, will emerge. Since no studies have yet followed transracially adopted children to adulthood, the issue is unresolved.

What has been, however, overlooked in this discussion is that in order to interpret the findings about transracially adopted children, comparable studies of children from the same backgrounds living with their families of origin are required. We shall argue that these studies have not yet been carried out with adolescents, but that where they have been completed with young children many points of similarity with the findings about transracially adopted children have emerged. We will go on to argue that the concept of a 'positive black identity' is, in any case, problematic and imprecise, and requires further analysis.

STUDIES IN RACIAL IDENTITY IN CHILDREN[1]

Considerable research has been carried out over the past five decades concerned with the racial identity of young black children living with their own parents. Much of it has used the 'doll' technique, developed by two black USA psychologists, Kenneth and Mamie Clark.

In their classic study the Clarks (1947) presented three- to seven-year-old black, then called 'negro', children with dolls which had identical physiognomies and differed only with respect to skin and hair colour. The basic findings were that by the age of three the black children could correctly select the doll that looked 'like a white child' and the one that looked 'like a coloured child'; but, when asked 'Give me the nice doll', half chose the white doll. A cause of particular concern was that a third of the black children chose the white doll in response to the question 'Give me the doll that looks like you', and half chose the black doll when asked 'Give me the doll that looks bad'. In contrast, white children overwhelmingly preferred the white doll, selected the black doll as bad, and accurately identified the white doll as looking most like them. These findings were replicated by many other researchers, in a number of countries.

The studies were interpreted as evidence that black children experience self-rejection and low self-esteem because they internalise white people's negative view of their race. Their identity confusion (misidentifying themselves as white) was said to result from a denial of their own colour. The research was used to argue for the desegregation of USA schools in the 1954 case of *Brown v. The Board of Education*, on the grounds that segregation damaged the racial identity of negro children. Whether the doll research did demonstrate this relationship, and whether desegregation led to an increase in self-esteem, is discussed in Murphy, John and Brown (1984).

During the 1970s replications of the studies showed a sharp drop in the proportion of children misidentifying themselves as white (cf. summary in Davey, 1987). Many writers link this reported development to the changes in black consciousness engendered by the Black Power and civil rights movements in the 1960s and 1970s (for example, Davey, 1987; Hraba and Grant,

)0; Milner, 1983). An alternative interpretation is that the changes reflect the use of more realistic dolls and photographs. Black children in the earlier studies misidentified themselves as white, it has been argued, not because of identity confusion, but because black dolls were at that time unfamiliar and the dolls used did not look like Afro-Americans or Afro-Caribbeans, but had European features and hair type, with very dark hair and skin. Whatever the explanation, a substantial proportion of young black children continue to say that they prefer, or would prefer to be like, the white doll or photograph. Davey and Norburn (1980), for example, found that only a third of their seven-year-old West Indian sample in London and Yorkshire, and two-thirds of their ten-year-old sample, chose the photograph of the child in their own racial group as the one 'they would most like to be'. The proportion of Asian and West Indian children who made 'own group choices' at both age levels was very similar. But white children of the same age still showed an over-whelming level of 'own group preference'.

Even though the findings of the doll and photograph studies do not directly attest to racial identity, researchers who use these techniques are convinced by the children's spontaneous verbalisations and other evidence that their responses do reflect genuine attitudes to race (Davey and Norburn, 1980; Milner, 1983; Wilson, 1987). Support for this view comes from almost the only study which has directly questioned young children about their acceptance of their race. Only 57 percent of a sample of five- to ten-year-old West Indian children in London said that they did not want to change their skin colour, compared with 88 percent of white children (Bagley and Coard, 1975).

Hardly any studies with adolescents have directly addressed the issue raised in the doll studies; that is, preference for one's own race. But a Jamaican study in the 1960s found a tendency for high school students to prefer European features, although most of them did not hanker for blonde hair or blue eyes. They admired straight noses, hair straight or wavy (and, in the case of girls, long), and a skin colour one or two shades darker than white. These adolescents were particularly likely to express dissatisfaction with their own hair and noses, the more so the darker their skin (Miller, 1969).

MIXED-RACE CHILDREN AND IDENTITY CONFLICT

The critics of transracial adoption argue that no distinction should be made between children with one white and one black parent and those with two black parents, since 'in this society any child who has the slightest taint of black is seen by the majority as black' (Small, 1986, p. 92). Adoption by white parents would give the child 'a white mask', and prevent 'exposure to his or her own self'. This view of the needs of people of mixed race was advanced fifty years ago by Stonequist (1937), one of the first theorists of 'marginality'. He saw them as caught between conflicting cultures, unable to feel a complete member of either, yet wishing to be a member of both. He believed that the turmoil, pain and confusion arising from this conflict may be lifelong, unless peace of mind is found by assimilating with the black group. Although another sociologist, Park (1937), stressed that there is a positive aspect to marginality, in that it provides insight into two communities, the negative view has been much more often heard.

The issue has become increasingly relevant because people of mixed white and Afro-Caribbean parentage constitute a steadily growing sector of the British population. The 1984–86 Labour Force Surveys showed that 27 percent of married and cohabiting Afro-Caribbean men aged under thirty and 28 percent of married and cohabiting Afro-Caribbean women of the same age had white partners[2] (Central Statistical Office, 1988). The children of these unions seem to be greatly over-represented amongst those entering care. They form, in fact, apart from white children, the largest group of those entering care.[3] In considering the fostering and adoption of these children, it seems important to understand the development and the identity of mixed-race children living with their own parents. Whilst it is certainly true that these children will have to come to terms with racial discrimination because they will not be accepted as white, what is contentious is the argument that they will only find happiness with black parents, and a black identity.

Unfortunately, very few studies of mixed-race children have been carried out. In the USA, moreover, mixed white and Afro-American children are now regarded as black, and not studied separately. Ann Wilson recently published a study of 51 six- to nine-year-old British mixed-race children, with one white and one African or Afro-Caribbean parent, living with their natural mothers. Half the mothers were single, and most, but not all, were white (1987). The study raises important issues, but it is difficult to know how far the findings are generalisable. This is because half the sample were members of Harmony, an organisation for interracial families, and were thus, as the author points out, highly reflective about racial issues. The research showed that a number of mixed-race children had an intermediate racial identity. They saw themselves as neither black nor white, but as half-caste, or brown. The great majority of the children – over 80 percent – picked the photograph of a mixed-race child as the one most like themselves, and the majority chose a mixed-race child's photograph as their preferred companion for a variety of activities. However, 70 percent of the children gave some indication of a preference for being white or, in a few cases, black. A clear mixed-race identity seemed to be associated with living in a multiracial area. Wilson suggests that this is because there may be sufficient numbers of mixed-race people to make 'mixed race' a viable racial identity.

There is also some evidence that casts doubt on the belief that mixed race children are rejected by both black and white people. A survey of friendship choices of junior school children in Manchester found that, on the contrary, children of mixed white and Afro-Caribbean parentage were popular with both racial groups. Children of Asian and Afro-Caribbean origin chose them as friends more often than they chose white children, whilst white children chose them more often than they chose children with two Asian or Afro-Caribbean parents. The mixed-race children themselves showed a strong preference for friends who were also of mixed race (Durojaiye, 1970). This study was carried out in a multiracial area and, like Wilson's, suggests that the identity of mixed-race children may be considerably influenced by whether or not they have contact with children 'like themselves'.

RACIAL IDENTITY AND SELF-ESTEEM

Those opposed to transracial adoption argue that, as a consequence of their negative attitude to their race, the self-esteem and mental health of trans-racially adopted children will be damaged. According to Small: 'If a healthy personality is to be formed, the child must first recognise and accept that he or she has a black psychic image' (1986, p. 88). The argument seems unrelated to the large amount of research that has been carried out on the self-esteem of black Afro-American and Afro-Caribbean children living with their own parents. These findings are, on the face of it, conflicting. As pointed out above, the results of the 'doll' studies which showed that young black children tended to misidentify themselves as white, and to choose a white doll as 'the nice one', were universally interpreted at the time as evidence of self-hatred, resulting from an almost inevitable damaging internalisation of racism. Initially, therefore, there was much surprise when, in the next decade, numerous direct assessments of self-esteem amongst black American adolescents showed that their self-esteem was similar to, or higher than, that of white adolescents (see review in Porter and Washington, 1979).

There are several possible interpretations of the apparent conflict of evidence. According to some, the discrepancy is caused by the change in the political climate between the heyday of the doll studies and the adolescent self-esteem studies. Another possibility is that as black children move into adolescence, their self-esteem increases, or their attitude to their race changes. Or it may be that young black people can have negative feelings about their racial identity, and yet have a positive self-concept.

Unfortunately, few studies have been made of racial identity in adolescents, and fewer still have assessed both racial identity and self-esteem in the same children. However, in those that have, the two have not been consistently related. This suggests that the assumption that self-esteem is inextricably linked with attitudes to one's race may be incorrect. An alternative theory is that self-esteem, and other aspects of mental health, are mainly developed in the context of an individual's most significant relationships, which in child-hood are within the family. In contrast, the racial identity of black children, whilst still influenced by the family, develops out of relationships with the white majority (see discussion in Jackson *et al.*, 1981). If this conceptualisation is correct, both black children living with their own parents, and those transracially adopted, may have some negative feelings about their racial identity, but high self-esteem and good mental health. Equally, other children of the same colour, but with poor family relationships, may have a high opinion of their blackness, but low self-esteem and serious psychological problems.

SURVIVAL SKILLS FOR BLACK CHILDREN

Opponents of transracial adoption argue that white families cannot provide black children with the skills to cope with racism. This argument seems compelling, but again we lack knowledge of the extent to which black parents, both Asian and Afro-Caribbean, provide their children with the means to cope with racism, or what the various coping mechanisms are, since these issues have rarely been studied. A small study of black American parents' views on helping their children to cope with racism found that they stressed the importance of instilling pride and self-respect in their children, and also pride in being black. Developing a tough skin, learning to put up with discrimination, and getting a good education were also mentioned. A number felt that they had not been prepared by their own parents to cope with racism (Peters, 1981).

Wilson, in her study of mixed-race children living with their natural mothers, described two ways in which some mothers helped children to cope with racism which appeared to be related to a realistic, i.e. 'intermediate', racial identity in the child (1987). These were: teaching them that the black community was collectively fighting discrimination, which was therefore not perceived as a personal problem for children to tackle on their own; and teaching them to divorce the experience of racism from self-esteem, that is, to understand that being discriminated against did not reflect shortcomings on their part. Wilson found that some white mothers taught these coping mechanisms, and some black mothers did not. However, her sample of black mothers was very small, and, like the Peters' sample, Wilson's sample over-represented parents with a particular interest in racial issues.

RELATING TO BLACK CULTURE

A further objection that has been raised to transracial adoption is that the children will be rejected by black people as 'not black enough in culture and attitude' (Small, 1986, p. 93). If transracial adoption does occur, then adoptive parents are urged to develop in the child 'cultural and linguistic attributes for functioning effectively in the black community', and to 'help or allow the child to develop a black personality' (Small, 1986, p. 97). It is certainly important that transracially adopted black children should be able to feel comfortable with other black people. But, apart from the impossibility of a person in one culture being able in any meaningful way to transmit another culture, the argument assumes the existence of a homogeneous black culture and community, distinct and different from a supposedly homogeneous white culture.

This is patently not true if the term 'black' is being used to include Asian cultures. But if in this context it means 'Afro-Caribbean' it is also unlikely to be correct. Social class is an important mediator of culture in black as it is in white communities. Generation is also an important influence on culture. Whilst an older generation may see their identity in terms of their island of origin, there is some evidence that many young people of Afro-Caribbean origin are relatively ignorant of Caribbean culture, and often do not define their identity in terms of their Caribbean origin. A study in London of children aged five to fourteen of Afro-Caribbean origin found the extent of their knowledge of Caribbean culture and history 'disappointingly low' (Bagley and Coard, 1975, p. 328). Hutnik (1985) found that, in describing themselves, adolescents of West Indian origin in the Midlands did not refer to the West Indies, unlike adolescents of South Asian origin, who tended to define themselves in terms of their country of origin. This does not, of course, mean that black youth has assimilated into white culture. A variety of black youth cultures have developed in Britain, some strongly influenced by the USA, others by Africa, others by the Caribbean. Because of their high prestige amongst young people, these black cultures have adherents amongst sectors of white youth, some of whom have acquired facility in Creole (Hewitt, 1986; Jones, 1988). Equally, it seems likely that sectors of aspirant black British youth are mainly oriented to white, middle class British culture, as appears to be the case in the USA (Banks, 1984; Troyna, 1979). Certainly, social class, generation, religion, region and neighbourhood are all likely to have a powerful influence on the culture of individual black families and young people. There is a clear need for further research on these issues, but meanwhile one must question whether the concept of a homogeneous black culture and a black personality is defensible.

THE CONCEPT OF A 'POSITIVE BLACK IDENTITY'

At the heart of the argument about transracial adoption is the concept of a 'positive black identity'. Each of the three terms in this concept is problematic, as is the simplistic either/or mode in which they are conceived. Underlying the concept is the assumption that people either have or have not a positive view of their identity: that they see themselves as either black or white; that they identify or do not identify with their racial group. We shall argue that this prescriptive view of psychological functioning is remote from the complex, ambivalent and shifting attitudes of real life. The first term, 'positive', in this context implies that it is unacceptable for any black child to feel other than proud of being black. We have shown above that research suggests that this may not be the attitude of many black children. Further, everyday experience suggests that our attitudes to the social groups of which we are members are often complex. One may, for example, on balance feel positive (although not 'proud') about being middle class, whilst wanting to dissociate oneself from some aspects of this identity, and seeing some disadvantages to it. Ambivalence of this kind is particularly likely to be felt by members of minority groups, who have to confront not only discrimination and abuse, but also the negative images of their group in the majority culture. For this reason, as Jackson *et al*. suggest, the relevant and important question is likely to be not 'Is the child's attitude positive or negative?', but 'What is the balance of their positive and negative feelings towards their group, and to what extent do they identify with the positive rather than the negative images they have of their group?' (1981).

The second term, 'black', is also problematic. Its use to refer to anyone who is not white has a clear justification, reflecting but rendering positive white society's division of the world into 'whites' and 'non-whites'. Because racism results in the social construction of black people as inferior to white people, for black children the development of racial identity in a racist society is likely to be an emotionally charged and painful process (Fanon, 1986). The discourse of race itself can constantly remind black children of how inferiorised their group is:

> I know that in my case I first discovered my Africanness when I learned that I was not only black but non-white. From that day onwards I began to regard the prefix non with absolute hostility . . . it vividly brought to mind the crude fact that in the eyes of the world my life represented something negative, something non. (Nkosi, 1983, pp. 44–5)

Although Nkosi is in this instance talking about South African society, the common use of the term in Britain (together with the absence of the term 'non-black') also represents the negative comparison of black people with white people here.

 ✳ Asian and Afro-Caribbean children are separated from white children by their experience of racism, and this experience forms an important part of their identity. However, it does not follow from their realisation that they are not white that they think of themselves as 'black'. As Modood (1988) has emphasised, this usage of black is aspirational, i.e. it has been adopted to promote a positive identity. But it is by no means clear how many people so designated by political activists use this term to describe themselves. There is evidence that many Asians in Britain do not do so (Banton, 1987; Modood, 1988), although it seems likely that the majority of young people of Afro-Caribbean origin do. On the other hand, some of their elders resent the fact that to white people West Indians and Africans are seen as an undifferentiated group, whilst they themselves feel the two groups have little in common, apart from their experience of racism (Benson, 1981). Wilson appears to be the only researcher to have elicited the racial labels that children and their mothers themselves use (1987). She found that half the mothers of mixed-race children, and a fifth of their children, used the terms 'half-caste', other children referring to themselves as 'half-and-half' or 'brown'. The term 'black' was understood by both mothers and children in several different ways, and many of the children and mothers preferred the term 'coloured'.

It is clearly worrying if children misidentify themselves, in the sense of believing that they look white, or that they are white, when they are not. But this issue is distinct from the issue of how they label themselves. There seems no valid reason to expect children to label themselves as 'black', if this is not how they are labelled by their family, peers, neighbourhood community, or the media. There is also no reason to believe that the label children give themselves has implications for their mental health.

Problematic issues also arise in relation to the concept of 'identity'. It is much too simple to suggest that one either identifies or does not identify with a social group of which one is a member. Any social identity, involving as it does not only awareness of group membership, but also the way in which one represents membership of a group to oneself, is a complex phenomenon, with many dimensions (Tajfel, 1978). Recent research on gender identity has delineated three of these dimensions, which also seem relevant to racial identity. These are: the extent to which one's identity is based on perceived similarities between oneself and others in the group; the extent of awareness of a common fate (that what happens to others in the group will affect oneself); and the extent to which membership of the group is central to the way one thinks of oneself (Gurin and Townsend, 1986). Women were found to occupy different positions on these dimensions. Comparable research on racial identity is much needed.

In discussions of black identity, it often appears that identity is to be viewed not only as a unidimensional, and bipolar, characteristic, but also as a fixed characteristic. But since identity is formed in social interaction, most social psychologists regard it as dynamic in content and organisation, and subject to change throughout the life cycle (Breakwell, 1986). This is obvious in the case of some social identities, for example those to do with age and occupation. In the cases of gender and race, group membership does not usually change, but its meaning is subject to change. As black children encounter new experiences, for example on leaving school or on entering new peer groups, changes in the meaning they give to their racial identity are to be expected. Such experiences may lead transracially adopted children as they grow older towards a closer identification with black people, or the reverse may occur. Either way, it is unlikely that their identity will remain fixed throughout childhood and adolescence.

CONCLUSION

The psychological arguments on which much of the opposition to transracial adoption is based rest on assumptions about the identity of black and mixed-race children living with their own parents. Since this chapter first appeared, the authors have carried out research with a sample of such young people, and found that more than half generally thought of themselves as 'mixed' or 'brown', rather than black (Tizard and Phoenix, 1993). Whether or not they had a black identity, the majority felt positive about their mixed background. Whether they lived with a white parent only, or with both parents, was not significantly associated with having a black identity, or a positive racial identity – other factors, such as the racial composition of their school and the extent of their politicisation, were more important.

There is no convincing evidence that self-esteem and mental health are necessarily tied to attitudes to race, and the notion that there is a 'black culture' which must be transmitted to transracially adopted children is unconvincing, given the plethora of contemporary black British lifestyles.

Finally, we would take issue with the tendency to reify racial identity as of unique importance to the individual. As Gilroy has argued, this tendency 'reduces the complexity of self-image and personality formation in the black child to the single issue of race/colour' (1987, p. 66). It leads, as discussed above, to equating 'positive black identity' with 'positive identity'. As we have shown, this equation cannot be justified on the basis of existing research, and its theoretical basis is contentious. It also inevitably results in the neglect of other important social identities, such as gender, social class, occupation, peer and neighbourhood groupings. Whilst the experience of racism impinges on the identity of all black people, other social identities may sometimes be more central and of greater salience to them.

One may or may not agree with the political objections to transracial adoption, and we would certainly agree that more black people should be encouraged and helped to come forward as adoptive and foster parents. But we would contend that the psychological objections to transracial adoption are not well grounded in either empirical data or theory. Differences are certainly to be expected in the identity of black children growing up in white and black adoptive families, but there are not at present sufficient reasons to believe that the race of the adoptive parents should necessarily override other considerations in determining placement.

NOTES

1. Whilst aware that the term 'race' is socially constructed and contentious, we have found no alternative to its use in a society where it has deep political and psychological meaning.
2. Although consensual unions are treated as marriages in the Labour Force Survey, 'informal cohabiting liaisons' are not recorded. These are known to be frequent amongst people of Afro-Caribbean origin, and there is some evidence that they are even more likely than legal marriages to be interracial (Community Relations Commission, 1976).

3. See two unpublished reports; *Child Care Placements – Patterns and Outcomes* (1988) by Jane Rowe, Marion Hundleby and Louise Garnett, a report to DHSS. *A Need Indicator of In Care Services for Children* (1988) by A. Bebbington and J. Miles, Personal Social Services Research Unit Discussion Paper 574, University of Kent.

REFERENCES

Bagley, C. and Coard, B. (1975) 'Cultural knowledge and rejection of ethnic identity in West Indian children', in G.K. Verma and C. Bagley, eds *Race and Education Across Cultures*. London: Heinemann, pp. 322–31.

Bagley, C. and Young, L. (1979) 'The identity, adjustment and achievement of transracially adopted children: a review and empirical report', in G.K. Verma and C. Bagley, eds *Race, Education and Identity*. London: Macmillan, pp. 192–219.

Banks, J.A. (1984) 'Black youths in predominantly white suburbs: an exploratory study of their attitudes and self-concepts', *Journal of Negro Education* 53(1): 3–17.

Banton, M. (1987) 'The battle of the name', *New Community* XIV (1/2): 170–5.

Benson, S. (1981) *Ambiguous Ethnicity*. Cambridge: Cambridge University Press.

Breakwell, G. (1986) *Coping with Threatened Identities*. London: Methuen.

Central Statistical Office (1988) 'Percentage of husbands and wives married to white persons: by ethnic group and age', *Social Trends* 18. London: Her Majesty's Stationery Office.

Clark, K.B. and Clark, M.K. (1947) 'Racial identification and preference in Negro children', in T. Newcomb and E. Hartley eds *Readings in Social Psychology*. New York: Holt, Rinehart and Winston, pp. 169–78.

Community Relations Commission (1976) *Between Two Cultures*. London: Community Relations Commission.

Costin, L.B. and Wattenburg, S.H. (1979) 'Identity in transracial adoption: a survey of parental dilemmas and family experiences', in G.K. Verma and C. Bagley, eds *Race, Education and Identity*. London: Macmillan, pp. 220–35.

Davey, A.G. (1987) 'Insiders, outsiders and anomalies: a review of studies of identities – a reply to Olivia Foster-Carter', *New Community* XIII (3): 447–82

Davey, A.G. and Norburn, M.V. (1980) 'Ethnic awareness and ethnic differentiations amongst primary school children', *New Community* VIII (1/2): 51–60.

Durojaiye, M.O.A. (1970) 'Patterns of friendship choices in an ethnically-mixed junior school', *Race* XIII (2): 189–200.

Fanon, F. (1986) *Black Skins, White Masks*. London: Pluto Press.

Gill, O. and Jackson, B. (1983) *Adoption and Race: Black, Asian and Mixed Race Children in White Families*. London: Batsford/BAAF.

Gilroy, P. (1987) *There Ain't No Black in the Union Jack*. London: Hutchinson.

Gurin, P. and Townsend, A. (1986) 'Properties of gender identity and their implications for gender consciousness', *British Journal of Social Psychology* 25: 139–48.

Hewitt, R. (1986) *Black Talk, White Talk: Inter-Racial Friendship and Communication Amongst Adolescents*. Cambridge: Cambridge University Press.

Hraba, J. and Grant, G. (1970) 'Black is beautiful: a re-examination of racial preference and identification', *Journal of Personality and Social Psychology* 16: 398–402.

Hutnik, N. (1985) 'Aspects of identity in a multi-ethnic society', *New Community* 12(2): 298–309.

Jackson, J.S., McCullough, W.R. and Gurin, G. (1981) 'Group identity development within black families', in H.P. McAdoo, ed. *Black Families*. London: Sage, pp. 252–63.

Jones, S. (1988) *Black Culture, White Youth: The Reggae Tradition from Jah to UK*. London: Macmillan Education.

McRoy, R.G. and Zurcher, L.A. (1983) *Transracial and Inracial Adoptees*. Springfield, IL: Charles C. Thomas.

Miller, E.L. (1969) 'Body image, physical beauty and colour among Jamaican adolescents', *Social and Economic Studies* 4: 72–89.

Milner, D. (1983) *Children and Race: Ten Years On*. London: Ward Lock Educational.

Murphy, J., John, M. and Brown, H. (1984) *Dialogues and Debates in Social Psychology*. London: Lawrence Erlbaum Associates.

Modood, T. (1988) '"Black"', racial equality and Asian identity', *New Community* XIV (3): 397–404.

Nkosi, L. (1983) *Home and Exile*. Oxford: Blackwell.

Park, R. (1937) 'Introduction', in E. Stonequist, *The Marginal Man*. New York: Scribners.

Peters, M.F. (1981) 'Racial socialisation of young black children', in H.P. McAdoo and J.L. McAdoo, eds *Black Children*. London: Sage, pp. 159–73.

Porter, J.R. and Washington, R.E. (1979) 'Black identity and self-esteem: A review of studies of black self-concept 1968–1978', *Annual Review of Sociology* 5: 53–74.

Simon, R.J. and Altstein, H. (1977) *Transracial Adoption*. New York: Wiley Interscience.

Simon, R.J. and Altstein, H. (1981) *Transracial Adoption: A Follow-up*. Lexington, MA: Lexington Books.

Simon, R.J. and Altstein, H. (1987) *Transracial Adoptees and their Families*. New York: Praeger.

Small, J. (1986) 'Transracial placements: conflicts and contradictions', in S. Ahmed, J. Cheetham and J. Small, eds *Social Work with Black Children and their Families*. London: Batsford, pp. 81–99.

Stonequist, E. (1937) *The Marginal Man*. New York: Scribners.

Tajfel, H. (1978) 'Social categorisation, social identity and social comparison', in H. Tajfel, ed. *Differentiation between Social Groups*. New York: Academic Press, pp. 61–76.

Tizard, B. and Phoenix, A. (1993) *Black, White, or Mixed Race?* London: Routledge.

Troyna, B. (1979) 'Differential commitment to ethnic identity by black youths in Britain', *New Community* VII (3): 406–14.

Wilson, A. (1987) *Mixed Race Children: A Study of Identity*. London: Allen & Unwin.

6 ATTACHMENT

SUSAN GOLOMBOK

There is a growing body of evidence to show that the course of a child's social and emotional development is closely related to the quality of the child's attachment relationships with parents. This chapter will examine the processes by which infants and parents become attached to each other, and the consequences of failure to form attachment relationships. The implications for intraracial and transracial adoptive families will then be considered. Although the following discussion focuses on mother–child attachment, it is acknowledged that children may also develop attachments to fathers, childminders, grandparents, and other people in their lives who are important to them.

ATTACHMENT FORMATION

By far the most accepted and comprehensive explanation of the processes involved in the development of attachment relationships comes from the ethological theory put forward by Bowlby (Bowlby, 1969, 1973, 1980) and Ainsworth (Ainsworth, 1972, 1982; Ainsworth *et al.*, 1978). According to this view, attachments develop through interactions between the mother and the infant; infants' innate behaviours such as sucking, grasping, crying, smiling, babbling, the tendency to listen to a human voice and the tendency to look at anything that moves, cause the mother to attend to the infant, engage in social interaction with the infant and remain nearby. As mothers and infants learn to interact with each other they develop synchronised routines so that they each begin to respond to the other in turn. An example of a sequence of synchronised interaction might involve the infant looking at the mother, followed by the mother looking at the infant, followed by the infant babbling, followed by the mother talking to the child, and so on. According to Bowlby and Ainsworth, synchronised interactions form the basis of attachment relationships, and as infants and mothers develop this ability they become mutually attached.

Infants pass through a series of stages in becoming attached to their mother. By six weeks they begin to show a preference for social rather than inanimate stimuli, and until six or seven months they enjoy attention from anyone, even a stranger. Infants become specifically attached to their mother at around seven months. At this time they begin to protest when they are separated from her (separation anxiety) and to become distressed when approached by an unfamiliar person (stranger anxiety).

Much controversy has surrounded the issue of how best to assess an infant's attachment to the mother. In their study of Scottish infants from early infancy to eighteen months, Schaffer and Emerson (1964) considered a child to be attached to the mother if separation from her consistently caused the child to protest. However, Ainsworth (1972, 1982) disagreed with the use of this criterion, arguing that a high level of protest in a situation of minor separation might indicate that the child is insecure in his or her relationship with the mother, and that a low level of protest does not necessarily mean that the child is insecurely attached. Ainsworth maintains that one of the most important criteria for healthy attachment is the child's ability to use the mother as a secure base from which to explore the world.

Ainsworth devised the Strange Situation Test to examine the child's use of the mother as a secure base from which to explore, as well as the child's response to the mother leaving and returning to the room and the child's response to a stranger (Ainsworth and Wittig, 1969). The Strange Situation Test begins with the mother and infant together in an unfamiliar room with toys, and then proceeds through a series of different situations each lasting about three minutes; a stranger joins the mother and infant, the mother leaves the infant with the stranger, the mother returns, the baby is left alone, the stranger returns and finally the mother returns. By analysing the infant's responses to the different situations in terms of the infant's exploratory activities, reaction to the stranger, reaction to separation and reaction to being reunited with the mother, the child is categorised as either securely or insecurely attached.

According to Ainsworth, a child of twelve to eighteen months who can explore freely in a strange situation using the mother as a secure base, who is not distressed by a stranger when the mother is present, who shows awareness of the mother's whereabouts during her absence and who greets her on her return, is securely attached, even when the child is distressed by the mother's absence. Insecure attachment can take one of two forms. Anxious/resistant attachment is demonstrated by an anxious child who doesn't explore when the mother is present, who is extremely distressed when the mother leaves the room, who tends to resist contact on the mother's return although remaining near to her, and who is wary of strangers even in the mother's presence. Anxious/avoidant attachment is characterised by a child who is uninterested in exploring when the mother is present, who shows little distress when separated from the mother, who avoids contact with her when she returns, and who is not particularly wary of strangers but may avoid or ignore them. Waters (1978) has also addressed the question of which is the best index of security of attachment, and concluded that this is the behaviour which the infant directs, or fails to direct, to the mother on reunion following separation, with securely attached infants greeting their mother positively on her return, approaching her, and being comforted by her when upset by the separation.

Ainsworth (1979) believes that the type of attachment which an infant develops to the mother largely depends upon the quality of interaction between the mother and the child. She describes mothers of securely attached infants as responsive from birth, sensitive to the infant's signals, and emotionally expressive (i.e. often smiling, using her voice expressively and frequently touching the infant). Mothers of anxious/resistant infants tend to misinterpret the infant's signals, fail to establish synchronised routines of interaction and are inconsistent in their responses (sometimes positive, sometimes negative), although they may provide close physical contact and care for their babies. In contrast, mothers of anxious/avoidant infants are characterised by impatience with their infant, resentment of the infant for impinging on their activities and unresponsiveness to the infant's signals.

Recent research provides empirical evidence in support of Ainsworth's view that the infant's development of secure or insecure attachment is associated with the quality of mother–infant interaction (Grossmann *et al.*, 1985; Isabella and Belsky, 1991; Izard *et al.*, 1991; Pederson *et al.*, 1990; Smith and Pederson, 1988). For example, it has been demonstrated that the development of secure attachment relationships is related to synchronous interactions in the infant's first year and, more specifically, that secure attachments are fostered by synchronous interactions in which mothers are responsive to their infant's vocalisations and distress signals (Isabella *et al.*, 1989).

Some mothers have difficulty in becoming attached to their infants. For example, mothers who are depressed interact less with their baby and are less responsive to the baby's social signals than non-depressed mothers, and this appears to have a negative effect for the child who is likely to have problems in becoming securely attached to the mother. When depressed and non-depressed mothers were compared with respect to patterns of mother–child attachment relationships, insecure attachments were found to be common for children whose mothers were clinically depressed (Radke-Yarrow, 1991; Radke-Yarrow *et al.*, 1985).

In other cases, characteristics of the infant rather than the mother can hinder the development of secure attachment. These include extreme irritability or unresponsiveness. This is demonstrated in a study of the relationships between infant irritability, maternal responsiveness, social support and attachment in 48 mother–infant pairs (Crockenberg, 1981). The results showed that the more irritable the infant, the less responsive the mother, and that unresponsive mothers who lacked social support were most likely to have insecurely attached infants. The importance of social support suggests that external environmental factors as well as the quality of interaction between the mother and her child are important for the formation of secure attachment relationships. In an investigation of individual differences in infant sociability, children who were unsociable at three months were found to be less likely than sociable children to be securely attached to their mother at one year (Lewis and Feiring, 1989). Differences in infant characteristics are believed to affect attachment by altering the nature of mother–infant interaction, thus indirectly affecting the quality of attachment (Sroufe, 1985).

Do infants who are securely attached to their mother develop differently from insecurely attached infants? Many investigations have addressed this question and, taking the findings as a whole, it seems that securely attached children do better in a variety of ways (Lewis et al., 1984; Londerville and Main, 1981; Lutkenhaus et al., 1985; Matas et al., 1978; Pastor, 1981; Slade, 1987; Sroufe et al., 1983; Youngblade and Belsky, 1992). For example, it has been shown that children who are securely attached are more sociable with their peers, more popular and more sociable with strange adults. They also have higher self-esteem, are less aggressive, show fewer behavioural problems and are more empathetic towards others. But although the quality of an infant's attachment to the mother appears to be important for healthy social and emotional development, the quality of infant–mother attachment is not fixed for life and can change for better or worse according to family circumstances (Thompson et al., 1982; Vaughn et al., 1979). So insecurely attached infants can become more secure over time if, for example, the mother experiences less stress. The opposite is also possible if the mother's situation makes her less accessible and less responsive to the child.

Whilst studies of attachment have traditionally focused on the development of attachment in infancy using the Strange Situation Test – a behavioural measure – as a means of classifying infants as securely or insecurely attached, in recent years attention has turned to the examination of attachment relationships in the pre-school and school-age years. As a result, interest has grown in representational aspects of attachment. Through their early experiences with attachment figures, children are believed to form internal representations of their attachment relationships (Bowlby, 1969, 1973, 1980). Bowlby refers to these internal representations as 'internal working models'. According to Bowlby, the child's internal working model of an attachment figure, for example as available and responsive in the case of securely attached children, or as unavailable and unresponsive in the case of insecurely attached children, will influence the child's expectations of, and behaviour towards, that person. The child's internal working models of attachment relationships are also believed to influence the child's internal representation of the self. Thus a child who represents attachment figures as responsive and emotionally available is likely to hold an internal model of the self as lovable, whereas a child with internal models of attachment figures as unresponsive and unavailable is likely to represent the self as unworthy of being loved. The child's internal representations of attachment figures and of the self are believed to have a profound influence on the individual's relationships with others in childhood and in adult life.

Techniques which focus upon thought, language and other representational processes have recently been developed to assess children's internal representations of their attachment figures. These include adaptations of the Separation Anxiety Test (Grossman and Grossman, 1991; Klagsbrun and Bowlby, 1976; Shouldice and Stevenson-Hinde, 1992; Slough and Greenberg, 1990) and a Family Drawing Task (Fury, 1993; Grossman and Grossman, 1991). In the Separation Anxiety Test, children are asked to respond to a series of photographs of a same-sex child experiencing separation from the parents; they are asked how the pictured child would feel and what the pictured child would do on separation. In the Family Drawing Task, children are asked to draw their family doing something. Responses to both tests have been validated against behavioural measures of attachment. Studies which have used these representational measures provide empirical evidence in support of Bowlby's view that individuals form internal models of their attachment relationships (for example Main *et al.*, 1985). It has also been demonstrated that a connection exists between working models of attachment figures and the working model of the self (Cassidy, 1988).

Although this chapter focuses on the child's attachment to the mother, it is important to point out that children also form attachments to their father and to other caregivers. According to Bowlby, children have a principal attachment figure, usually the mother, to whom they are especially attached, as well as subsidiary attachment figures. When upset, children tend to prefer to seek comfort from the principal attachment figure, and major separations from the principal attachment figure cause more distress than major separations from a subsidiary attachment figure.

In recent years, more attention has been paid than previously to children's attachments to their father (Lamb, 1986). Studies which have examined children's attachments to their father as well as to their mother have used the Strange Situation Test first with one parent and then with the other. These studies have found a similar proportion of infants to be securely attached to the father as to the mother (Fox *et al.*, 1991). Just like mothers, fathers who engage in frequent social interaction with their babies, and who respond readily and sensitively to them, have strongly attached infants (Cox *et al.*, 1992). But it remains the case that mothers are much more involved than fathers with their children. It is not because fathers are incompetent and insensitive parents that they are less important attachment figures than mothers, but because in most cultures they interact with their children less (Bowlby, 1988).

ATTACHMENT FAILURE

What happens when infants fail to form attachments in the first year or two of life? This most commonly occurs when infants are raised in institutions where they have little contact with their caretakers, but may also happen to infants raised at home by severely neglectful parents. Studies of rhesus monkeys raised in isolation during infancy have shed some light on this issue (Harlow and Harlow, 1977). After three months of isolation, they avoided other monkeys, appeared to be extremely fearful, and showed a number of abnormal behaviours such as biting themselves and rocking backwards and forwards. Those who had been isolated for six months, in addition to avoiding monkeys of the same age, failed to exhibit the aggressive play which is typical of monkeys at one year old, and when attacked by others they did not defend themselves or fight back. Monkeys who had experienced 12 months of social deprivation were extremely withdrawn, showed no social interaction and were in danger of being seriously injured or even killed by other monkeys during aggressive play.

The monkeys who had experienced three months' deprivation recovered and developed normal social relationships in adolescence and adulthood. However, those who had been exposed to at least six months of deprivation demonstrated unusual social and sexual behaviour as they grew up. On the basis of these findings, it was argued that the first six months of life are a critical period for the social development of infant monkeys, and that those who are deprived of a normal social environment during this time will be unable to develop appropriate social and emotional relationships.

Later investigations showed that the effects of early deprivation can be reversed. When isolated monkeys were given 'therapy' which involved touching and playing with younger, non-aggressive monkeys, they recovered and showed normal social behaviour (Novak, 1979). It is now generally agreed that there is no evidence for a critical period for attachment, i.e. that the effects of deprivation are permanent and irreversible. Instead, the first six months of life are thought to be a time when normally reared monkeys become attached to their mother, and when social deprivation interferes with the attachment process this results in social and emotional disturbance – but recovery is possible with appropriate therapy.

Studies of the effects of social deprivation on human infants have focused on children raised under conditions not too far removed from those experienced by the Harlows' monkeys. These children had little interaction with adult caretakers, were left alone in their cot for most of the time and rarely played with toys or other children. Although they showed normal behaviour for the first six months of life, they then stopped crying and babbling, developed rigid body postures, showed delayed language development, appeared to be depressed, and lost interest in social contact. Such children were followed up over a 12-year period by Goldfarb (1943, 1947). Children who were fostered during the first year of life ('foster children') were compared with children who spent their first three years in an orphanage ('institutional children'). The 'institutional' children showed much slower developmental progress than the 'foster' children on measures of IQ and language development. The 'institutional' children also showed a higher rate of behavioural problems such as temper tantrums, aggression and destructive behaviour. They were incapable of forming close attachments and by adolescence they were loners.

In a more recent comparison of early-adopted and institutional children (Hodges and Tizard, 1989a, 1989b; Tizard and Hodges, 1978), the 'institutional' children had access to many caretakers and thus were not socially deprived. Staff turnover was high, however, with children aged four years having experienced around 50 different caretakers. As a result, they rarely formed attachments during their first few years of life. By eight years, the children were socially outgoing and had normal levels of intellectual functioning, but those who had spent at least four years in an institution showed more behavioural problems at school, such as attention-seeking, disobedience and poor peer relationships, than early-adopted children. At age sixteen, these children still showed evidence of behavioural and emotional difficulties. The authors concluded that in spite of the improvements in institutional care since Goldfarb conducted his study, the children showed lasting effects from failing to form attachments early in life, and that this remained the case even when they formed strong attachments to their adoptive or foster parents.

The issue of whether or not there is a critical period for human infants to become attached to their mother has received much attention in the literature. Bowlby (1973) argued that attachment has to develop in the first two years of life for social and emotional development to proceed normally. However, the children in the investigation by Tizard and Hodges (1978) failed to form attachments in infancy but did develop attachments to their adoptive parents even when adopted after four years of age. So it seems that attachments can occur in children as late as four to six years, suggesting either that a critical period does not exist or that it extends beyond two years. But these children did show emotional problems, indicating that although attachments can still develop after two years, optimum social development may depend on the early attachment of the infant to the mother. It is now generally believed that infancy is a sensitive period, rather than a critical period, for the development of attachment (Rutter, 1981); that is, attachments may develop after infancy if appropriate social conditions are present and will lead to considerable recovery, but completely normal social and emotional development will be less likely if attachments are not established early in life.

ATTACHMENT AND ADOPTION

Do attachment relationships in adoptive families differ from those in non-adoptive families? The answer to this question has both theoretical implications for the understanding of the attachment process and practical implications for the wellbeing of adoptive families. It seems that the most important factor for a child's development of secure attachments is the quality of interaction between the attachment figures and the child. Adopted children, therefore, would be expected to develop secure attachments to their new parents providing the parents are responsive to them. Brodzinsky *et al.* (1987) discuss the various aspects of adoptive family life which may upset this process. Firstly, for adoptive parents who have not come to terms with their infertility, problems may arise in their relationship with each other and with their adopted child. Secondly, the uncertainty surrounding the timing of the adoption, together with an intrusive screening procedure by the adoption agency, may create difficulties for adoptive parents and undermine their confidence as parents thus disrupting the attachment process. In addition, some adoptive parents receive less support from family, friends and the wider community than non-adoptive parents, which may also have a negative impact.

Surprisingly few studies have examined attachment relationships in adoptive families. One notable exception is Singer *et al.*'s (1985) comparison of the attachment relationships of adoptive and non-adoptive infants. Using the Strange Situation Test, no differences were found between the two groups of infants in the proportion showing secure versus insecure attachments to the mother. Similar findings were obtained in a comparison between adopted and non-adopted four- to eight-year-old children using the Separation Anxiety Test (Golombok *et al.*, 1993). These findings show that mothers can develop a close emotional bond with their adopted child in spite of their lack of contact with the newborn infant. Thus the widely held view, initiated by Klaus and Kennell (1976), that interaction with the infant in the hours following birth is crucial for the mother to bond to the child – a view which implies that adoptive mothers would have difficulty in forming a close attachment because they lack this experience – is not supported by the evidence.

A factor which is often considered to be associated with quality of attachment to adoptive parents is the child's pre-placement history. Children adopted after they reach six months, the age at which attachments are formed, are thought to be more at risk for insecure attachment to their adoptive parents than early-adopted infants. Indeed, the findings discussed in the previous section provide evidence to support this view. The development of secure attachment relationships with adoptive parents may also be at risk in situations where the child had become attached to biological or foster parents before being placed with the adoptive family. Bowlby argues that when attachments are severed, long-lasting difficulties in forming new attachment relationships may result. In a study of late-adopted children who had experienced highly disrupted pre-placement relationships, it was found that difficulties remained for these children and their adoptive families one year after permanent placement (Rushton *et al.*, 1988). Family relationships had improved somewhat, with the majority of parents reporting that their adopted child had developed a genuine attachment to them, suggesting that reattachment may be possible, at least to some extent. The quality of the child's attachments to the adoptive parents was not assessed directly in this study.

ATTACHMENT AND TRANSRACIAL ADOPTION

What are the implications of existing knowledge about attachment for transracial adoption? Empirical data on attachment relationships in transracial adoptive families come from Singer *et al.*'s (1985) study in the United States which, in addition to the intraracial adoptive families, examined a group of families with infants of a different race from the adoptive parents. No difference in the quality of attachment was found between the intraracial and the transracial adoptive infants. However, there was a higher incidence of insecure attachment to the mother amongst the transracial adoptive infants than amongst the non-adopted infants. In a replication of this study with a larger sample in the Netherlands (Rosenboom, 1993), no differences in security of attachment to the mother were found between intraracial and non-adoptive families. The different outcomes of the two studies may result from the more negative attitudes towards transracial adoption in the United States, which may delay the formation of secure attachment relationships for these families.

It is generally agreed that the best placement for a child is with a same-race family from the outset. However, this situation cannot always be achieved. Current policy has resulted in ethnic minority children either being moved from one foster home to another or remaining in a foster home for several years until a same-race adoptive family is found. Both of these circumstances are likely to be harmful for the attachment process. Children who experience a number of foster homes in their early years may fail to form attachments. As already discussed, the most important determinant of secure attachment relationships for children is the sustained presence of responsive attachment figures. If children are denied such relationships, they fail to form attachments and this may lead to lasting negative effects. It is generally believed that infancy is the optimal period for the development of secure attachment relationships. Although children who fail to form attachments during that time may develop attachments later in childhood if placed in better circumstances, these later attachments may never completely compensate for the absence of attachment figures in infancy. For children who have been raised in a single foster home, the disruption of existing attachment relationships with the foster parents produced by moving a child to a same-race family is also likely to have negative consequences for the child.

In deciding where to place an ethnic minority child it is crucial that the child's attachment history is taken into account and considered alongside the advantages of growing up in a same-race adoptive family. If a child is denied the opportunity to form secure attachments whilst waiting for an appropriate adoptive family, or if existing attachments with foster parents will be broken, the benefits to the child may be outweighed by the costs incurred as a result of attachment failure or disruption. If greater priority is given to ethnic matching than to other factors which are important for the child's development, the outcome may not be in the best interests of the child.

REFERENCES

Ainsworth, M.D.S. (1972) 'Attachment and dependency: a comparison', in J.L. Gewirtz, ed. *Attachment and Dependency*. New York: Wiley.

Ainsworth, M.D.S. (1979) 'Attachment as related to mother–infant interaction', in J. Rosenblatt, R.A. Hinde, C. Beer and M. Busnel, eds *Advances in the Study of Behavior*, vol. 9. Orlando, FL: Academic Press.

Ainsworth, M.D.S. (1982) 'Attachment: retrospect and prospect', in C.M. Parkes and J. Stevenson-Hinde, eds *The Place of Attachment in Human Behavior*. New York: Basic Books.

Ainsworth, M. and Wittig, B. (1969) 'Attachment and exploratory behaviour of one-year-olds in a strange situation', in B.M. Foss, ed. *Determinants of Infant Behaviour*, vol. 4. London: Methuen.

Ainsworth, M.D.S. Blehar, M., Waters, E. and Wall, S. (1978) *Patterns of Attachment*. Hillsdale, NJ: Erlbaum.

Bowlby, J. (1969) *Attachment and Loss*, vol. 1, *Attachment*. London: Hogarth Press.

Bowlby, J. (1973) *Attachment and Loss*, vol. 2, *Separation: Anxiety and Anger*. London: Hogarth Press.

Bowlby, J. (1980) *Attachment and Loss*, vol. 3, *Loss*. London: Hogarth Press.

Bowlby, J. (1988) *A Secure Base: Clinical Applications of Attachment Theory*. London: Routledge.

Brodzinsky, D.M. (1987) 'Adjustment to adoption: a psychosocial perspective', *Clinical Psychology Review* 7: 25–47.

Cassidy, J. (1988) 'Child–mother attachment and the self in six-year-olds, *Child Development* 59: 121–34.

Cox, M. J., Owen, M.T., Henderson, W.K. and Margand, N.A. (1992) 'Prediction of infant–father and infant–mother attachment', *Developmental Psychology* 28: 474–83.

Crockenberg, S. (1981) 'Infant irritability, mother responsiveness, and social support influences on the security of infant–mother attachment', *Child Development* 52: 857–65.

Fox, N.A., Kimmerly, N.L. and Schafer, W.D. (1991) 'Attachment to mother/attachment to father: a meta-analysis', *Child Development* 62: 210–25.

Fury, G. (1993) 'The relation between infant attachment history and representations of relationships in school-aged family drawings'. Poster presented at the 60th meeting of the Society for Research in Child Development, New Orleans.

Goldfarb, W. (1943) 'The effects of early institutional care on adolescent personality', *Journal of Experimental Education* 12: 107–29.

Goldfarb, W. (1947) 'Variations in adolescent adjustment in institutionally reared children', *Journal of Orthopsychiatry* 17: 449–57.

Golombok, S., Cook, R., Bish, A. and Murray, C. (1993) 'Families created by the new reproductive technologies: quality of parenting and social and emotional development of the children', submitted to *Child Development*.

Grossmann, K.E. and Grossmann, K. (1991) 'Attachment quality as an organizer of emotional and behavioural responses in a longitudinal perspective', in C.M. Parkes, J. Stevenson-Hinde and P. Marris, eds *Attachment across the Life Cycle*. London: Routledge.

Grossman, K.E., Grossmann, K., Spangler, G., Suess, G. and Unzer, L. (1985) 'Maternal sensitivity in northern Germany', in I. Bretherton and E. Waters, eds *Growing Points of Attachment Theory and Research. Monographs of the Society for Research in Child Development* 50: 233–56.

Harlow, H.F. and Harlow, M.K. (1977) 'The young monkeys', in *Readings in Developmental Psychology Today*. Del Mar, CA: CRM Books.

Hodges, J. and Tizard, B. (1989a) 'IQ and behavioural adjustment of ex-institutional adolescents', *Journal of Child Psychology & Psychiatry* 30: 53–75.

Hodges, J. and Tizard, B. (1989b) 'Social and family relationships of ex-institutional adolescents', *Journal of Child Psychology & Psychiatry* 30: 77–97.

Isabella, R.A. and Belsky, J. (1991) 'Interactional synchrony and the origins of infant–mother attachment: a replication study', *Child Development* 62: 373–84.

Isabella, R.A., Belsky, J. and von Eye, A. (1989) 'Origins of infant–mother attachment: an examination of interactional synchrony during the infant's first year', *Developmental Psychology* 25: 12–21.

Izard, C.E., Haynes, M., Chisholm, G. and Baak, K. (1991) 'Emotional determinants of infant–mother attachment', *Child Development* 62: 906–17.

Main, M., Kaplan, N. and Cassidy, J. (1985) 'Security in infancy, childhood and adulthood: a move to the level of representation', in I. Bretherton and E. Waters, eds *Growing Points of Attachment Theory and Research. Monographs of the Society for Research in Child Development* 50, Serial No. 209 (1–2): 66–104.

Klagsbrun, M. and Bowlby, J. (1976) 'Responses to separation from parents: a clinical test for young children', *British Journal of Projective Psychology* 21: 7–21.

Klaus, H.M. and Kennell, J.H. (1976) *Maternal–Infant Bonding*. St Louis, MI: Mosby.

Lamb, M.E. (1986) *The Father's Role: Applied Perspectives*. New York: Wiley.

Lewis, M. and Feiring, C. (1989) 'Infant, mother, and mother–infant interaction behaviour and subsequent attachment', *Child Development* 60: 831–37.

Lewis, M., Feiring, C., McGuffog, C. and Jaskir, J. (1984) 'Predicting psycho-pathology in six-year-olds from early social relations', *Child Development* 55: 123–36.

Londerville, S. and Main, M. (1981) 'Security of attachment, compliance, and maternal training methods in the second year of life', *Developmental Psychology* 17: 289–99.

Lutkenhaus, P., Grossmann, K.E. and Grossmann, K. (1985) 'Infant–mother attachment at twelve months and style of interaction with a stranger at the age of three years', *Child Development* 56: 1538–42.

Matas, L., Arend, R.A. and Sroufe, L.A. (1978) 'Continuity of adaptation in the second year: the relationship between quality of attachment and later competence', *Child Development* 49: 547–56.

Novak, M.A. (1979) 'Social recovery of monkeys isolated for the first year of life: II. Long term assessment', *Developmental Psychology* 15: 50–61.

Pastor, D.L. (1981) 'The quality of mother–infant attachment and its relation-ship to toddlers' initial sociability with peers', *Developmental Psychology* 17: 326–35.

Pederson, D., Moran, G., Sitko, C., Campbell, K., Ghesquire, K. and Acton, H. (1990) 'Maternal sensitivity and the security of infant–mother attach-ment: a Q-sort study', *Child Development* 61: 1974–83.

Radke-Yarrow, M. (1991) 'Attachment patterns in children of depressed mothers', in C.M. Parkes, J. Stevenson-Hinde and P. Marris, eds *Attach-ment across the Life Cycle*. London: Routledge.

Radke-Yarrow, M., Cummings, E.M., Kucznski, L. and Chapman, M. (1985) 'Patterns of attachment in two- and, three-year-olds in normal families with parental depression', *Child Development* 56: 884–93.

Rosenboom, L. (1993) 'Patterns of attachment of interracial adopted children in a Dutch sample compared to an American sample'. Paper presented at the 60th Meeting of the Society for Research in Child Development, New Orleans.

Rushton, A., Treseder, J. and Quinton, D. (1988) *New Parents for Older Children*. London: BAAF.

Rutter, M. (1981) *Maternal Deprivation Reassessed*. Harmondsworth: Pen-guin, 2nd edn.

Schaffer, H.E. and Emerson, P.E. (1964) *The Development of Social Attach-ments in Infancy. Monographs of the Society for Research in Child Development* 29, Serial No. 94

Shouldice, A. and Stevenson-Hinde, J. (1992) 'Coping with security distress: the separation anxiety test and attachment classifications at 4.5 years', *Journal of Child Psychology & Psychiatry* 23: 331–48.

Singer, L. M., Brodzinsky, D.M., Ramsay, D., Steir, M. and Waters, E. (1985) 'Mother–infant attachment in adoptive families', *Child Development* 56: 1543–51.

Slade, A. (1987) 'Quality of attachment and early symbolic play', *Developmental Psychology* 23: 78-85.

Slough, N.M. and Greenberg, M.T. (1990) 'Five-year-olds' representations of separation from parents: responses from the perspective of self and other', *New Directions for Child Development* no. 48, pp. 67-84.

Smith, P.B. and Pederson, D. (1988) 'Maternal sensitivity and patterns of infant–mother attachment', *Child Development* 59: 1097-1101.

Sroufe, L.A. (1985) 'Attachment classification from the perspective of infant–caregiver relationships and infant temperament', *Child Development* 56: 1-14.

Sroufe, L.A., Fox, N.E. and Pancake, V.R. (1983) 'Attachment and dependency in developmental perspective', *Child Development* 54: 1615-27.

Thompson, R.A., Lamb, M.E. and Estes, D. (1982) 'Stability of infant–mother attachment and its relationship to changing life circumstances in an unselected middle-class sample', *Child Development* 53: 144-8.

Tizard, B. and Hodges, J. (1978) 'The effect of early institutional rearing on the development of 8-year-old children', *Journal of Child Psychology & Psychiatry* 19: 99-118.

Vaughn, B., Egeland, B., Sroufe, L.A. and Waters, E. (1979) 'Individual differences in infant–mother attachment at 12 and 18 months: stability and change in families under stress', *Child Development* 50: 971-5.

Waters, E. (1978) 'The reliability and stability of individual differences in infant–mother attachment', *Child Development* 59: 483-94.

Youngblade, L.M. and Belsky, J. (1992) 'Parent–child antecedents of 5-year-olds' close friendships: a longitudinal analysis', *Developmental Psychology* 28: 700-13.

7 THE LAW AND TRANSRACIAL FAMILIES

JENNIFER CRAVEN-GRIFFITHS

The subject of transracial families involves various areas in both the civil law and the criminal law. The civil law involves disputes between individuals, or between individuals and authorities, whereas the criminal law involves the police and the determination of guilt or innocence of criminal wrongdoing. Both of these aspects will be dealt with, although it is the civil law which is relevant in the overwhelming majority of cases concerning transracial families.

THE CIVIL LAW

Administrative bodies such as local authorities both draw their authority from, and act within, a legal framework. This is known as acting *intra vires* (within the powers). Actions taken which are *ultra vires* (outside the powers) can be challenged in the High Court using the procedure known as Judicial Review.[1] It is therefore important to examine both the wider legal framework and the particular legal rules which relate to children in substitute families, including the question of race.

THE LEGAL FRAMEWORK

Local authority Social Service Committees are set up under an Act of Parliament,[2] which also specifies that a director must be appointed.[3] The Committee has the powers and duties under various statutes (contained in Schedule 1 of the Act as amended). Under the Adoption Act 1976 s.1, local authorities must also run an adoption service. The powers and duties are set out in the statutes, and are further explained and defined in the case law of the High Court, Court of Appeal and the House of Lords. Further to this are the Regulations and Rules published under the Acts, which also have the force of law. These include the Adoption Rules 1984 and the Foster Placement (Children) Regulations 1991. Departmental advice and professional rules, from whatever source, are *not* rules of law, and can only be pleaded in a legal case as possible evidence of good professional practice. In contrast, a breach of statutory rules or a failure to carry out a statutory duty may result in an allegation of unlawfulness.

In considering this area of law, it is important to realise that it is essentially taking place in public civil law, as opposed to privately contested civil law or criminal law. Individual families and children may find themselves caught in a complex web of rules, both legal and non-legal (i.e. purely administrative). Some cases will be dealt with outside the local authority framework, for example, where the dispute is between the natural parent(s) and the foster parents of a privately fostered child.

THE PUBLIC LAW

All administrative bodies are obliged in law to carry out their legal powers and duties in a manner in which a 'reasonable' authority would do so. To do otherwise is to act *ultra vires*, whereby the decision may be open to a judicial declaration as being of no effect. In law, a 'reasonable' decision is one which a 'reasonable' authority may come to. To put it the other way round, an *unreasonable* decision is one which no reasonable authority could *ever* make. It is therefore perfectly lawful for an authority to make a decision with which the judge (or judges) would not agree, providing it is one which the judge believes a reasonable authority could possibly have made.[4]

Included in the powers of authorities is the power to make policies. However, in law, a policy is an overall objective and an administrative rule of convenience, which *must*, to be lawful, be tempered in the light of each individual case.[5] Individual cases must be decided in the light of the facts of each case, taking into account relevant matters and carefully excluding irrelevant matters, including political ideologies. This has been upheld in a series of decisions, from *Roberts v. Hopwood* (1925),[6] where a policy of equal pay for women was declared to be an irrelevant consideration, to the GLC. 'Fares Fair' case.[7]

When relating these rules to children's cases, there are further considerations, since the law imposes duties to protect children whilst minors, mainly by way of the wardship jurisdiction in the High Court and the statutory powers and duties vested in local authority Social Service Committees. Furthermore, the law has, as a central objective, a duty not only to protect children, but to make decisions which are in children's interests. There are specific areas of law where children's interests are not central, but in relation to the care and upbringing of a child, the law requires that decisions are made in the interests of the child. Whilst this might seem to coincide with social work practice, it cannot be assumed to do so, since the law will prescribe its own meanings and proofs on the question of the child's best interests.

The welfare of the child is 'paramount' only in those Court hearings which relate to the upbringing of the child or the child's property,[8] and wardship disputes. This now includes orders in public cases.[9] In these hearings, the paramountcy of the child's welfare is such that it can even override the (usual) rights of a parent.[10]

In contrast to this, in adoption law the welfare of the child is the 'first consideration'.[11] The difference in meaning may seem small, but it does ensure that in adoption the natural parents' rights cannot easily be set aside. In public care cases, there is also a proviso which can override the usual criteria, where the child or another might be liable to 'serious injury'[12] or 'significant harm' or injury.[13]

Three questions then need consideration in children's disputes:

1. What is meant in law by 'welfare of the child' (and therefore, in this context, how does the issue of 'race' relate to that)?
2. What legal and other procedures may be used, and by whom?
3. What priority does 'the welfare of the child' have?

THE WELFARE OF THE CHILD

Judicial interpretation of this phrase varies, but certain common elements can be deduced from leading decisions. It is generally considered that, where possible, children should live with a parent, preferably the mother in the case of a young child. Children should live with siblings,[14] and their wishes, whilst important, should not outweigh other, possibly more important, criteria.[15] The courts have also clearly demonstrated support for the concept of the 'status quo' in private law cases, such as custody disputes and wardship cases, and have given judicial backing to the need for security in a child's life, especially a young child. In this way, the social parents of a child may be able to establish a better case for keeping the child than a natural parent. As it was aptly put by Ormrod LJ in the adoption case *Re H*,[16] 'Once the child has been placed with the adopters, time begins to run against the mother . . . '.

THE QUESTION OF RACE

The Children Act 1989 specifically requires local authorities to consider race, not only in making decisions on placements, but also in the *recruitment* of substitute families, where they must have regard to the different racial groups to which children in their area belong. The Act requires that local authorities consider 'the child's religious persuasions, racial origin and cultural and linguistic background'.[17] Similarly, these are considerations when deciding the suitability of daycare and foster arrangements, and in relation to the adequacy of a childminder.[18]

It seems quite clear that not only will local authorities be *entitled* to consider race as an important factor in child placement, they will be *required* to consider race *as well as* religion, cultural background and language, as of equal importance. The current policy will then be superseded by a *duty* to consider these factors, which, theoretically, would then be open to challenge in Judicial Review by a person qualified as having sufficient 'interest' in a case (or in an Attorney-General relator action).

The Foster Placement (Children) Regulations 1991,[19] which govern the placement and supervision of children in public care in foster homes, require the local authority to consider in relation to the foster parent and his/her family: 'his religious persuasion . . . capacity to care for a child from any particular religious persuasion'[20] and 'his racial origin, his cultural and linguistic background and his capacity to care for a child from any particular origin or cultural or linguistic background'.[21] In relation to the child the authority must include information relating to 'personal history, religious persuasion and cultural and linguistic background and racial origin'.[22]

It can be seen, therefore, that race is an important part of the consideration in placement, but it does not have legal *priority* over other criteria. By implication, race is therefore a part of the evaluation of 'the welfare of the child'. When considering case law, it can also be seen that this is an important factor.[23] The law has therefore taken note of race as an issue in family placement, but not necessarily as having an overriding priority.

Children's wishes can be considered as an important aspect of the 'welfare of the child' in both private and public law. In *private law cases*, such as residence disputes, children of about nine years and older will have their wishes considered by the court.[24] Where the child is a teenager, the court will normally attempt to concur with the child's wishes.[25] The case of Gillick[26] now suggests that a child of 'understanding' may be totally competent to make such decisions for themselves. In *public law*, the Children Act[27] directs the local authority to 'give due consideration having regard to his age and understanding, to such wishes and feelings of the child as they have been able to ascertain'. It would be reasonable to conclude that the child's wishes and feelings on their placement should be taken into account, unless they can be shown to conflict with their welfare. It should also be noted that under the Children Act 1989, children may bring their own actions for residence and/or contact.[28]

LEGAL PROCEDURES

These might include Section 8 (of the Children Act 1989) Applications, Adoption, Wardship and Judicial Review. There is now legal authority that applications to Court to review *contact* decisions by local authorities will supersede their discretion to place children for adoption. This may be a possible legal challenge therefore for both natural parents and foster parents (who had had the child for three years).[29]

Section 8 Applications

These are for Residence, Contact, Prohibited Steps or Specific Issue Orders.

Applicants

These may include non-relatives who have had the care of a child for at least three years (within the previous five) preceding the application. In relation to a child in the care of a local authority, only a *residence* order may be made;[30] in the case of other children (i.e. privately fostered), the applicant may apply for a residence or contact order.[31] Where a residence order is made, the care order will terminate.[32]

Adoption

This is available as a procedure only where (for non-relatives) there is either an adoption agency placement or an application to the High Court. Foster parents (private or public) who lack an agency placement are therefore forced to apply to the High Court, unless they have had the child for five years.[33] Neither can a foster parent keep a child in their (actual) custody without the consent of the person (or agency) having legal custody, unless they are qualified to and do apply for residence, adoption (the three- and five-year rules), or are able to make the child a ward of court).

Adoption Placements

The 'same-race' policy presents enormous difficulties for white families wishing to adopt, who would until relatively recently have been considered suitable for children of colour, particularly of mixed race, or siblings with different ethnic backgrounds. Whilst nothing in the law *or* guidelines prevents such placements, *providing* they are made with first consideration to the welfare of the child or children concerned, there is considerable evidence that such placements are at best discouraged or even prohibited in many areas. In *Re 41* of 1974,[34] Lord Denning gave judgement returning a child of about 14 months to its Indian mother from white prospective adoptive parents, partly on the grounds that the child would be best growing up within its own culture. However, he also remarked that a child of such an age could be moved without psychological harm or damage, a conclusion which might nowadays be considered questionable.

The law on adoption placements is relatively clear: *any* placement must be in the child's welfare, although not necessarily in the *paramount* interests of the child. However, this requirement is to protect the interests of the natural parents, and not the policy needs of the local authority. Decided cases reiterate this, as in the leading decision of *Re W*,[35] where it is made clear that in deciding the reasonableness of parental refusal to agree to adoption, a parent can be found to be withholding agreement unreasonably *without* being culpable. That is, the 'unreasonable parent' test is an objective one, which does not require the actual parent to have committed any wrongful act.

The Natural Parents

Any parent who has parental responsibilities, or a father without such rights who has paid maintenance for his child, *must* 'agree' to the adoption. This agreement has to be made formally, and *either* given in relation to the placement or as part of the 'freeing for adoption' procedure. Other than this, a placement can be made without parental agreement by a local authority where a child is in the compulsory care of the authority or where the High Court authorises the placement. Nevertheless, unless agreement has already been given, or set aside in the judicial hearing for 'freeing', the parent(s) must still agree or have that agreement set aside in the (judicial) adoption hearing. Natural parents therefore do have some rights in relation to the placement of their children, even if these are limited to attempting to influence placement by suggesting what they would or would not object to. Indeed, where a child has been 'freed' for adoption, the natural parents *must* be informed if the child has not been successfully placed or whether or not the child has been adopted after a year. It has also been decided that where a placement *fails*, the parent(s) must be informed, even where the child is not moved from the failed placement.[36]

Equally, if a child not yet 'freed' waits in care for placement, then the parents are entitled to ask what is happening to their child, particularly if the authority are considering or have terminated parental access to the child. Although the natural parent cannot impose conditions when their child is adopted, their views will be considered by the court, and this fact may therefore be used to influence the adoption agency's plans. This aspect was considered in *Re S*,[37] where information on the prospective adoptive father's health was denied to the natural mother.

The Adopters

The situation of would-be adopters who are not even considered for a placement is very difficult, since there is no 'right' to adopt as such, only the 'right' to apply and, at best, a legitimate expectation to be considered 'fairly'. This means that any decision to reject should be made *without arbitrariness or prejudice*,[38] although a *policy* is quite lawful, providing it is not based on irrelevant considerations, or used as a rule to the *exclusion* of consideration of relevant evidence. Even this right of challenge (in judicial review) is difficult to establish in the area of medical/social 'treatment', as demonstrated in the case of Harriott,[39] where a woman unsuccessfully challenged the refusal of the hospital's ethical committee to allow her to have IVF treatment on the grounds that she was socially unsuitable. It may be that a couple who would *otherwise* be suitable adopters could successfully challenge a refusal to consider them in relation to, for example, mixed-race children, especially where they could bring evidence to show that they were experienced in coping with such children. This may be a possible challenge, but it would seem unlikely that any couple would want to be a test case of this kind, in addition to the difficulty of obtaining funding for such an action. Thus, the reality for such couples is that they should perhaps concentrate on finding an authority or other adoption organisation who are prepared to consider them on their merits, rather than impose the 'same-race' policy in an inflexible manner.

Judicial challenge to the *policy* may be best considered by natural parents rather than by would-be adopters, and it may be that this will now happen, where the natural parents are unhappy for their child to wait for, or even be placed at all with, a black or mixed-race family, especially where there are other factors, such as religion, involved.[40]

The Adoption Review

The current review of adoption seems likely to recommend that children's contacts with natural families are maintained post-adoption, as in *Re C*,[41] and this could be one way in which would-be adopters with transracial families can assist their children to maintain racial identity.

It is notable that in some of the reported wardship cases where foster parents have prevented natural parents (often black) from removing the child, the High Court has refused adoption to the foster parents. The child has been kept in wardship, so as to protect the status quo throughout the child's minority, but also to protect the child's right to access from the family of origin. There is, in fact, a provision in adoption law which enables the court to attach *conditions* to an adoption order.[42] The difficulty of such a condition is that it can only be sanctioned by the threat of contempt of court (and ultimately imprisonment). This may sound sufficient, but it is nothing compared to the true ultimate consequence of disobedience in wardship, that is losing the child, since in wardship the court remains the guardian of the child, whereas in adoption, the adopter is the child's guardian. However, in recent cases, the House of Lords has sanctioned the use of adoption with a condition of access (to a member of the family of origin), where the court is satisfied that all the parties accept that this is for the welfare of the child and are prepared to cooperate. In *Re C* (1987),[43] an adoption was made, subject to a condition of access to a brother of the adopted child. It may be that this procedure is a useful one when considering the placement for adoption of some 'children of colour', where contact with a member of the family of origin (such as a grandparent or father) might be for the welfare of the child and enable a wider choice of potential adopters.

It is likely that adoption law will be amended so as to include specifically a consideration of religion, race, cultural background and language. What is unlikely is a *requirement* to place children in 'racially matching' families or to give first priority to such 'racial matching' over other matters, including religion, etc. Thus the current dilemmas are unlikely to be resolved by any new adoption rules. What might be done is to encourage the placement of children with 'good enough' adopters after an initial attempt at placement has failed, thus placing upon adoption agencies the duty to place a child within a reasonable time (such as six months), rather than search without time limit for the perfect racial match, even where such a match can be reasonably described as 'in the best interests of the child'.

WARDSHIP

Wardship, where the applicant *by applying* makes the minor a ward of court, freezes the status quo: no change in the minor's life can be made without the consent of the court whilst s/he remains a ward. Applications are to the High Court, where wardship is regarded, in modern law, as the protection of the minor's welfare, first and paramount.

By making a minor a ward, the foster parents are able to have a hearing based entirely on a consideration of the child's welfare, all other considerations being secondary, including parental rights,[44] economic cost,[45] and the freedom to publish.[46] The great difficulty with wardship is that the court may decide to keep the minor in permanent wardship (as in *Re N*[47]), so that the foster parents *never* attain parental responsibilities in relation to the child.

Previously it was possible for a local authority foster parent to persuade the authority to allow the case to be heard in wardship (as in *Re P*[48]), since the courts would not otherwise allow the application to proceed.[49] However, although recent cases did suggest that local authorities were beginning to allow such disputes to be decided by the High Court in Wardship, the Children Act 1989 has now barred such applications.[50] Thus Wardship is now only available in private fostering cases. All other applications must be brought (if possible at all) in Judicial Review.

JUDICIAL REVIEW

This is the most cumbersome and difficult procedure to use, since it involves an initial application to the High Court for permission to proceed, followed by an application for the Review itself.[51] In this procedure, the applicant must be a person 'interested' in the outcome,[52] who is asking the court to consider the procedural correctness of how the decision was made, rather than the merits as such. Clearly, in this jurisdiction, the welfare of the child is only a consideration in so far as the authority have failed to carry out their statutory duties.

The advantage of this procedure is that *any* person with an interest can commence such an action, including a local councillor,[53] or a council tax payer,[54] or possibly by the use of an Attorney-General relator action, where the Attorney-General gives consent for his status to be used to allow a trial of a matter 'in the public interest'.[55]

CASE EXAMPLES

Private Fostering

The privately fostered child's case can be dealt with in the wardship jurisdiction, where the child's welfare is paramount. Reported cases where the child has been fully integrated into the family have resulted in decisions leaving the child in the care of the foster parents. Whilst this principle, supporting the integrity of the child's status quo with the foster parents, can apply equally to a child of any race (as indeed it did in *J v. C*,[56] where all the parties were Caucasian), in a series of reported cases from the early 1970s onwards,[57] the child has been black, often West African in origin. This may reflect a social problem of clashing cultural practices, which the courts have tended to resolve by giving care and control to the foster parents, but which current social work policy might suggest should be resolved by moving the children back, possibly with specialist assistance, to their black communities.[58]

This essential conflict was very sharply seen in the case of *Re N*,[59] involving a Nigerian child who had been privately fostered with a white family since she was three weeks old. The mother lost contact but the child's father kept in touch, although he worked in America. The father had attempted to have the child to live with him, but he had been unable for some time to obtain a visa for her because she was illegitimate. At the age of four-and-a-half, the father was able to make firm plans to take her to America, but by then the foster parents wanted to adopt her. In the wardship hearing brought by her father, he asserted that her long-term welfare was to be with him and to have a black identity, which was not possible if she was adopted. He proposed that she be transferred to his care by way of specialist black foster parents. The foster parents brought expert evidence to show that serious, long-term emotional damage would result to the child from being moved. Mr Justice Bush said: 'the emphasis on colour rather than on cultural upbringing can be mischievous and highly dangerous when you are dealing in practical terms with the welfare of children'. He rejected adoption and ordered wardship to continue, with care and control to the foster parents and reasonable access to the father, to take place in England. No leave was given for any future applications, the implication being that this situation was likely to continue throughout the child's minority. Both parties were effectively warned by the judge in his decision to cooperate for the child's welfare. The fact that the judge preferred to keep the child in wardship indicated that he saw a need for the court to keep control of the child's life.

This is not to suggest that the courts will ignore blood ties or race and cultural issues. In *Re K*,[60] private foster parents who had taken a baby believing the arrangement to be on a permanent basis, brought wardship proceedings when the parents wanted the child returned. The judge granted care and control with a view to adoption by the foster parents. The child was by then seven-and-a-half months old. The Court of Appeal reversed the decision for the following reasons: the natural family was not 'so unsuitable' that the child's welfare positively demanded the displacement of 'parental responsibility'; rehabilitation should be tested; and 'the differences between the natural parents and the foster parents of age, and culture . . . should not be discounted . . . [foster parents were fifty-five and forty-seven years old, Orthodox Christians, and of Greek Cypriot origin. The wife spoke imperfect English. The natural parents were Irish Catholics.] . . . a child of a few months, or indeed, under two, can move relatively easily' [*sic*]. This child was placed back with her natural parents, but under a Care Order in favour of the local authority, to enable them to remove the child if at risk.

This is a complex case and is not authority for suggesting that any particular factor will sway a court, but it does suggest that couples who are particularly unsuitable as long-term carers will not be successful in keeping a very young child against the wishes of the natural parent(s) or social workers. However, where would-be adopters are *otherwise* suitable, differences of race are not a legal impediment as such. The advantage that private fosterers have is in being able to use wardship.

Public Care

Where a child is in public care, the case cannot now be heard in wardship. This leaves foster parents of local authorities in a very vulnerable situation, since they will have agreed, as foster parents, to 'hand back' the children upon request. The only statutory rights of the foster parents in this situation are to apply for residence or adoption after having had the care of the child for three years (or periods amounting to three years) or for five years respectively. If, therefore, foster parents have had the care of a child for some time, and either cannot use or choose not to use these rights, and if the local authority intend to move the child to another placement *on the grounds of race alone*, then the foster parents can only challenge legally the local authority by way of Judicial Review in the High Court. Previously, the local authority could acquiesce in a wardship hearing, as in *Re P* (1990).[61] Here, the issue was *not*, as portrayed by the media, one of upholding the social work policy as opposed to a consideration of the welfare of the child. In *Re P*, the foster mother had five children by her first husband, had only just married her second husband, and had recently been rejected by the local authority Adoption Panel as an adopter. The Social Services department gave evidence that she had never been considered by them as anything other than a short-term foster mother.

B and J took full account of all these factors, and his decision in favour of the local authority suggests that although the child was apparently thriving with the foster mother, the court may have been unlikely to allow her to have a permanent placement of the child as an adoptive mother. The child here was about seventeen months old and of mixed race. She had been with the family since she was six days old. The racial element was one factor in the decision, although for the local authority it may have been the decisive one.

Judicial Review has been used recently in 'care' cases other than 'race' ones; for example, in a series of cases involving the closure of children's homes, the courts have allowed the applicants (in Judicial Review) to plead that, *as a part of their statutory duty*, the local authority must consider the welfare of each child separately where the children's home in which they live is to be closed.[62] Thus, whilst this procedure cannot demand that the case be heard on its merits, i.e. the court will *not* substitute its own decision for that of the authority, it can force authorities to consider each part of the evidence correctly before coming to a final decision.

Under the previous law, the strict refusal in public care cases to allow the initiation of wardship by parents (and others) against local authorities, together with the suggestion of Judicial Review as the proper forum, was followed in several cases, including *In re L* (1990),[63] where grandparents were unable to invoke the wardship jurisdiction to challenge the termination of their access to their grandchild; although they could appeal to the Crown Court on the matter of termination of the *Care* Order, that Court had no jurisdiction to hear the issue of access. It was said in the Court of Appeal that the Crown Court could hear the additional evidence of the grandparents, and 'the local authority would, as much as the Court, have an obligation to consider that evidence and to see whether it altered their present approach'.

This case demonstrates how the courts are determined to keep within and to support the statutory framework as far as possible.[64] Nevertheless, cases taken in Judicial Review can be very useful: the court has held[65] that in deciding whether or not to allow a child home on trial where there were unsubstantiated allegations against the parents, the local authority had to have a fair procedure which gave the parents the chance to make representations and call evidence. Similarly, the courts did insist[66] that local authorities complied with the *objectives* of the Child Care Act 1980, s.12(a)–(e)[67] in allowing parental challenge to the decision of the local authority to terminate access to the child.

In relation to the issue of *race*, therefore, a challenge may be made in Judicial Review, for example where the Wednesbury Principles have not been followed. This would include where the placement decision in relation to a child was made according to a pre-ordered 'rule' of 'black children to black families', rather than according to the welfare of the child in the case in question. However, the limitations of using Judicial Review must be understood, as can be seen in two recent (unreported) cases, involving a Birmingham couple and a Lancashire couple.

In the Birmingham case *Re JK*,[68] Mr and Mrs Fenton were finally allowed to proceed to an adoption hearing for their foster child of Asian origin. After two years, the local authority had wanted to move the child to Asian foster parents, pending permanent placement. The decision was made in wardship proceedings, i.e. the welfare of the child was paramount. Sir Stephen Brown, President of the Family Division, speaking in the High Court in Birmingham, 29 March 1990, said:

> After a three-day hearing I have today given judgement in wardship proceedings concerning a child of Asian origin, who, from shortly after birth, had lived with foster parents of a non-Asian origin in Birmingham. I have considered all the relevant factors involved, among others the child's attachment and bonding to her foster parents, the parental capabilities of the foster-parents and the child's racial background. I have borne in mind throughout the paramount importance of the welfare of the child. I have made an order that the child continue as a ward of the court and that she should remain living with her foster parents and that they should have leave to commence adoption proceedings.

It is important that, in this case, the child's welfare was paramount (because it was heard in Wardship), a consultant psychiatrist reported that the child (three years old by the time of the hearing) would probably suffer a lasting psychological scar if she were to be moved from the foster parents, that after three years the authority still could not find a Sikh family willing to adopt her, and that the foster parents were 'tolerant, wise people, capable of loving children of whatever race, and they would assist the child to follow her own Sikh traditions and culture and . . . seek assistance if necessary'. These factors combined to give the foster parents an extremely good case.

Contrast this with a case involving Lancashire County Council[69] where, in Judicial Review, the foster parents lost their mixed-race foster child, after also having had the child for nearly two years, because ' . . . no court could say that Lancashire County Council had acted unreasonably'. The judge had declared that in order to find their actions 'unreasonable', there would have to be 'a reasonable prospect of the High Court viewing the decision as so unreasonable that no council could have acted as Lancashire County Council did'.[70] The critical problem here was having to bring their case in Judicial Review, where the welfare of the child is merely incidental, although this does not mean the couple here would have otherwise been successful, since they were judged by the social worker to be 'colour blind' to the child's mixed-race origin, and to have other children in their care 'competing' for attention. The adoptive parents to whom the child was moved were also white, but had two other mixed race children and had 'openly addressed' the issues of background and origin.

The critical issue may well be jurisdiction: cases heard in Wardship or under the Children Act 1989 making the child's welfare paramount. Local authority foster parents who have not had the child for three years have no rights of application under the Children Act, but *may* apply (for leave to apply) for a residence order with the leave of the authority,[71] as in the past, where authorities gave leave for foster parents to seek wardship, so they could be persuaded to allow applications in relation to residence orders. This could be fruitful in particular cases, since the case of *Re B* makes it clear that the courts may and will intervene on matters of *contact*, even in adoption placement decisions.[72]

COMPLAINTS

Under the authority of the Children Act 1989, the 1991 Representations Procedure Regulations provide for a two-stage complaints procedure for children and young people, their parents and other interested parties, such as foster parents, against decisions made on services provided. The first stage consists of a review of the complaint by the authority which must contain an independent member. The result must be notified within 28 days. A further written appeal may then be made to a panel of three people, one of whom must be independent, who must meet within 28 days of the appeal. A written decision must be made within 24 hours.

GOVERNMENT GUIDELINES AND ADVICE

Following media attention and discussion, the Government issued new guidelines[73] to directors of Social Services in January 1990, headed 'Issues of Race and Culture in the Family Placement of Children'. It should be noted that the status of mere guidelines is of advice, which could probably be relied upon as evidence of good practice, but not as legal authority for any decisions or actions taken by a local authority.[74] The guidelines are useful, since they do show how the Government's intentions and policies in this area are developing. Over-reliance on any such guidelines can be problematic if this interfered with the discretionary nature of the decision-making process. The guidelines require social services departments to 'address and seek to meet the needs of children and families from all groups in the community'.[75] The explanation follows calls for 'awareness, sensitivity and understanding of the different cultures of groups in the local community', and directs departments to 'identify sources of advice and help'. The need to avoid children coming into care unnecessarily is highlighted, especially where there may be over-representation of some ethnic groups in care. Paragraph 5 suggests that 'sustained efforts may be needed' to recruit substitute families from particular groups, 'and of that religion'. This paragraph also draws attention to the need for assessment and training to be available for *all* foster parents.

The guidelines warn against 'simplistic assumptions of similarity between different ethnic groups', but also advises directors of the need to anticipate the extension of the Foster Placements (Children) Regulations' requirements as to religion, culture, linguistic background and racial origin, to all decisions regarding children being looked after by local authorities. Local authorities will also have to have regard to the racial groups to which children belong when needing day care or fostering services. The guidelines state:[76] 'These requirements will formalise in relation to child care an approach which should already be an indispensable element in both child care and adoption practice.' Nevertheless, social services departments are reminded that it is the welfare of the individual child which is important. No one factor is to be given such primacy as to override all other factors. Thus, all these matters are to be considered in placement decisions, but,

> there may be circumstances in which placement with a family of different ethnic origin is the best choice for an individual child. In other cases, such a placement may be the best available choice . . . The importance of religion as an element of culture should never be overlooked . . . [77] Also, special care is needed where placement with a family of different ethnic origin is being considered . . . [78] and . . . choice will be influenced . . . , as with all placement decisions, by the child's wishes and feelings.[79]

Social services departments are reminded of the need for good planning, including 'clear agreements' and 'careful reviews'. Departments are advised that 'children should not be removed from placements which are otherwise satisfactory solely because the ethnic origin of the foster parents does not accord with the requirements of general policies'.[80] The guidelines remind social services departments of the good practice reasons for policies which include considerations of race, culture, language and religion in children's work, but also carefully point out the legal basis of such work and the need to temper policies and objectives with discretion when making decisions in relation to individual children.

THE CRIMINAL LAW

ABDUCTION AND REFUSAL TO HAND BACK

The crime of abduction is committed by a non-parent who removes a minor from the actual care of a parent (or a person either with legal custody or the consent of a custodian) without lawful authority.[81] It should be noted that this crime requires the removal or detention of a minor under the age of sixteen 'so as to keep him out of the lawful control of any person entitled to lawful control of the child'.[82] An abduction which is carried out in such a way as to cause alarm or assault may constitute *kidnapping*[83] – a very serious offence.

Criminal offences are also committed where any person removes a child from the care of a local authority without the consent of the authority. Even a parent may not remove the minor where the minor is in compulsory care.[84]

Refusal to hand back can incur criminal penalties where the child is in compulsory care. The local authority may bring a Place of Safety Order,[85] or may invoke search powers and penalties.[86] Such situations, i.e. disputed care as opposed to abduction, have been said not to be suitable for *habeas corpus* proceedings.[87]

RACE RELATIONS LAW

A policy of 'same-race' placement enforced by a local authority social services department probably does not contravene the Race Relations Act because foster parents are exempt from the discrimination provisions.[88]

INCITEMENT TO RACIAL HATRED

The criminal law relating to this offence is now to be found in the Public Order Act.[89] Racial hatred must be either intended or likely to be stirred up against a racial group. Mere abuse is not 'racial incitement', which is deemed to be a more serious matter, although abuse can be within the offences of threatening, abusive or insulting words or behaviour.[90] Racial hatred offences may only be prosecuted by, or with the consent of, the Attorney-General.[91] These criminal offences are unlikely to be very important in the context of transracial families.

CONTEMPT OF COURT

It should be remembered throughout this discussion of the law that disobedience of an order of the court, including the magistrates' court, can be punished as contempt of court. While an order *can* be postponed whilst an appeal is heard, permission to do so must be sought from the court. Contempt of court can always result eventually in imprisonment, even if the matter is an entirely civil one.

SUMMARY

It is likely that the outcome of recent and forthcoming legislation and rules, together with new emphasis in social work training, will be that there will continue to be a considerable emphasis on race criteria in substitute family placements, including transfer of children who are considered to be incorrectly placed. These practices are lawful, providing that, in every case, it can be shown that the policy was reviewed in the actual child's welfare, and not superimposed whatever the cost to the child. Potential adopters should be made aware of these policies and should only accept or become involved in transracial placements where the parameters are agreed and accepted by all the parties. For parents already in a transracial situation, there is a need to clarify the intentions of the natural parents and social workers involved. If they are threatened with removal of the child, they should consider using the local authority's own appeal process, including intervention in case conferences involving the child. Once any legal application has been decided upon, the applicants must remember that they will have to prove their case. This means bringing explicit, factual, objective evidence in relation to the specific child and family. This can include medical, psychiatric and social evidence, using, for example, general practitioners, specialist consultants, independent social work evidence, nursery or health visitor reports, etc. In the case of Judicial Review, the burden of proof is very high, and it will be necessary to show that the decision is one that no *reasonable* local authority could have made. Finally, the usefulness of *negotiation* using skilled mediators should not be under-estimated. Is the situation hopeless, or is there room for negotiation and possible compromise? The assistance of experienced people will be advisable.

Although there are many complex legal aspects to the whole question of transracial families, it is possible to summarise it as follows:

1. The 'racial' element in child care decisions is *one* of the elements which, together, make up the 'welfare of the child'.
2. Decisions by local authorities in relation to a child in their care *must* make the welfare of that child the paramount consideration.
3. A local authority *policy* in relation to placement of children, for example, a 'same-race' policy, is *not* a rule of law, and is only lawful if it does not, in any individual case, override other equally important factors such as religion and cultural background.
4. Natural parents are entitled to be informed about their children until a successful adoption takes place.
5. Natural parents (and other relatives) may be able to have a contact order made in their favour, even if the child's welfare is best served by living with another family.
6. Foster parents who have had the child living with them for three or five years may apply *without* the consent of the local authority or parent for residence or adoption (respectively).
7. Foster parents who have privately fostered may apply to make the child a ward of court.
8. Local authority foster parents may be able to obtain the local authority's leave to apply for a residence order (even if the local authority opposes them, they may agree to facilitate a hearing[92]).
9. Local authority foster parents can use the internal review system to 'appeal' against decisions, and obtain an independent hearing, which the local authority will have to take into account.
10. Foster parents who have been unable or unsuccessful in using other procedures may be able to invoke Judicial Review to challenge local authority decisions which have apparently *not* been made in the first consideration of the welfare of the child. This procedure may also be

available to natural parents in relation to their child, and to councillors and council tax payers in relation to the policy as such.

It can be seen that although challenge to the local authority is not easy or straightforward, some procedures are available. Where a reasonable case can be made out, and where the applicant is within the financial limits, legal aid may be available for a judicial challenge. Unfortunately, financial assistance is unlikely to be available for disputes or appeals within the local authority structure, despite the fact that professional advice is always advisable in these cases.

NOTES

1. Judicial Review of Administrative Action.
2. Local Authorities Social Services Act 1970 s.2.
3. *Ibid*, s.6.
4. *Associated Provincial Picture Houses Ltd. v. Wednesbury Corporation* [1948] 1 KB 223. The guidelines set out in this case are commonly known as the Wednesbury Rules.
5. *R v. Sec. of State for the Environment ex p. Brent L.B.C.* [1982] QB 593.
6. *Roberts v. Hopwood* [1925] AC 578.
7. *Bromley L.B.C. v. G.L.C.* [1983] 1 AC 768.
8. Children Act 1989 s.1(1).
9. Children Act 1989 s.1(4)b.
10. *J v. C* [1970] AC 668.
11. Adoption Act 1976 s.6.
12. Children Act 1989 s.22(6).
13. Children Act 1989 s.25(1)(ii).
14. *Re C* [1980] 2 FLR 163.
15. See notes 24–7.
16. *Re H* [1977] 1 WLR 471.
17. Children Act 1989 s.22(5)(c).
18. *Ibid*, s.74(6) and Schedule 2(11).
19. S.I. 1991/910.
20. *Ibid*, Schedule 1 Reg. 3(4)(b) 5.
21. *Ibid*, Schedule 1 Reg. 3(4)(b) 6.
22. *Ibid*, Schedule 3 Reg. 5(6)(b).
23. *Re N* [1990] 1 FLR 58, *Re P* (1989) 'The Independent' 1 September 1989 (CA).
24. Practice Direction of 2 November 1982 (1983) 13 Fam. Law 5 (as extended by Registrar's Directions of 23 September1983 and 31 October1984) suggests that a child of nine or over should accompany parents on referral to conciliation of custody and access cases.
25. *M v. M* [1987] 2 FLR 146.
26. *Gillick v. W. Norfolk & Wisbech Area Health Authority* [1986] AC 112.

27. Children Act 1989 s.22(5)(a).

28. Children Act 1989 s.10(8). Children must apply for leave and to the High Court. [1993] 1 FLR 668.

29. *Re B* 1993 1 FLR 543.

30. Children Act 1989 s.9(1).

31. Children Act 1989 s.10(5)(b).

32. Children Act 1989 s.91(1).

33. Adoption Act 1976 s.28.

34. *Re Application No 41* of 1974, reported in *The Times*, 30 April 1975.

35. *Re W* [1971] AC 682.

36. *R v. Derbyshire C.C. ex p. T* [1990] FL 141; Adoption Act 1976 s.19.

37. *Re S* 17 December 1992 (CA).

38. *R v. Liverpool Corporation ex p. Liverpool Taxi etc. Association* [1972] 2 QB 299.

39. *R v. Ethical Committee, St. Mary's Hospital, Manchester ex p. Harriott* [1988] 18 FL 165.

40. This was an issue in a case involving Liverpool's social services department, which has apparently now been resolved.

41. *Re C* [1987] 2FLR 383.

42. Adoption Act 1976 s.12(6).

43. *Re C* [1987] 2 FLR 383. Note that Adoption proceedings are now part of Family Proceedings: this may encourage *contact* orders being made alongside adoption orders, although the court is likely to insist on the consent of all the parties.

44. *J v. C* [1970] AC 668.

45. *Re B* [1981] 1 WLR 1421.

46. *X County Council v A and another* [1985] 1 All ER 53.

47. *Re N* [1990] 1 FLR 58.

48. *Re P* (1989) *The Independent*, 1 September 1989 (CA).

49. *A v. Liverpool C.C.* [1982] AC 363; *W v. Nottinghamshire C.C.* [1986] 1 FLR 565.

50. Children Act 1989 s.100.

51. Supreme Court Act 1981 s.31(3).

52. In law, this is known as *locus standi*. The right to bring a case is generally interpreted liberally today; see, e.g., *Covent Garden Community Association Ltd v. G.L.C.* [1981] JPL 183.

53. *Attorney-General ex rel Tilley v. Wandsworth L.B.C.* [1981] 1 All ER 1162, CA.

54. *R v. I.R.C. ex p. Nat. Fed. of Self-Employed and Small Businesses Ltd.* [1982] AC 617.

55. As in, e.g., *Tilley*, quoted in n. 53.

56. *J v. C* [1970] AC 668.

57. E.g., in *Re E O*, *The Times* Law Report, 15 February 1973, and in *Re A* [1978] 8 FL 247.

58. Note the estimate by the Save The Children Fund that there may be up to 9,000 West African children privately fostered in this country.
59. *Re N* [1990] 1 FLR 58.
60. *Re K.* [1991] 1 FLR 57.
61. *Re P* (1989) *The Independent* 1 September 1989 (CA).
62. *R v. Solihull M.B.C. ex p. C* [1984] FLR 365.
63. *In re L* [1991] 1 FLR 14.
64. This case would now be able to be heard under the Children Act 1989.
65. *R v. Hertfordshire C.C. ex p. B* [1987] 1 FLR 239.
66. *R v. Bolton M.B.C. ex p. B* [1985] FLR 345.
67. Now s.34 of the Children Act 1989.
68. *Re JK* 1991 2FLR 340.
69. *R v. Lancashire County Council ex p. M.*
70. Lord Justice Balcombe, 12 April 1991.
71. Section 9(3) of the Children Act 1989.
72. See above.
73. CI (90) 2, issued by the Chief Inspector, Social Services Inspectorate, Department of Health.
74. Note that the various 'Codes' published by Ministers are generally admissible in court as evidence of good practice, e.g., Codes published under the Police and Criminal Evidence Act 1984. Contrast these with Statutory Instruments which have the force of statute law.
75. *Ibid*, para. 4.
76. *Ibid*, para. 7.
77. *Ibid*, para. 10.
78. *Ibid*, para. 11.
79. *Ibid*, para. 12.
80. *Ibid*, para. 14.
81. Child Abduction Act 1984 s.2.
82. *Ibid*, s.3. These offences may only be prosecuted by or with the consent of the Director of Public Prosecutions.
83. *R v. D* [1984] 3 WLR 186 (HL), where the child's father was convicted of kidnapping after he had acted in defiance of the court and with considerable aggression.
84. Children Act 1989 s.49.
85. Children and Young Persons Act 1933 s. 40.
86. A Recovery Order, under s.50 of the Children Act 1989.
87. *Krishnan v. L.B. of Sutton* [1969] 3 All ER 1367.
88. Race Relations Act 1976 s.23(2).
89. Public Order Act 1986 ss.17–29. Section 17 defines racial hatred as hatred against a group of persons in Great Britain defined by reference to colour, race, nationality (including citizenship) or ethnic or national origins.
90. *Ibid*, s.4, s.5.
91. *Ibid*, s.27(1).

92. As in *Re A and W* [1992] 2 FLR 154, where the foster mother was allowed to apply for leave by the local authority who successfully opposed the grant of leave.

BIBLIOGRAPHY

Ahmed, S., Cheetham, J. and Small, J., eds (1986) *Social Work with Black Children and Their Families*. London: Batsford.

Bagley, C. and Young, L. (1982) 'Policy dilemmas and the adoption of black children', in J. Cheetham, ed. *Social Work and Ethnicity*. London: Allen & Unwin.

Bartholet, E. (1991) 'Where do black children belong? The politics of race matching in adoption', *University of Pennsylvania Law Review* 139(1163): 1207–26.

Black and In Care Steering Group (1986) *Black and In Care: Conference Report*. London: Children's Legal Centre.

Brown, C. (1984) *Black and White Britain: The Third PSI Study*. London: Heinemann.

Celestin, N. (1986) *A Guide to Anti-Racist Childcare Practice*. London: Voluntary Organisations Liaison Council for Under Fives.

Commission for Racial Equality (1988) *Equal Opportunity Developments in Social Services Departments – Report of a Survey*. London: CRE.

Commission for Racial Equality (1990) *Adopting a Better Policy: The Race Dimension*. London: CRE.

Coombe, V. and Little, A. (1986) *Race and Social Work*. London: Tavistock.

Costin, L. and Wattenberg, S. (1979) 'Identity in transracial adoption: A study of parental dilemmas', in G. Verma and C. Bagley, eds *Race, Education and Identity*. London: Macmillan.

Dominelli, L. (1988) *Anti-Racist Social Work*. Basingstoke: Macmillan.

Ely, P. and Denney, D. (1987) *Social Work in a Multi-Racial Society*. Aldershot: Gower.

Gill, O. and Jackson, B. (1983) *Adoption and Race: Black, Asian and Mixed Race Children in White Families*. London: Batsford/British Agencies for Adoption and Fostering.

Jervis, M. (1990) 'Balancing the damage', *Social Work Today*, 8 Feb., pp. 16–17.

London Borough of Wandsworth Social Services Department Adoption and Fostering Unit (1985) *White Workers' Common Misgivings or Misconceptions about Black Families*. London: Wandsworth Social Services.

Tizard, B. and Phoenix, A. (1989) 'Black identity and transracial adoption', *New Community* 15(3): 427–37.

8 TRANSRACIAL ADOPTION: THE AMERICAN EXPERIENCE

RITA J. SIMON

Transracial adoptions started in the United States following the end of World War Two when there were thousands of homeless children in Europe and Asia. But it did not get underway on a large scale until the mid-1960s when it was accompanied by major changes in social work and adoption agencies' policies. Two categories of children were most affected by these changes: blacks and native Americans.

Organised opposition to transracial adoption, begun in the early part of the 1970s, was formidable enough by 1975 to bring about a reversal in policy on the part of major adoption agencies in most states throughout the country. The opposition was led and organised primarily by black social workers and leaders of black political organisations who saw in the practice an insidious scheme for depriving the black community of its most valuable future resource – its children.

Opposition also came from some of the leaders of American Indian groups who labelled transracial adoption 'genocide' and who also accused white society of perpetuating its most malevolent scheme, that of seeking to deny the Indians their future by taking away their children.

Both the black and Indian groups who were opposed to transracial adoption agreed that it is impossible for white parents to rear black or Indian children in an environment that would permit them to retain or develop a black or Indian identity. Even if some white parents might want their adopted children to grow up Indian or black, they lack the skills, insights and experience necessary to accomplish such a task.

To a large extent these arguments proved effective in bringing to a halt or greatly reducing the number of transracial adoptions. But it left unsolved the problem that gave rise to the practice in the first place: the presence of large numbers of non-white children in public institutions.

This chapter describes the rhetoric and goals of the groups that opposed and supported transracial adoption in the United States. It also shares the results of a longitudinal study of families who adopted children of a different race. The thrust of the study, which began in 1971, was to trace the racial identities and attitudes of the transracially adopted children and the biological siblings in the families over time, and to examine the extent to which the family members were committed to each other.

OPPOSITION TO TRANSRACIAL ADOPTION

Since 1972, the National Association of Black Social Workers (NABSW) has been the largest and most outspoken critic of transracial adoption. In that year, the president of the NABSW, William T. Merritt, announced 'Black children should be placed only with black families, whether in foster care or for adoption' (Simon and Alstein, 1987, p. 9). In his testimony before a Senate Committee on 25 June 1985 Merritt stated:

> We are opposed to transracial adoption as a solution to permanent placement for Black children. We have an ethnic, moral and professional obligation to oppose transracial adoption. We are therefore *legally* justified in our efforts to protect the right of Black children, Black families and the Black community. We view the placement of Black children in White homes as a hostile act against our community. It is a blatant form of race and cultural genocide. (Simon and Altstein, 1987, p. 143)

By the early 1970s committees of Native Americans had joined in the denunciation of transracial adoption. In 1972 a group of American Indians issued the following statement:

> The identity crisis of adolescence is likely to be especially traumatic for the Indian child growing up in a White home. When they are old enough to realise that they're different there is likely to be real trouble, especially if White parents haven't made serious efforts to expose them to their own cultural heritage . . . And trouble will come from the White family too. The White man's hatred of the native American may be forgotten when he's a cute helpless baby or child, but it will show up when the child becomes an adolescent and able to think and act as an individual. (Simon and Altstein, 1977, p. 68)

By 1978, Congress had passed the Indian Child Welfare Act which was designed to prevent the decimation of Indian Tribes and the breakdown of Indian families by transracial placement of native American children. Title I of the Act stated:

> Section 105 (a) In any adoptive placement of an Indian child under State law, a preference shall be given, in the absence of good cause to the contrary, to a placement with (1) a member of the child's extended family; (2) other members of the Indian child's tribe; or (3) other Indian families. (b) In any foster care preadoptive placement, a preference shall be given, in the absence of good cause to the contrary, to a placement with (1) a

member of the Indian child's extended family; (2) a foster home licensed, approved, or specified by the Indian child's tribe; (3) an Indian foster home licensed or approved by an authorised non-Indian licensing authority; or (4) an institution for children approved by an Indian tribe or operated by an Indian organisation which has a programme suitable to meet the Indian child's needs. (Simon and Altstein, 1981, pp. 69–70)

In essence, the leaders of black and Indian organisations argued that non-white children who are adopted by white parents are lost to the communities into which they had been born. The experience of growing up in a white world makes it impossible for black and Indian children ever to take their rightful place in the communities of their birth.

ARGUMENTS IN FAVOUR OF TRANSRACIAL ADOPTION

The North American Council on Adoptable Children (NACAC), which represents a broad coalition of individuals and adoptive parent groups, is the leading advocate of transracial adoption. At a 1980 White House conference on families, NACAC's president testified:

> We believe every child has the right to a loving, 'forever' family of his or her own. For a great many children now in foster or institutional care, permanency and love can only be found through adoption . . .
>   We are not talking here about the adoption of racially-matched infants by white, middle-class couples. That is not adoption today . . . 'Adoptable children' today include many who are older, who are of school age, who are emotionally troubled, physically handicapped, of mixed or minority race, or members of sibling groups. These are 'special needs' adoptable children. They need special families . . . We know such families exist . . . (Simon and Altstein, 1981, p. 71)

NACAC acts as an advocacy group for children and families by providing information and public education on adoption: intercountry, transracial, subsidised and single-parent.

The Council on Adoptable Children (COAC) also favours transracial adoption as a means to achieve permanence for children. It was founded in Michigan in the late 1950s by a biologically fecund family who, after four years and 22 rejections, finally adopted a hard-to-place child. COAC was established when they joined with other adoptive families to find prospects for available children.

In addition, there are smaller citizens' groups throughout the United States and Canada that support transracial adoption. They include the Open Door Society, Families Adopting Children Everywhere (FACE), Room for One More, and Plan Loving Adoptions Now (PLAN).

THE ROLE OF THE COURTS

By 1985, transracial adoption was a legal form of child placement in every state. Nevertheless, when adoptions or custody petitions are interracial, they are often denied by the court, initially or on appeal, for no other reason than race. In a 1968 law review article, Susan Grossman argued that decisions against transracial placements, based solely on the criterion of race, are a violation of the Fourteenth Amendment: 'No state shall . . . deprive any person of life, liberty or property without due process of law; nor deny to any person within its jurisdiction the equal protection of the laws' (Simon and Altstein, 1987, p. 12). The test of the equal protection standard is 'essentially one of reasonableness; the equal protection clause requires the states to exercise their powers so as not to discriminate between their inhabitants except upon some reasonable differentiation fairly related to the object of regulation'. Thus, regarding transracial adoptions, the courts have been charged with the task of deciding if the use of race as a factor in adoption proceedings is reasonable in the light of the judicial purpose, which is to determine the best interests of the child.

In 1980, the ruling in the Iowa case of *Kramer v. Kramer* began to limit the use of race as a factor in child custody (pp. 14–15). A divorcing white couple were disputing the custody of their two minor children. The court considered it relevant that shortly after the couple separated, the husband returned to the family home and found a black man sleeping on the couch. The wife stated that she had sexual relations with the man and that he had moved to the couch when the daughter had come into the bedroom. She stated that she had sexual relations with the man on two or three occasions. At the time of the divorce trial, she testified that she had not seen the man for over five weeks and that she had no intentions of marrying him. The court stated that to allow a 'biracial relationship . . . to exist in the presence of the children is not in their best interest and is going to make their lives in the future much more difficult'. Custody of the children was awarded to their father.

The Supreme Court of Iowa, upon appeal, ruled that 'the trial court erred in basing its custody decision on racial considerations' and that race cannot be a decisive factor in questions of custody (p. 14). The custody award remained with the father, however, because the court found the mother's emotional instability a more compelling reason not to reverse the original custody decree.

In addition to ruling on the specifics of that case, the Kramer decision began to develop an outline for 'reasonable' uses of racial considerations in adoption decisions. The outline provided by the Kramer court stated:

1. Unsubstantiated judicial predictions concerning the effects of racial prejudices in the community are not to dictate the disposal of child custody issues.
2. Child custody decisions shall not be affected by the existence of racial

tension unless it can be clearly demonstrated that this tension is relevant to the decision.
3. Simply proving the existence of racial tension or prejudice in the community is not sufficient to show relevancy.
4. Even when race is proven to have some demonstrated relevancy, the factor of race should serve only as one consideration, to be weighed together with all other considerations.
5. The proof that race is relevant to a child custody decision must be garnered from the evidence specific to each particular case. (p. 14)

Another 1980 case involved a dispute between two white parents over custody of their minor daughter (p. 15). The court found relevant the mother's plans to marry a black man. It then predicted continuous adjustment difficulties for the child if she were to live with parents of differing races and awarded custody to the father.

The decision was appealed and the appellate court determined that in establishing the best interests of the child, race should be ignored as a factor. In its decision, the court wrote:

There has been a marked increase in the United States in recent years of interracial marriages and transracial adoptions, and sociological studies establishing that children raised in a home consisting of a father and a mother who are of different races do not suffer from this circumstance. (p. 15)

This statement, which acknowledged that transracial adoptions cause no detrimental effects to a child's welfare, supported the growing judicial proposition that the use of race as a factor is unreasonable and should not be allowed.

In *Farmer v. Farmer*, a 1981 New York case, race was once again viewed by the court as only one factor among a host of others to be considered in rendering its decision (p. 15). A divorcing interracial couple (black husband, white wife) each sued for custody of their six-year-old daughter. The father's petition asserted that his daughter would be identified by American society as black – an undisputed claim – and that therefore she should be reared in a black environment which he, a black person, could provide. In arguing that his daughter would experience identity problems if awarded to her mother, he claimed that 'social and psychological problems can result from the unresolved internal conflicts which are the product of confused identity' (p. 16). One of the father's expert witnesses opined:

What I'm trying to say, a black youngster who is raised in a black home, of course a possibility exists that the youngster will still grow up with problems. I [am] trying to put things into perspective. If I'm a black youngster raised in a black home, if I clearly know who I am, if I have all sorts of role models around me, even though there may be a number of slings and arrows thrown at me from without, at least I can sustain myself within the groups. (p. 16)

Witnesses for the child's mother argued:

Nurturing is the relationship between parent and child that accords the child a sense of security, stability, warmth, love and affection. . . . Economic stability is valuable; emotional stability is crucial. . . . How the parent related to the child, the parents' communication with the child, which includes the sharing of emotions, is crucial . . . race has low priority on the scale of values determining best interests. The colour of the custodial parent is immaterial to the child . . . this child is white as well as black and what will be important to her is how her parents' sensitivity to her will affect her. (pp. 16–17)

The court concluded that

race is of little or no significance where the issue is custody. . . . It is simply one of many factors which may be considered in a contest between biological parents for custody of an interracial child . . . That the best interests of this child . . . compel the award of custody to him [the father] because society will perceive her to be black must be rejected. (p. 17)

In February 1984, the US Supreme Court, despite its traditional avoidance of litigation involving domestic arguments, reluctantly heard *Palmore v. Sidoti* (pp. 19–20). The Court emphasised its usual procedure concerning domestic cases: 'The judgement of a state court determining or reviewing a child custody decision is not ordinarily a likely candidate for review by this Court' (pp. 19–20).

Palmore v. Sidoti encapsulated all the controversies and processes historically identified with child custody when the racial identity of any family member is a factor. The child of a divorcing white couple was awarded to her mother, who entered into a relationship with a black man whom she subsequently married. The child's father petitioned for custody of his daughter, citing the mother's marriage. The court agreed with the father even though 'there is no issue as to either party's devotion to the child, adequacy of housing facilities, or respectability of the new spouse of either parent' (pp. 19–20). It then somewhat paradoxically continued:

This court feels that despite the strides that have been made in bettering relations between the races . . . it is inevitable that [the child] will, if allowed to remain in her present situation and [if she] attains school age and [is] thus more vulnerable to peer pressures, suffer from the social stigmatisation that is sure to come. (p. 20)

The child's mother appealed to the Supreme Court. Acknowledging that the lower court established the competency of either parent to care for their daughter, the Court rejected the father's plea that court custody should revert to him. The Court additionally recognised the lower court's exclusive use of race as a determining factor, in favour of the father. In reversing the decision, the Court stated:

> A core purpose of the Fourteenth Amendment was to do away with all governmentally-imposed discrimination based on race. Classifying persons according to their race is more likely to reflect racial prejudice than legitimate public concern; the race, not the person, dictates the category . . . Whatever problems racially-mixed households may pose for children in 1984 can no more support a denial of constitutional rights than could the stresses that residential integration was thought to entail in 1917. The effects of racial prejudice, however real, cannot justify a racial classification removing an infant child from the custody of its natural mother found to be an appropriate person to have such custody. (p. 20)

Clearly, the developments in 1984 did not end the controversies surrounding child placement when there are racial differences among the participants. Indeed, one wonders what it will take to convince lower courts that when race alone is defined as a significant factor in deciding child custody, those decisions are overturned on appeal. As the Supreme Court indicated in *Palmore v. Sidoti*, 'Reality of private biases and possible injury they might inflict are not permissible considerations under the equal protection clause' (p. 20).

Writing in the *Notre Dame Law Review*, Margaret Howard argued strongly against placing non-white children into white adoptive homes (p. 20). Admitting that the number of parentless non-white children exceeds the availability of non-white families willing to accept them, Howard urged: 'The alternative to transracial adoption . . . is not inracial adoption but non-adoption, i.e. continued institution or foster care' (p. 20). She stated: 'If the goal is to maximise the possibility of healthy emotional growth, then our best information tells us that a stable family is of paramount importance, and the transracial placement should be made. If, however, cultural identity is more important, then transracial adoption should not be permitted' (pp. 20–1). And in conclusion, Howard posited: 'There is little to recommend transracial adoption – except that the alternatives are so often worse' (p. 21).

In spite of all the courts' decisions and precedents, the issue of race in child custody remains as powerful an influence today as at any other time. For example, in 1985 in Detroit, Michigan, when white foster parents wanted to adopt their seventeen-month-old biracial (black-white) foster daughter with Down's Syndrome, who had been placed in their home at the age of one month, the County Department of Social Services dissuaded them on the grounds that racial matching of children and adoptive parents is a significant factor in the child's later adjustment. The foster parents were also told that the child 'had the racial identity of her "non-Caucasian" parent' (p. 21). After seeing the child's picture in the newspaper, a black couple filed a petition for adoption and were selected in a competition with fifteen other families. Upon petition by the foster parents, the court ordered that the adoption should be postponed until the Department of Social Services could complete an investigation as to which couple would be the most suitable adoptive family. The county circuit court awarded temporary custody of the child to the foster parents pending a recommendation to the probate court by the Department of Social Services.

A second case also involved litigation initiated by white foster parents. Social workers abruptly removed a two-and-a-half-year-old black child from the couple's care solely because they were white. The child had been with them since the age of fourteen months, having been in seven prior foster homes (p. 21). The foster parents sued the State Department of Social Services for 'invidious racial discrimination' (p. 21). The American Civil Liberties Union (ACLU) joined the suit on the grounds that the department's policy of racial matching was unconstitutional. The court ordered the child returned to the foster parents. The judge described the department's policies as 'absolutely and utterly absurd'. (p. 21)

The cases cited above show a common theme. The courts have attempted to clarify some difficult issues regarding transracial adoptions. By and large, they have determined that race may neither serve as an automatic classification nor as a decisive and determinative factor in child custody. But some of the decisions still allow for discretion in agency use of racial factors and thus mitigate against any predictability. It is this lack of predictability that continues to fuel legal battles in which transracial adoption is the major issue.

WHAT DO THE DATA SHOW?

In 1975, the federal government stopped collecting data on the number of adoptions. Thus, no individual, group, or institution has reliable national figures on the number of adoptions, inracial or transracial, that have occurred in the United States since then. The data that are available (pre-1975) indicate that there were 831 transracial adoptions in that last year. The high point for transracial adoptions occurred in 1971, when 2,574 placements were made. Looking at data from 1968 to 1975, and then at some estimates that were made for 1976 to1978 and subsequent years, our guess is that there are about 25,000 transracial adoptions in the United States today. This figure does not include Korean, Vietnamese and other intercountry adoptions.

The remaining portion of this chapter describes the findings from a longitudinal study of white parents who had adopted American Black, Indian and Korean children in the late 1960s. My colleague Howard Altstein and I first met these families in 1971, when they agreed to our request that we interview the parents and each of the children (those adopted and those born to them) in their homes. When we first met these families, their adopted children were between the ages of three and seven years. They lived in five cities in the mid-west: Chicago, Illinois; St Louis, Missouri; Minneapolis, Minnesota; Ann Arbor, Michigan; and Madison, Wisconsin. There were 204 families with 167 biological children and 199 adopted children, 157 of whom were transracially adopted. The focus of our first and subsequent encounters with these families was the racial identity, awareness and attitudes of the adopted non-white children and their white siblings.

The most important finding that emerged from our first encounter with the families (see Simon and Altstein, 1977) was the absence of a white racial preference or bias on the part of the white and non-white children. Contrary to other findings that had thus far been reported, the children reared in these homes appeared indifferent to the advantages of being white, but aware of and comfortable with the racial identity imposed on them by their outward appearance. By and large, the parents of these children were confident that the atmosphere, the relationships, the values and the lifestyle to which the children were being exposed would enable successful personal adjustments as adults. In writing about the results of our study in 1977, we emphasised that transracial adoption appeared to provide the opportunity for children to develop awareness of race, respect for physical differences imposed by race, and ease with their own racial characteristics, whatever they may be.

When we returned to these families in 1979, we contacted only the parents by mail and telephone. We felt it was important to have even such an abbreviated contact because most of the children were about to enter adolescence or were already young teenagers and it was a propitious time to take a second reading. We learned in 1979 that the 'extremely glowing, happy portrait' that we had painted seven years earlier now had some blemishes on it. It showed signs of stress and tension. We noted that

> for every five families in which there were the usual pleasures and joys along with sibling rivalries, school-related problems and difficulties in communication between parent and child, there was one family whose difficulties were more profound and were believed by the parents to have been directly related to the transracial adoption. (1977, p. 28)

The serious problem most frequently cited by the parent was the adopted child's (usually a boy) tendency to steal from other members of the family. We described parents' accounts of the theft of bicycles, clothing, stereos, and money from siblings' rooms, so that brothers and sisters had resorted to putting locks on their bedroom doors. Another serious problem was the parents' rather painful discoveries that the adopted children had physical, mental or emotional disabilities that were either genetic or the results of indifferent or abusive treatment received in foster homes.

Our most recent encounter with these families occurred in 1984. By this time we could locate or arrange to interview only 96 of the original 204 families. Between 1971 and 1979 we were unable to find 61 families. Of the

143 that we located in 1979 all but ten agreed to participate in the second phase. By 1984, 28 of the 133 families had relocated and could not be found. Of the remaining 105 families, 11 (roughly 10 percent) declined to be interviewed.

Amongst the 11 couples who did not wish to be interviewed, two of them had been divorced since 1979. The family members were separated, and some of them did not wish to 'get involved'. Three families had been interviewed by other researchers and felt that 'enough was enough'. One said, 'They [the children] have gone through a number of family problems recently and this is not a good time for them.' The other five families gave no reason.

In total, the 96 families had 394 children, 213 boys and 181 girls; 256 were still living at home, and 34 were away at school (higher education) but considered the parents' home their home. The others had moved away, were working, or were married. 43 percent of all the children had been transracially adopted.

We interviewed 218 children representing 55 percent of the total number of children born to or adopted by the parents and 85 percent of the children still living at home. 54 percent of those at home were transracially adopted. Amongst the transracially adopted children, we interviewed 61 boys and 50 girls, or 80 percent of those at home. 89 of the 111 transracially adopted children are American black. The others are Korean, native American, Eskimo and Vietnamese. We also interviewed 48 males and 43 females who are born into the families and 4 males and 12 females who are white adoptees.

What did we find now that the children were adolescents and young adults? First of all, almost all the parents said that if they had to make the decision today about whether to adopt transracially, they would do it again, and they would recommend it to other families. They believe that they and the children born to them have benefited from their experiences. Their birth children have developed insights, sensitivity and a tolerance that they could not have acquired in the ordinary course of life. Their transracial adoptee may have been spared years in foster homes or institutions. They have had the comfort and security of loving parents and siblings who have provided them with a good home, education and cultural opportunities, and the belief that they are wanted.

We found that almost all the families made some changes in their lives as a result of their decision to adopt. Most of the time, however, the changes were not made merely because of their decision to adopt a child of a different race, but because they decided to add another child to the family. Thus, the parents talked about buying a bigger house, adding more bedroom space, having less money for vacations and entertainment, and allowing less time for themselves. In retrospect, most of the parents do not dwell on what they wished they had done but did not do; nor do they berate themselves for things they did and wished they had not done. Most of them feel that they did their best. They worked hard at being parents and at being parents of children of a different race.

In the early years, many of them were enthusiastic about introducing the culture of the transracially adopted children's backgrounds into the family's day-to-day life. This was especially true of the families who adopted American Indian and Korean children. They experimented with new recipes; sought out books, music and artefacts; joined churches and social organisations; travelled to the South-West for ceremonies; and participated in local ethnic events. The parents of black children primarily introduced books about black history and black heroes, joined a black church, sought out black playmates for their children and celebrated Martin Luther King's birthday. In a few families, a black friend is the godparent to their transracially adopted child. One mother told us: 'Black parents regard us as black parents.'

But as the years wore on, as the children became teenagers and pursued their own activities and social life, the parents' enthusiasm and interest for 'ethnic variety' waned. An increasing number of families lived as their middle and upper-middle class white neighbours did. Had the children shown more interest, more desire to maintain ethnic contacts and ties, most of the parents would have been willing to follow the same direction. In the absence of signals that the activities were meaningful to their children, the parents decided that the one-culture family was an easier route.

Almost all the parents said that they were affected by the stance of the National Association of Black Social Workers and that of the Native American Councils in the 1970s *vis-à-vis* the adoption of black and Indian children by white families. Almost all the parents thought that the position taken by those groups was contrary to the best interests of the child and smacked of racism. They were angered by the accusations of the black social workers that white parents could not rear black children, and they felt betrayed by groups whose respect they expected they would have. Race, they believed, was not and should not be an important criterion for deciding a child's placement. In their willingness to adopt, they were acting in the best interest of a homeless, neglected, unwanted child. One parent said: 'Our children are the ones no one wanted. Now they are saying you are the wrong family.'

The discussion thus far has been derived largely from the parents' interviews. We report now on findings from the children's data. All the children in the study were asked to complete a Self-Esteem Scale, which in essence measures how much respect a respondent has for himself or herself. A person is characterised as having high self-esteem if he/she considers him/herself a person of worth. Low self-esteem means that the individual lacks respect for him or herself. Because we wanted to make the best possible comparison amongst our respondents, we examined the scores of our black transracially adopted children separately from those of the other transracially adopted children, and from those of the white born and white adopted children. The scores for all four groups were virtually the same. No one group of respondents manifested higher or lower self-esteem than the others.

The lack of difference amongst our respondents on the Self-Esteem Scale reminds us of the lack of difference we reported for these children in the first study when we asked them to choose dolls of different races. A child received one point each time he or she selected the white doll in response to: 'Which doll would you: (a) like to play with the best? (b) think is a nice doll? (c) think is a nice colour?' and did not select the white doll as the doll that looked bad. The scores obtained demonstrated that none of the children manifested a white racial preference. Out of a possible score of four, which would have meant that the white doll was selected in response to each question, the average score was 1.7. Such a score indicated that none of the children selected the white dolls even half the time.

On the basis of all the responses to the items in which dolls were used to measure racial attitudes, racial awareness, and racial identity, we found no consistent differences amongst the adopted and non-adopted children and amongst the black and other transracially adopted children. We wrote in our first volume:

There was no consistent preference for the white doll among the black, white and Indian or Oriental children. There was no indication that the black children had acquired racial awareness earlier than the white children, and there was no evidence that the white children were able to identify themselves more accurately than the non-white children. (Simon and Altstein, 1977, pp. 147–8)

Our 1977 study was the first to report that there were no white racial preferences amongst American black and white children. The responses suggested that the unusual family environment in which these children were being reared might have caused their deviant racial attitudes and resulted in their not sharing with other American children a sense that white is preferable to other races. We noted that the children's responses also demonstrated that their deviant racial attitudes did not affect their ability to identify themselves accurately.

Both sets of responses, those obtained in 1971 and in 1984, consistently portray a lack of difference between black and white children in these special, multiracial families, when differences have been and continue to be present between black and white children reared in the usual single-racial family. Something special seems to happen to both black and white children when they are reared together as siblings in the same family.

The lack of differences amongst our adolescent responses is again dramatically exemplified in our findings on the Family Integration Scale which included such items as: 'People in our family trust one another; my parents know what I am really like as a person; I enjoy family life'. The hypothesis was that adopted children would feel less integrated than children born into the families. But the scores reported by our four groups of respondents (black transracial adoptees, other transracial adoptees, white born, and white adopted) showed no significant differences and, indeed, amongst the three largest categories (not including the white adoptees), the mean scores measuring family integration were practically identical: 15.4, 15.2 and 15.4.

Turning to the matter of perceptions about race and racial identities, we reported that 71 percent of the transracial adoptees said that they had no problem with the fact that they were the only black or Korean or Indian person in the family. By the time of our study in 1987, they simply took it for granted. And the same percentages of transracial adoptees as white children answered 'No' to the item that asked, 'Have there been times in your life when you wished you were another colour?' We did find, however, that when we asked them to identify themselves so that someone whom they had never met would recognise them at a meeting place, many more of the transracial adoptees than white children mentioned race. Such a choice, though, may have more to do with the practicalities of the situation than with any sense of 'affect' or evaluation. If one is black or Korean or Indian in a largely white area, recognition is much easier.

Eleven percent of the transracially adopted children told us directly that they would prefer to be white, and 27 percent of the parents believe that their transracially adopted children identify themselves as white. According to the parents, all of these children are of mixed backgrounds. The above-mentioned discrepancy between the children and the parents concerning the former's racial identity should not be assumed to represent the parents' lack of insight or recognition regarding their children's beliefs and desires. Some part of that 27 percent of parents who believe that their transracially adopted children identify themselves as white could well reflect wish-fulfilment by the parents. Most of those children look as if they are white; the parents might like to believe that the children also consider themselves to be white, like the rest of the family.

Some evidence for this hypothesis may be seen in the parents' and adolescents' estimates about the adolescents' future. For example, a greater number of transracial adoptees said that they would opt to live in a racially mixed community than did parents, more of whom thought the transracially adopted children would choose to live in a community like the one in which they were reared, which was predominantly white. Interestingly, about 25 percent of both the parents and children thought the children would marry exogamously. Thus, the evidence we have for parental ambivalence over having a child of a different race is the 16 percent difference between the parents' and adolescents' responses on the item about racial identity, together with the expectations on the part of more transracial adoptees than parents that the former would live in racially mixed rather than predominantly white communities. Neither of these issues, however, is directly tied to the sense of integration or cohesion felt by the parents and children about their relationship.

CONCLUDING REMARKS

We reported in the first study (Simon and Altstein, 1977), when the children were between three and eight years old, that all but three percent of the parents said that they would urge a family to adopt. Seven percent answered that as a matter of principle they would not advise anyone on such a personal, complicated issue. In the most recent study, in 1987, which was conducted when the transracial adoptees were adolescents and young adults, six percent of the parents said that they would advise against such a decision, one percent were uncertain about the advice that they would give, and eight percent would not offer advice as a matter of principle. Eighty-five percent would urge a family to adopt transracially.

Is 85 a high percentage? Compared to what – to families who have adopted inracially; to families who have only had birth children? Would more than 85 percent advise other couples to bear children? Would there not be some small percentage who would believe, as a matter of principle, that they should not advise people on such a personal issue; and would there not be a small category of, say, seven percent who would feel, for many different reasons, that having children had been a mistake for them and who would be willing to generalise their experiences to others? In the end, whether 85 percent is a large or small proportion of families, whether it is an indicator that families believe transracial adoption was a success or failure, is up to the reader to decide.

To conclude, I believe it is important to emphasise that our studies show that transracial adoption causes no special problems amongst the adoptees or their siblings. We have observed black children adopted and reared in white families and have seen them grow up with a positive sense of their black identity and a knowledge of their history and culture. We are not saying that all adoptions involve plain sailing for the adoptees and their parents, or that there are no emotional and psychic costs to adoption. Our data show that the transracial aspect does not involve special problems, traumas, or heartbreak. There was, for example, not a single instance of a disrupted adoption amongst the families we studied.

REFERENCES

Simon, R.J. (1993) *Family Bonds: Adoption and the Politics of Parenting*. New York: Praeger.

Simon, R.J. and Altstein, H. (1977) *Transracial Adoption*. New York: Wiley-Interscience.

Simon, R.J. and Altstein, H. (1981) *Transracial Adoption: A Follow-Up*. Lexington, MA: Lexington Books.

Simon, R.J. and Altstein, H. (1987) *Transracial Adoptees and Their Families: A Study of Identity and Commitment*. New York: Prager.

9 RACE MATCHING IN ADOPTION: AN AMERICAN PERSPECTIVE

ELIZABETH BARTHOLET

This chapter* focuses on the policies that make race a central factor in determining placement for black as well as for white children born in the United States. The tradition in the adoption world has been to categorise as 'black' all children and prospective parents with any identifiable black African heritage and to place all such children with black parents. The label 'transracial' has been applied to any adoption involving placement with white parents of a biracial child, or indeed of any child having any identifiable black heritage. Although I find the terminology problematic, I will use the terms 'black' and 'transracial' in this chapter in the way they have generally been used in this context.

Most public and private adoption agencies are governed by powerful race-matching policies in making placement decisions. There is very general agreement amongst adoption agency policy-makers that children should be placed inracially 'if possible', and transracially only 'if necessary' or as a last resort. There is, however, significant variation among adoption agencies. Some of the private agencies are quite open to transracial adoption, and private agencies as a group are generally more open to such adoption than the public agencies. But public matching policies control to a significant degree private agencies, either through the regulatory process or through contracts for services. Public agencies also have under their jurisdiction a disproportionate share of the minority children available for adoption. Recognising the variety amongst agencies, I will try to give a sense of the nature of the policies that govern placement in most public and traditional private agencies.

Unfortunately, there has been no systematic documentation of the specifics of current racial matching policies and how these specific policies affect children in terms of delay in, or denial of, permanent adoptive placement. This

---

* A longer version of this chapter, containing extensive documentation of the sources, appeared in the *University of Pennsylvania Law Review* (1991) 139(5): 1163-1256.

is particularly problematic because of the hidden nature of the policies at issue. They are generally unwritten, and what is written may give few clues or even false clues as to the unwritten reality. In addition, those in a position to know what today's racial matching policies look like are often reluctant to disclose what is going on for fear of attack by people on different sides of the matching issue.

Although a study systematically documenting the nature and impact of existing racial matching policies would be extremely useful, it is possible without that study to get a general sense for these matters. My own investigation has included interviews with a wide array of leaders in the adoption world and experts on racial matching policies, together with a review of the relevant literature.

This investigation has made clear to me that race is used as the basis for official decision-making in adoption in a way that is unparalleled in a society that has generally endorsed an anti-discrimination and pro-integration ideology. This investigation has also made clear that current policies have a severe impact on minority children, often causing serious delays in or permanent denial of adoptive placement. Later in this chapter I will flesh out my findings in more detail.

An initial order of business for most adoption agencies is the separation of children and prospective parents into racial classifications and sub-classifications. Children in need of homes are typically separated into black and white pools. The children in the black pool are then classified by skin tone – light, medium, dark – and sometimes by nationality, ethnicity, or other cultural characteristics. The prospective parent pool is similarly divided and classified. An attempt is then made to match children in the various 'black' categories with their parent counterparts. The goal is to assign the light-skinned black child to light-skinned parents, the Haitian child to Haitian parents, and so on. The white children are matched with white prospective parents.

This matching scheme confronts a major problem in the fact that the numbers of children falling into the black and the white pools do not 'fit', proportionately, with the number of prospective parents falling into their own black and white pools. In 1987, 37 percent of the children in out-of-home placement were black as compared with 46 percent white. Although no good statistics are available, the general understanding is that a very high percentage of the waiting adoptive parent pool is white. In addition, many whites interested in adopting do not bother to put themselves on the waiting lists because of their understanding that there is such a limited number of children available to them.

The matching policies of today place a high priority on expanding the pool of prospective black adoptive parents so placements can be made without utilising the waiting white pool. As discussed below, programmes have been created to recruit black parents, subsidies have been provided to encourage them to adopt, and traditional parental screening criteria have been revised.

Nonetheless, the numbers mismatch continues. There are many more black children than there are waiting black families. There is a large pool of waiting white families. In recent years both the number of children in foster care and the proportion that is black have been growing.

Today's matching policies generally forbid the immediate placement of black children available for adoption with waiting white families. These policies, discussed below, tend to preclude such placements, either implicitly or explicitly, for periods ranging from 6 to 18 months to several years or longer. In many instances the policies preclude placement altogether.

The matching process surfaces, to a degree, in written rules and documented cases. But it is the unwritten and generally invisible rules that are central to understanding the nature of current policies. Virtually everyone in the system agrees that, all things being equal, the minority child should go to minority parents. Thus by the universal rules of the official game, race matching must be taken into account in the placement process. But this vastly understates the power of racial matching policies in the official adoption world. The fact is that the entire system has been designed and redesigned with a view towards promoting inracial placements and avoiding transracial placements. The rules generally make race not simply 'a factor' but an overwhelmingly important factor in the placement process.

In recent years, several states have written into law requirements that agencies exercise a same-race preference in placing children in adoptive families. Minnesota and Arkansas have laws specifying a preference for placement with a family of the same racial or ethnic heritage. If a same-race placement is not feasible, the preference shifts to 'a family of different racial or ethnic heritage from the child which is knowledgeable and appreciative of the child's racial or ethnic heritage'. California law similarly mandates a same-race placement preference and, in addition, it prohibits placement across racial or ethnic lines for a period of 90 days after a child has been relinquished or declared free for adoption. The law further prohibits such adoption after the 90-day period 'unless it can be documented that a diligent search' for a same-race family has been made, using all appropriate recruitment resources and services. Only on the basis of such documentation can a child be placed across racial or ethnic lines with a family 'where there is evidence of sensitivity to the child's race, ethnicity, and culture'.

Other states have regulations or written policies that similarly provide for racial preference in the placement process. Some of these, like the California law, specify mandatory waiting periods during which children must be held in hopes of an inrace placement before a transracial placement can be considered.

The existence and the recent nature of these kinds of laws, regulations, and policy guidelines hint at the power and the current popularity of the racial matching policies that lie beneath the level of written policies; normally in our society there is a reluctance to put into written form requirements that race be a factor in decision-making. However, the unwritten policies are far more extreme in their promotion of racial matching than any written policies would suggest.

Numerous cases have surfaced in the media, in congressional hearings and in litigation, involving the removal of black children from white foster families with whom they have lived for long periods, often years. In some cases removal is triggered by the white family's expression of interest in adopting their foster child, and the agency intervenes to move the child to a same-race foster family which may or may not be interested in adoption. In other cases the agency removes the child simply because a same-race foster family has become available. The white parents have poignant stories to tell. Often they have been given a child in very poor physical or psychological shape, or with serious disabilities, and have nursed the child through hard times. The child has thrived under their care and feels a close attachment. They feel a similar attachment and want to adopt so that the child will be a permanent part of their lives. The agency can offer nothing but a shift to a new foster family as an alternative. Experts testify to the destructive impact that disruption of the only stable relationship the child has known will have. Adoption agencies may or may not be forced to back down in these cases, whether by public pressure or by court order. But either way, these cases reveal something of the power of the racial matching policies operating in the adoption agency world, since there is very general agreement among today's child welfare professionals that stable parent–child relationships should not be disrupted and that appropriate foster families should be given priority consideration for the adoption of children with whom they have formed such relationships. These cases are fought out in the public eye not because they are particularly extreme examples of the racial matching policies at work, but because the decision to remove the child, and the crucial role race plays in that decision, are highly visible.

Although these child removal cases tell us something about the powerful role race plays in agency decision-making, they do not tell us much about the specifics. It is not clear how common these policies ever were or are today. Racial matching policies apply to foster care placement as well as to adoptive placement, so that a relatively small number of black children are placed in white foster homes. In recent years there has been an even greater priority placed on racial matching in foster care, at least in part out of concern that transracial foster placements can lead to permanent adoption.

However, state welfare systems often have difficulty finding sufficient numbers of same-race foster homes for the increasing number of minority children in need of substitute care. Adoption workers often have no choice as they look for temporary homes for 'crack babies' and older children removed from their families, or surrendered, except to place them with white foster parents. Current policies often make it difficult or impossible for those parents to adopt and require the removal of the child for a same-race foster or adoptive placement, however bonded and committed the white family and its black foster child may become.

Agency policies typically involve holding black children in foster or institutional care for significant periods of time after they are, or could be, free for adoption if no same-race adoptive family is available. Consideration will not be given during this time to placement with available white families. Sometimes the policies specify a definite time period – 3 or 6 or 12 or 18 months – before a transracial adoption may be considered, or after which it must be considered. But even these time-specific policies give no real sense for the length of the holding period at issue since the time generally starts to run only from the date that a child becomes legally free for adoption. Adoption workers will often not begin the process of freeing a child for adoption until and unless there is a same-race family available. Assuming that an agency does eventually succeed in finding a same-race family for a waiting child, it may be several more years before the child can actually be placed. The court process terminating the biological parents' rights can easily consume two to four years, and the newly recruited family will generally have to go through the home study process before placement can occur.

Many policies simply require that children be held until active efforts to locate same-race families have proved fruitless, or until documentation has been submitted regarding such efforts and the unavailability of a same-race family. Many adoption professionals feel that under these non-time-specific policies black children are held for even longer periods.

Rules requiring social workers to provide documentation of their minority family recruitment efforts before transracial placements will be permitted place the social worker who contemplates making such a placement in the position of doing additional work and incurring the other costs involved in making an exception to the general rule. Such a social worker also risks invoking the wrath of the National Association of Black Social Workers (NABSW) and other vocal critics of transracial adoption. The overburdened and underpaid adoption worker has every incentive to avoid the multiple troubles promised by transracial placement.

Policies amounting to absolute or near-absolute bans on transracial adoption appear common. The NABSW continues to take an absolute stance against transracial adoption: 'NABSW steadfastly holds to the position that black children should not be placed with white parents under any circumstances . . .' (NABSW, 1986, p. 31). There appear to be many adoption workers who are either sympathetic with the NABSW position or feel intimidated by NABSW advocates and by others who oppose transracial adoption except in the most limited circumstances.

A sense of the extreme nature of current holding policies is revealed by the stories of some of the transracial adoptions that *are* allowed to take place. One director of an adoption programme for minority children in New York State told me that 99 percent of his agency's placements were inrace placements. He then described one of the few transracial placements he had facilitated. The child had been in the foster care system for 11 years and free for adoption for eight of those years. He was finally placed transracially at the age of 13 only because of concern that as a result of accumulated bitterness over the years he would be likely to exercise the option he would get at age 14 to refuse to accept adoption if it was offered. The director, a strong advocate of racial matching, felt that an exception was warranted in these unusual circumstances, but noted that he had to do battle with forces within the state and agency bureaucracies in order to implement the transracial placement.

The director of another programme with a specific focus on recruiting minority parents told me of one transracial adoption she had arranged. It involved 'John', a victim of fetal alcohol syndrome, who was mentally retarded. The director had held John for three years whilst she looked for a minority family by means that included listing him in a state-wide photo-listing register, or 'exchange', of children available for adoption. When a white couple volunteered their interest in adopting John, the director described herself as having hesitated, but having finally agreed to see them. She eventually placed the child with them, finding herself very impressed by their parenting credentials and the fact that they already had children from a variety of ethnic backgrounds. Another director told me of a transracial placement she made in a case involving hard-to-place minority siblings. The only available minority family was interested in adopting one but not the other. Since the director felt separation would be disastrous for the children, she placed them with a white couple. As a result she was subjected to intense criticism and pressure from the local chapter of the NABSW.

There is general agreement amongst adoption workers that an affirmative effort should be made to recruit black families so that there will be more such families for the available black children, although the resources actually devoted to recruitment vary enormously. There have been some notable efforts to form organisations and adoption agencies under black leadership and to involve black churches and the media in the recruitment attempt. These efforts have had some success in encouraging black families to consider adoption and move through the adoption process. State, regional, and national exchanges of black and other 'hard-to-place' children waiting for adoption have been created both as a means of making their availability more generally known, and as a way of recruiting parents not locally available.

There is, of course, no systematic recruitment of white families for waiting black children, since matching policies preclude transracial placement except as a last resort. Nor is there generally any effort to recruit white families even for children for whom there seems little prospect of ever finding black adoptive families. Older black children with very serious mental or physical disabilities constitute a hard core hard-to-place group. One leader in the world of 'special needs' placement told me that she had recently begun to wonder if it would not be appropriate to recruit white as well as black parents, in the interest of finding homes for some of these children, but had run into nothing but opposition from her colleagues.

Race-conscious recruitment and non-recruitment takes many forms. Agencies whose job is to find homes for minority children target their media and organisational efforts on minority communities. Adoption exchanges often specify with respect to the black children listed that the social worker is looking for a black family. 'Sunday's Child' or 'Wednesday's Child' advertisements that appear in newspapers and on television describing particular waiting children often contain similar specifications. And as indicated above, adoption workers may choose not to free minority children for adoption so that adoptive parents can be recruited, because of the dearth of minority families thought likely to be available.

Subsidies are very generally made available to minority couples and singles to enable and encourage them to adopt minority children. All states make some provision for subsidies to persons adopting certain 'special needs' children. The Federal Government encourages such subsidies by providing states with federal funds to match qualifying state subsidies. Minority status alone puts children in the 'special needs' category for federal law purposes, making them eligible for the subsidies so long as certain other conditions are met, including state eligibility requirements. These subsidies are provided on an ongoing basis until the child's maturity. Even though limited in amount, these subsidies are thought to have made a significant difference in encouraging large numbers of minority families to adopt.

Although white families are technically eligible for these subsidies, the fact that whites will rarely be allowed to adopt minority children means the subsidies operate primarily to facilitate inrace adoption. Indeed, it is clear that subsidy programmes have been designed to a significant degree to further the goal of expanding the minority parent pool. The federal subsidy legislation is written in race-neutral language which would seem to require that agencies make an effort to place children without regard to race with families that can afford to adopt without subsidy, before the child can be qualified as a 'special needs' child. However, the federal and related state subsidy programmes are administered within the context of a general understanding that no such efforts are in fact required since it is only same-race placements that are considered appropriate.

Agencies apply significantly different parental screening criteria to prospective black adoptive parents than they do to prospective white adoptive parents in order to increase the prospects for inrace placement. In efforts to increase the number of black prospective parents, agencies reach out to include the kinds of people traditionally excluded from the white parent pool, or placed at the bottom of the waiting lists for children – singles, older people in their fifties and sixties, and people living on welfare, social security, or similar marginal incomes. Critics of transracial adoption have condemned the traditional screening criteria as discriminatory against the black family, and they feel that agencies have not moved nearly far enough to remove this kind of discrimination.

They are right that traditional criteria, which emphasise economic stability, marriage, and middle-class American values, do function disproportionately to disqualify blacks. They are also right that agencies have not abandoned their traditional criteria altogether in screening black applicants. Nonetheless, most agencies have either significantly softened or radically departed from their traditional criteria in considering black adoptive applicants.

As a result, the pool of black adoptive parents looks very different in socio-economic terms from the pool of white parents. Black adoptive parents are significantly older, poorer, and more likely to be single than their white adoptive counterparts. A major study published in 1986 called the Westat Report (Westat, 1986) gives some indication of the differences: 50 percent of minority adoptive families had incomes below $20,000 per year, and 20 percent had incomes below $10,000 per year. By contrast, only 14 percent of non-minority families had incomes below $20,000, and only two percent had incomes below $10,000. Forty-five percent of the fathers in the minority families were age 45 or over, with 14 percent age 61 or over. Only 19 percent of the non-minority adoptive fathers were age 45 or over and only two percent were age 61 or over.

It is important to note that in altering screening criteria for black adoptive families, adoption workers have by no means repudiated the traditional criteria as irrelevant to determining parental fitness. Black and white parent candidates are still assessed and ranked by these criteria, with singles, older people, and economically marginal candidates placed at the bottom of the prospective parent lists. What adoption workers have done, in trying to expand what is an all-too-short black prospective parent list, is to seek out the kind of people they would normally exclude altogether from the white parent lists. Because of the importance attributed to the racial factor, those at the bottom of the black list are generally preferred over all those on the white list for any waiting black child.

THE IMPACT OF CURRENT POLICIES

A major issue is the degree to which racial matching policies result in delaying or denying permanent placement for minority children. What we know is that minority children are disproportionately represented in the population of children waiting for adoptive homes, they spend longer waiting than white children, and they are less likely to be eventually placed. Estimates indicate that of the population of children waiting for homes, black children make up over one-third and children of colour make up roughly one-half. The Westat Report (Westat, 1986) found that minority children waited for an average of two years, compared to an average one-year wait for non-minorities. Minority placement rates were 20 percent lower than non-minority placement rates. The minority children were comparable in age with the non-minorities and had other characteristics which, had race not been an issue, should have made it easier to find adoptive placements – they had fewer disabilities and fewer previous placements in foster care. The study concluded that racial status was a more powerful determinant of placement rate than any other factor examined (Westat, 1986, pp. x–xi, 3-7-3-8, 3-7-3-44). These findings are consistent with the general understanding. They of course do not conclusively demonstrate a relationship between the problems minority children face in finding adoptive placements and the racial matching policies described earlier. But it seems highly likely that there is significant linkage. Informed observers of the adoption scene – people who know the policies and see them in operation – believe there is a strong causal connection between the policies and the delays and denial of placement that minority children face.

The most adamant critics of transracial adoption argue that there are no good figures available on the children waiting for adoption. They say that even if minority children are particularly subject to delays and denial in placement, the solution lies in devoting more resources to the preservation and the reunification of black biological families, and to the recruitment of minority families for those children who must be removed from their homes. They argue that with such efforts, black homes could be found for all waiting children. They argue further that whites would not be willing to adopt the minority children who wait, noting that most of the children in foster care are older and that they suffer from a variety of physical and emotional problems.

But the fact is that the resources devoted to the goal of preserving black biological families and to making inracial adoption work *have* been limited and are likely to be limited in the foreseeable future. There are and almost certainly will be for some period of time too few black families available for the waiting black children. By contrast, there are many white families eagerly awaiting the opportunity to adopt. Although white adopters, like black adopters, tend to prefer healthy infants, 'special needs' recruitment efforts in recent years have demonstrated that whites as well as blacks are often willing to adopt older children and children with devastating disabilities. Current racial matching policies stand in the way of tapping this ready resource of homes for minority children. Moreover, the reason that so many of the waiting black children are older is in part because matching policies have kept them on hold.

Although it seems clear that racial matching policies cause delays and denial in placement for minority children, it is harder to get a sense of how common and how lengthy the delays are and how frequently minority children are permanently denied adoptive homes. The consensus among adoption professionals seems to be that black homes can be found for healthy young black infants; most children falling into this category are being placed. However, their placement may still require a recruitment process of many months. If the agency is not engaged in active minority family recruiting, years may go by whilst the agency waits for a same-race family. For young black children who must be freed for adoption by court proceedings terminating parental rights, there will often be additional years of delay. Whilst the months and years go by the children are pushed deeper into the hard-to-place category, as they get older and accumulate what are often damaging experiences in foster care. Delay thus puts the child at risk of yet more delay and, ultimately, the denial of placement altogether.

For children with severe disabilities and for older children, most of whom have some problems in addition to age that make them hard to place, the risks of lengthy delay and permanent denial of placement are even greater. Although agencies are generally somewhat more willing to consider transracial adoption for these children, they are still likely to treat it at best as a last-resort option to be considered only after minority families have been recruited and appropriate waiting periods exhausted. Accordingly, white adoptive parents are actively discouraged from finding out about or expressing interest in minority special needs children by the race-specific recruitment devices described above, and white parents' requests for consideration for specific minority children are often rebuffed.

Equally significant is the fact, noted above, that recruitment has not been used in a positive way to encourage white parents to adopt hard-to-place minority children. The lesson of the last two decades, during which children with special needs have for the first time been placed in significant numbers, is that active recruitment together with the use of subsidies and a relaxation of traditional screening criteria are essential to the goal of finding homes for these children. With such recruitment it appears that homes can be found for even the most seriously disabled.

Conversations I had with the director of the National Adoption Center give some sense of how different aspects of the inrace preference policies work together to limit chances that minority special needs children will find permanent homes. Funded by the Federal Government, the Center sponsors the only major national exchange that lists both hard-to-place children and prospective parents. Agencies from around the country use the exchange to list children for whom they have been unable to find what they consider appropriate placements locally. Most of the minority children have therefore already been waiting for placement with a minority family for a significant period of time before they are placed on the exchange. The Center tries to match children listed on its exchange with appropriate parents who are on its list, and it also recruits parents in the minority community for the waiting minority children. The Center will not consider a transracial placement until a child has been listed on the exchange for six months. At that point, the Center might consider couples in which one member is of the same race as the child, or even a white family that specifically requested a particular minority child. But the Center makes no effort then or at any subsequent point to look for white families for waiting minority children. Even when the Center is willing to consider a transracial placement, the local agencies, which have formal custody of the children, often remain unwilling. The Director described herself as a strong proponent of inracial placement, who believed transracial adoption should be considered only as a last resort. Nonetheless she revealed her concern with the delay children often experienced in getting listed on her exchange, with the reluctance to consider white families as an option even after a minority child had been listed for six months, and with the failure actively to recruit white families.

We know that many minority children never receive adoptive homes, and many others spend years waiting in foster care or institutions. We know that while most prospective white adopters prefer to adopt healthy white infants, many are interested in adopting black children and many are interested in adopting older children with serious disabilities. There can be no doubt that the current racial matching regime, by barring and discouraging white parents from transracial adoptions, rather than welcoming them in the agency doors, denies adoptive homes to minority children.

The racial matching policies also mean that black children who can be placed inracially go to families that are as a group significantly different in socio-economic terms from typical white adoptive families and rate significantly lower according to traditional parental screening criteria. Some are of course going to middle-class black couples who look like the classic white adoptive family. But recruitment has never produced enough such couples for the minority children in need. As a result, black children are being placed, on a wholesale basis, with families for whom the limited subsidies available are a necessary precondition for adoption and with families that would be screened out by traditional criteria regarding economic and social stability.

The important question here is whether placements are being made on a frequent basis with families that should be seen as sub-standard or as significantly less fit to provide appropriate parenting than waiting white adoptive parents. The current system creates obvious pressures for such placements. Adoption workers unable to arrange a same-race match are left with a child for whom the official system provides no other acceptable alternative – long-term foster care and transracial adoption are both seen as system failures. Recruitment can be used to pressure people who have no genuine interest in parenting to adopt children for whom they are told no home is available. Subsidies can be used to encourage people who have very real financial needs but no real interest in a child to agree to an adoptive placement. Many of those I spoke to voiced their fears that racial matching policies had in fact produced, on a widespread basis, placements with families that were not capable of or interested in providing appropriate parenting.

It is true that traditional screening criteria are seriously flawed and based on a narrow vision of the ideal family form – the white, middle-class nuclear family of some mythical past. But we should not leap to substitute an idealised vision of the black family when dealing with black children. We should not romanticise about what it is like to live on the social and economic margins of society. It is one thing to argue, as I have, for the elimination of the traditional system for screening and rating parental fitness in favour of a system which looks to the motivation to parent as a primary indicator of parental fitness (see Bartholet, 1993). I favour a system that would establish only minimum criteria for parental fitness for black and for white adopters and then rely on counselling to educate and socialise prospective adoptive parents. I am prepared to assume that those who push forward to pursue adoption under these circumstances will, as a general matter, be at least as committed and fit a parent group as non-adoptive parents, many of whom fall into parenting without any conscious choice whatsoever. But it is quite another thing to use financial inducements to recruit, as adoptive parents, people who may have no particular interest in parenting and whose social and economic circumstances make parenting extremely difficult, in a context in which the assumption is that the children have no other viable alternative.

THE EMPIRICAL STUDIES

A number of research studies (see Bartholet, 1991) have attempted to assess how well transracial adoptions work from the viewpoint of the adoptees and their adoptive families, analysing such factors as adoptee adjustment, self-esteem, racial identity, and integration into the family and community. The nature of the studies that exist reflects a bias on the part of those responsible for funding, sponsoring and conducting research. The early studies tend to look at transracial adoption as an exception to the accepted racial matching norm and ask questions as to whether the kinds of problems adoption professionals might anticipate have developed. The later studies tend to look at the claims made by the NABSW and other critics of transracial adoption to determine whether there is evidence to support their arguments that transracial adoptees will not develop 'appropriate' racial identities or adequate 'survival skills'. The general emphasis is thus on the potential negatives in transracial adoption. Few studies ask questions designed to assess the potentially positive aspects of transracial adoption. Almost none ask questions designed to assess the potentially negative aspects of current matching policies. As indicated above, there have been no systematic attempts to measure the degree to which racial matching policies result in delay in and denial of adoptive placement. There have been no systematic attempts to evaluate on a comparative basis the experience of children placed immediately with waiting white families to the experience of children held in foster or institutional care on a temporary or permanent basis for same-race placement. There have been no attempts to assess the experience of those black children placed inracially pursuant to current policies with the same critical approach used to assess the experience of those placed transracially.

Despite this bias in the design of the research, the studies provide an overwhelming endorsement of transracial adoption, as is described more fully below. The studies were conducted by a diverse group of researchers that included blacks and whites, critics and supporters of transracial adoption. With astounding uniformity their research shows transracial adoption working well from the viewpoint of the children and the adoptive families involved. The children are doing well in terms of such factors as achievement, adjustment, and self-esteem. They seem fully integrated in their families and communities, yet have developed strong senses of racial identity. They are doing well as compared to minority race children adopted inracially and minority race children raised by their biological parents.

This is not to say that the studies in themselves should resolve the debate about transracial adoption.The issue of how these adoptions and how current matching policies affect the welfare of children is only one piece of that debate. Another piece involves issues as to the values of preserving and promoting black families and black communities and black culture, and related issues as to the role of black political power and black nationalism. The studies provide some evidence that black children raised in white families tend to develop a different sense of their relationship to black and to white communities from black children raised in black families. How one reads this evidence depends largely on one's political perspective on these issues. Nonetheless, most participants in the debate claim they are motivated largely or entirely by their concern with the welfare of the children at issue. The adoption professionals, the legislatures, and the courts which will jointly be responsible for resolving the debate are all bound by principles that require, in matters regarding children, enormous deference to 'the best interest of the child'.

Again, the studies do not definitively resolve the issue of what serves the children's interests. It may be that studies are incapable of measuring the value to a black child of being raised by black parents as part of a black community with a sense of its unique black cultural heritage. One can criticise the studies as relying unduly on the subjective views of the adoptive parents involved, or reflecting the value judgements of the researchers as to how to measure adjustment or racial identity, or how to establish indicators of adoptive success.

But the studies constitute the only evidence we have as to what has actually happened when children are placed transracially. They are often relied on by critics of transracial placement, by legislators, by the media, and by courts as indicative of the problems for children inherent in such placement. The studies in fact provide *no basis* for concluding that placement of black children with white rather than black families has any negative impact on the children's welfare. The studies may not definitively prove anything, as few studies relating to the happiness of human beings do. But in a world of limited information, they provide persuasive evidence that transracial adoption serves the interests of children.

At the same time, there is no real need for comparative studies of the impact of current matching policies to know that these policies are likely to cause serious harm to minority children. We know that these policies regularly delay and often prevent permanent placement. To the degree we know anything in the child welfare world, we know this harms children. We have many studies and decades of professional experience demonstrating that continuity and stability in a child's family relationships are central to wellbeing, that permanent adoptive homes are far better for children than temporary foster homes, and that delay in adoptive placement reduces the chances for a successful adoptive adjustment.

A number of studies have looked at transracial adoptees and their families and tried to assess adjustment or adoptive success by examining such factors as self-esteem, educational achievement, levels of satisfaction expressed by family members, behavioural problems, and adoption disruption. These studies consistently show transracial adoptees doing well according to the measures of successful adjustment chosen by the researchers. In many of these studies the transracial adoptees are compared to control groups of black inracial adoptees; in others they are compared to black children raised in their biological families or to white children raised in white adoptive or biological families. Other studies focus in the first instance on study samples that include inracial as well as transracial adoptees and analyse the degree to which the racial matching factor appears to be related to adoptive success. All of these comparative studies show transracial adoptees doing generally as well as the other groups of children in terms of various traditional measures of social adjustment.

Despite the positive findings, there is often a cautious and negative tone to the researchers' characterisations. Many of the studies emphasise that although the evidence looks positive so far, problems may well show up as the transracial adoptees reach some later stage of development. The early studies focused on adolescence as the point when the anticipated problems might manifest themselves. But as successive studies have followed the children through adolescence and into early adulthood, they find that the children continue to feel good about themselves, to enjoy good relationships with their families, and to do well in the outside world.

Three of the most significant of these recent studies are those conducted by Ruth McRoy and colleagues (1982, 1983), by Shireman and colleagues (1988) in conjunction with the Chicago Child Care Society, and by Rita Simon and Howard Altstein (see Chapter 8, this volume). The McRoy study compared a group of black adolescents adopted by white families to a group of black adolescents adopted by black families. There was rough comparability between the two groups in terms of such factors as age at placement and socio-economic level, with some differences in parents' education and employment levels. The study focused initially on the development of self-esteem, in part because the critics of transracial adoption had argued that the adoptees would experience problems in this area. The researchers concluded:

> This exploratory study indicated that there were no differences in overall self-esteem between the sampled transracially and inracially adopted children. Furthermore, the level of self-esteem of the adoptees was as high as that reported among individuals in the general population. This suggests that positive self-esteem can be generated as effectively amongst black children in white adoptive families as in black adoptive families. (McRoy *et al.*, 1982, p. 525)

The Chicago Child Care Society has followed a small cohort of black children since the 1970s, comparing those placed transracially with those placed inracially as well as with black children raised in their biological families. The most recent of several follow-up reports, published in 1988 (Shireman, 1988), looks at the children in their teen years and concludes that the transracial adoptees are generally doing well and are generally doing comparably with the other adoptees and with the non-adopted children. The report also assesses the way in which the adoptive families are functioning, concluding that for transracial families as for other adoptive families, 'the data of this study fit the common pattern of other research . . . in showing family systems which have accepted the adopted child and are functioning well' (Shireman, 1988, p. 34).

The Chicago study also shows transracial adoptees developing a strong sense of black identity and racial pride and feeling more comfortable than the inracial adoptees with other black Americans. The main difference revealed by the evidence is that transracial adoptees appear more positive than blacks raised inracially about relationships with whites, more comfortable in those relationships, and more interested in a racially integrated lifestyle. There is also evidence that they think race is not the most important factor in defining who they are or who their friends should be. Studies have found some transracial adoptees describing themselves as biracial or American or 'human', rather than black. Most of them are, incidentally, genetically biracial and relatively light rather than dark-skinned, as these are the kind of 'black' children that have generally been placed transracially.

The Chicago Child Care Society's study concludes:

> As far as we can tell with our measures, there has developed a positive black self-image, combined with a mixed black-white pattern of social interaction. It seems to us that this pattern may be one which will allow these young people to move with equal comfort in both black and white worlds, allowing them to cull what they wish from each culture, and perhaps creating bridges which will be of use to an even wider world. (Shireman, 1988, pp. 36–7)

The research evidence does indicate some significant differences between black children raised inracially and the transracial adoptees in connection with attitudes about race and race relations. Some of the researchers interpret this evidence as problematic, and they rely on it in drawing relatively negative or cautious conclusions regarding some aspects of transracial adoption. Critics of transracial adoption cite this evidence and these conclusions as supportive of their position.

But conclusions that this evidence is positive or negative in its implications for transracial adoption depend entirely on one's political perspective. From the perspective of one who believes that blacks and whites should be learning to live compatibly in one world, with respect and concern for each other, with appreciation for their racial and cultural differences as well as their common humanity, the evidence is positively heart-warming. And there is no evidence that the differences in racial attitudes have any negative bearing on the welfare of the transracial adoptees themselves.

The evidence shows clearly that transracial adoptees develop a strong sense of black identity, contrary to many of the claims made about the evidence. Questions on this issue were raised by some of the earlier research that relied on anecdotal descriptions of certain transracial adoptees who allegedly over-identified with their white families. But more sophisticated comparative research (Womack and Fulton, 1981) indicates that transracial adoptees essentially have as strong a sense of black identity and racial pride as other minority children. Indeed, some of the evidence indicates that transracial adoption may even have a positive impact in terms of black children's sense of comfort with their racial identity.

The fact that there are some differences in the racial attitudes developed by transracial adoptees is not surprising. It is completely consistent with what one would expect from the evidence as to general adjustment described above. These children have grown up in white families who tend to live in either relatively white or integrated communities. The adjustment evidence indicates that the children have felt a comfortable part of their white families and have flourished in what have been significantly white worlds. It is understandable that they will have developed a sense of the meaning of race that is very different from that of black children living in a state of relative isolation or exclusion from the white world.

This evidence is understandably problematic from a black separatist or nationalist perspective. One of the claims made by the critics of transracial adoption is that it prevents black children from developing the survival skills necessary for life in a racist society – skills they say can only be fostered by black parents who have themselves developed those skills. Although the evidence shows the transracial adoptees appear to be surviving very well, it could be argued that they have developed a naive and dangerous faith in their ability to get along in the white world, a faith that will serve them badly as they grow into the challenges of adulthood. In addition blacks who believe their group interests will be advanced by building a politically and otherwise powerful black community are likely to find cause for concern in the evidence that black children raised in white families are growing up to feel comfortable in the white community. The President of the NABSW wrote in the Association's Spring 1988 Newsletter:

> The lateral transfer of our children to white families is not in our best interest. Having white families raise our children to be white is at least a hostile gesture toward us as a people and at best the ultimate gesture of disrespect for our heritage as African people . . . It is their aim to raise black children with white minds . . . We are on the right side of the transracial adoption issue. Our children are our future. (NABSW Newsletter, 1988, pp. 1, 2)

The studies indicate that white families vary significantly in the degree to which they engage in deliberate socialisation efforts to make their black children feel part of a black cultural community and proud of a black heritage. Such efforts do seem to have an effect in producing a greater sense of race interest and race pride. But there is no evidence that black parents do a better job than white parents of raising black children with a sense of pride in their racial culture and heritage.

Nor is there any evidence that such differences as may exist in racial attitudes have any negative implications on the wellbeing of those raised transracially. The studies that have examined racial attitudes have found no relationship between measures of racial identity or racial integration of the child's social setting on the one hand, and measures of self-esteem or general adjustment on the other.

Feigelman and Silverman's report (1983) on their major comparative study of transracial adoptees concludes:

> It seems obviously desirable . . . to foster the development of a sense of racial pride and identification. Such attributes would seem to be valuable for the development of self-esteem and optimal psychological functioning. Yet, we were unable to find any connection between the possession of black self-identification and a variety of indicators suggesting optimal social and psychological adaptation . . . It is entirely possible that these represent independent dimensions of social and psychological life. It may be that a transracial adoptee can be well-adjusted and identified with the black community, white society, or both. (1983, pp. 118-19)

As noted above, the great body of research on transracial adoption has been structured to look for its negative and not its positive potential. But there is every reason to think there are advantages for children inherent in growing up in a transracial, transcultural family setting. Existing studies necessarily contain only fragmentary hints of what might be found if anyone chose to look for such possible advantages.

Critics of transracial adoption have claimed that only blacks can teach black children the coping skills needed for life in a racist society, but there seems at least as good an argument for the proposition that whites are in the best position to teach black children how to manoeuvre in the white worlds of power and privilege. Indeed, it seems clear that for black children growing up in a white-dominated world, there would be a range of material advantages associated with having white parents and living in the largely white and relatively privileged world that such parents tend to frequent.

There could be other, less material advantages for adoptees growing up in a transracial family. For example, it could be an advantage to enjoy the kind of comfort in both black and white worlds that the studies discussed above indicate transracial adoptees feel. It could also be an advantage for an adoptee to grow up in a family that is so obviously not fashioned in imitation of the biological model. Studies indicate that transracial adoptive parents are more open in discussing adoption with their children and that the children are more likely to identify themselves as adopted. These findings raise the interesting possibility that, in transracial adoptive families, the very obvious difference of race may encourage a healthier acceptance of the fact that their family is in various other ways not the same as a biological family. The Chicago Child Care study notes:

> All of the transracially adopted children were told of their adoption early; communication about this has been open in these families . . . Recognition of differences and maintenance of some distance between parents and child, may be associated with constructive handling of adoption . . . (Shireman, 1988, pp. 31-2)

There is a lot of evidence, and a strong consensus, on the costs to children of delays in adoptive placement and in permanent denial of an adoptive home. Child welfare professionals agree with virtual unanimity that children need continuity in the context of a permanent home in order to flourish. There is a significant body of studies demonstrating that children do better in adoption than in foster care, and that age at placement in an adoptive family is a central factor in determining just how well adoptees will do in terms of various measures of adjustment.

Moreover, to the degree that research studies have attempted to address the issue of whether delay in placement or racial match is a more significant factor in adoptive adjustment, they have found delay to be the key factor. Feigelman and Silverman (1983) did research that was specifically designed to answer the question whether 'race difference and racial isolation in an alien community pose a more potent determinant for a child's adoptive adjustment than the discontinuities and hazards associated with delayed placement'. In their study involving both black and white children placed with white parents, they found age at time of placement by far the most significant factor in explaining variations in adjustment measures. They concluded:

> The data . . . suggest that the deleterious consequences of delayed placement are far more serious than those of transracial adoption. The findings imply that when a choice must be made between transracial placement and continued foster or institutional care, transracial placement is clearly the option more conducive to the welfare of the child . . . If policy makers and social workers fail to consider [transracial adoption] as a possibility for homeless non-white children, then they are likely to condemn those who cannot be placed in black homes to significant and lasting psychological harm. (p. 93)

These studies provide powerful evidence that the delays in placement and denials of permanent adoptive homes that are a part of current inrace placement policies are seriously harmful to children.

In the context of a society struggling with the issue of how to deal with racial difference, the studies of transracial adoptive families are extraordinarily interesting. They do not simply show that black children do well in white adoptive homes. They do not simply show that we put black children at risk by delaying or denying placement while we await black homes. The studies show that black children raised in white homes are comfortable with their blackness and also uniquely comfortable in dealing with whites.

In addition, the studies show that transracial adoption has an interesting impact on the racial attitudes of the white members of these families. The parents tend to describe their lives as significantly changed and enriched by the experience of becoming an interracial family. They describe themselves as having developed a new awareness of racial issues. The white children in transracial adoptive families are described as committed to and protective of their black brothers and sisters. The white as well as the black children are described as exhibiting an unusual absence of white racial bias, and as unusually committed to the vision of a pluralistic, multicoloured world in which a person's humanity is more important than his or her race.

The studies show parents and children, brothers and sisters, relating to each other in these transracial families as if race was no barrier to love and commitment. They show the black adopted and the white birth children growing up with the sense that race should not be a barrier in their relationships with people in the larger social context. In a society torn by racial conflict, these studies show human beings transcending racial difference.

THE LAW

Current racial matching policies are in conflict with the basic law of the land on race discrimination. And they are anomalous. In no other area do state and state-licensed decision-makers use race so systematically as the basis for action. In no other area do they promote the use of race so openly. Indeed, in most areas of our community life, race is an absolutely impermissible basis for classification.

The Federal Constitution, state constitutions, and a mass of federal state, and local laws prohibit discrimination on the basis of race by public entities. Private entities with significant power over our lives are also generally bound by laws prohibiting discrimination on the basis of race. In the past 25 years this body of law has grown so that today there are guarantees against race discrimination not only in housing, employment, and public accommodations, but in virtually every area of our community life.

It is true that the anti-discrimination norm has been limited by the principles of respect for privacy and freedom of association. People are permitted to act on the basis of racial preference in choosing their friends and companions, and in forming truly private social clubs. But the state is not permitted to insist that race count as a factor in the ordering of people's most private lives. And so in *Loving v. Virginia* (388 U.S. 1 (1967)) the Supreme Court held it unconstitutional for the state to prohibit interracial marriage, and in *Palmore v. Sidoti* (466 U.S. 429 (1984)) the Court held it unconstitutional for the state to use race as the basis for deciding which of two biological parents should have custody of a child. Palmore involved the issue of whether a white child could be removed from the custody of its biological mother on the basis of the mother's relationship with a black man. The Court unanimously held that in this context reliance on race as a decision-making factor violated the equal protection clause of the 14th Amendment. The Court rejected arguments that removal of the child from a racially mixed household was justified by the state's goal of making custody decisions on the basis of the best interests of the child. Conceding that there was a 'risk that a child living with a step-parent of a different race may be subject to a variety of pressures and stresses not present if the child were living with parents of the same racial or ethnic origin', the Court nonetheless had no problem concluding that these were constitutionally impermissible considerations (466 U.S., p. 433).

The anti-discrimination principle has been interpreted to outlaw almost all race-conscious action by the state and by the agencies which control our community lives. There need be no showing that the action is designed to harm or that it results in harm. Race-conscious action has generally been allowed only where it can be justified on the grounds of compelling necessity, or where it is designed to benefit racial minority groups either by avoiding or preventing discrimination or by remedying its effects, as in the case of affirmative action. But these exceptions have been narrowly defined.

The 'necessity doctrine' was used to justify the exclusion for national security reasons of Japanese-Americans from military areas in this country during World War Two. But it is a sign of how limited this doctrine is that the Supreme Court decision upholding this exclusion as constitutional stands essentially alone in American constitutional jurisprudence and has been significantly discredited.

Affirmative action has always been controversial in the United States. The anti-discrimination norm has generally been expressed in individualistic and race-neutral terms – forbidding discrimination 'on the basis of race' or man-dating 'the equal protection of the laws' – and has accordingly been inter-preted to protect whites as well as blacks. Action designed to promote black group interests has often been challenged as discriminatory against whites. The courts have generally insisted that for affirmative action programmes to be upheld as legitimate they must be justified on the basis of a remedial rationale.

In recent years the Supreme Court has held that for federal law purposes, even 'benign' racial classifications are highly suspect and must be limited to narrowly defined situations. In *City of Richmond v. J.A. Croson Company* (488 U.S. 469 (1989)) the Court held that state and local programmes designed to benefit minority groups are subject to the same kind of strict constitutional scrutiny as programmes designed to burden such groups. It held further that affirmative action can be justified as constitutional only if shown to be absolutely essential to remedying prior discrimination.

The adoption world is an anomaly in this legal universe in which race-conscious action is deemed highly suspect and generally illegal. In agency adoptions, as we have seen, race-conscious action is one of the major rules of the child allocation game. The fact that race is a recognisable factor in decision-making is enough under the general anti-discrimination norm to make out a case of intentional discrimination. Adoption agency policies make race not merely a factor, but the overwhelmingly significant factor in the placement process.

The public adoption agencies, as well as many of the private agencies, are governed by legislative and constitutional provisions forbidding race discrimi-nation. The Federal Constitution's equal protection clause, and the related 'Croson' limit on legitimate affirmative action, apply to all state and local governmental entities, whether they be adoption agencies, adoption courts, or governmental bodies promulgating legislation, regulations, and other policies governing adoption. Title VI of the 1964 Civil Rights Act bans discrimination by adoption agencies, public and private, that receive federal funds. Accordingly, it applies to virtually all public and many private agencies. Many states have constitutional, statutory and regulatory provisions that broadly prohibit discrimination by public and private agencies.

But for some reason the anti-discrimination principle is thought to mean something quite different in the adoption area from what it means elsewhere. The federal policy guidelines clarifying the meaning of Title VI of the Civil Rights Act in the context of adoption and foster care (see Chavkin, 1981) are symptomatic of how differently the anti-discrimination norm is understood in this context.

The guidelines provide specifically that race can be used as a basis for decision-making in foster and adoptive placement so long as it is not used in any absolute or categorical way to prohibit consideration of transracial adoption altogether. They state: 'Generally, under Title VI, race, colour, or national origin may not be used as a basis for providing benefits or services. However, in placing a child in an adoptive or foster home it may be appropriate to consider race, colour, or national origin as one of several factors' (Chavkin, 1981, p. 1). The guidelines go on to emphasise that this exception applies only in these contexts: 'This policy is based on unique aspects of the relationship between a child and his or her adoptive or foster parents. It should not be construed as applicable to any other situation in the child welfare or human services area covered by Title VI' (p. 4).

Racial matching policies fit none of the recognised exceptions to the anti-discrimination norm. There is no compelling necessity for racial match-ing, on a level comparable to a national emergency threatening the survival of the nation. The black community within this nation is not threatened with extinction. The number of black children available for adoption is very small compared to the size of the black community; placing more of those available for adoption transracially poses no realistic threat to the existence of that community or the preservation of its culture. It is hard to see transracial adoption as more threatening to these interests than racial intermarriage or racial integration in public education. Official efforts to prevent such intermar-riage or to prevent black children from attending school with white children or being taught by white teachers have been held unconstitutional, and would be regarded as intolerable by blacks and whites alike in today's society.

Nor can racial matching policies be rationalised as programmes designed to eliminate or to remedy the effects of prior discrimination, or otherwise to benefit blacks as a group. It is easy to argue that there has been such discrimination. Traditional agency screening procedures and criteria can be criticised as having discriminated against prospective black parents, depriving them of an equal opportunity to adopt. Transracial adoption, which has operated to place black children but not white children across racial lines, can be criticised as having discriminated against the black children, depriving them of an equal opportunity to the benefits of a same-race upbringing. And transracial adoption can be seen as part of a continuing pattern of discrimina-tion against the black community. A vast array of social policies going back to the institution of slavery can be characterised as responsible for the fact that it is black families whose children are disproportionately available for adoption and white families who are disproportionately in a position to seek adoption.

Taking all these perspectives together, transracial adoption can be charac-terised, and indeed has been by the NABSW and others, as one of the ultimate forms of exploitation by whites of the black community and the black family. This understanding of the social and historical context gives meaning to the NABSW's description of transracial adoption as a form of racial genocide. The NABSW's goal of preventing transracial adoption and its current emphasis on efforts to preserve or reconstitute the biological family as an alternative to adoption, can thus be understood as based on remedial justifications in at least some broad sense.

The problem is that racial matching policies do not look like the kinds of remedial affirmative action programmes that the courts have accepted as legitimate. The policies are blatantly inconsistent with the Supreme Court's recent 'Croson' decision which places severe limits on legitimate affirmative action, requiring a near-exact fit between a given affirmative action programme and the discriminatory actions it is designed to remedy. 'Croson' prohibits the use of affirmative action that is designed more broadly to counter the effects of historical or societal discrimination.

But even putting 'Croson' to one side, the courts have generally insisted that affirmative action programmes look backward more than they look forward, be limited in duration, and be designed to help move society to a point where race can be eliminated as a decision-making factor. By contrast, racial matching policies seem to look forward at least as much as they look backward. They require race matching on an ongoing basis, without apparent limit in time. They are not designed to eliminate the role of race in agency decision-making in the future, but to perpetuate its importance.

Racial matching policies are in addition fundamentally inconsistent with traditional affirmative action rationales because racial matching promotes racial separatism rather than racial integration. Black leaders in the adoption world originally promoted racial matching in the historical context of the black nationalism movement that gained prominence in the latter part of the 1960s, with its calls for black power and black self-determination. Black leaders have argued for racial matching policies on the grounds that black people have the right to control the destiny of 'their' children and that racial matching promotes the integrity of the black community and black culture. This is part of why so many of the studies of transracial adoptees have focused on the issue of racial identity as a measure of adoptive success. White leaders in the adoption world developed their policies of matching parents with adoptive children who were biological look-alikes in a historical context in which racial intermarriage was universally frowned upon and often illegal. Racial matching policies serve to prevent racial integration in the intimate context of the family.

By contrast, affirmative action programmes that have had any general level of acceptance have been consistent with the orthodox view in this country on the nature of the racial problem and of appropriate solutions to that problem. That orthodox view holds that the problem lies in the segregation of an oppressed class, and the solution can be found in the integration of that class with those who have enjoyed the privileges of life in this society. Both anti-discrimination law and affirmative action programmes have been designed to break down barriers and to promote integration.

Many would argue that the problem of race has more to do with oppression and racial hierarchy than with separation. They would see the solution, either short term or long term, in black separatism and black self-determination. Many would argue that the preservation and promotion of a separate black culture and black community serves important interests independent of overcoming social stratification. But these views have not been incorporated in the basic law of the land on race.

In addition, and even more significant, race-conscious action that has any level of principled support in today's world relies on arguments that it benefits racial minorities. Even those courts and Supreme Court Justices most sympathetic to affirmative action have argued that allegedly benign racial classifications should be scrutinised carefully to ensure that they are truly benign in impact and do not serve to disadvantage their supposed beneficiaries. Racial matching policies are not clearly beneficial in any short-term or long-term sense to blacks as a group, and in fact, they seem quite harmful to a significant part of that group – the children in need of adoptive homes.

Thus, it is hard to understand racial matching policies as an affirmative action programme designed for the benefit of black parents as a group. Anecdotal evidence indicates that black birth parents who feel they have a choice among agencies often choose to surrender their children to private rather than public agencies, precisely because many of the private agencies have a reputation for putting a high priority on placing children without delay in whatever loving families are available, rather than delaying placement for same-race matching or other purposes.

For prospective black adoptive parents, racial matching policies represent a complex mix of burdens and benefits. It is true that blacks who are interested in adopting get priority consideration for black children. But the policies operate to limit black as well as white prospective parents to colour-matched children. Light-skinned blacks may be limited to light-skinned black children, dark-skinned blacks to dark-skinned black children, and interracial couples to those biracial children that are left over after same-race couples have been served. All of the above will almost certainly be precluded from consideration for a white child.

It is also hard to see black parents as seriously victimised by virtue of any exclusion from the formal adoption process since there is no evidence of a large, unmet demand by black parents for more adopted children, as there is, for example, for better jobs, housing, or schools. Many of the children available for adoption are older children with complicated histories of abuse and neglect or children with serious mental and physical handicaps. It is difficult to place these children even when traditional parental screening criteria are scrapped and affirmative efforts are made to recruit black parents and to subsidise the adoptions. The parents who adopt these children may experience their parenting as a special privilege. But the fact is that our society conceives of the parenting of special needs children as involving very significant financial and emotional burdens.

Racial matching policies make no more sense as affirmative action programmes if we focus on the larger black community rather than just the parents. There is no particular reason to believe that blacks as a group would support these policies. They are policies developed and promoted by the leaders of one black social workers' organisation in the absence of any evidence of general support in the black community and with limited vocal support from any other organisation. Reported surveys of black community attitudes indicate substantial support for transracial adoption and very limited support for the NABSW position or for the kinds of powerful matching principles embodied in today's adoption policies.

For example, a study designed to assess the black community's attitudes regarding the transracial adoption debate found significant support for transracial adoption and very limited support for the NABSW's position among a sample black population (Howard, Royse and Skerl, 1977). A majority (57 percent) had an 'open' attitude towards transracial adoptions, while 7 percent were 'most unfavourable' and 19 percent 'somewhat unfavourable'. Seventy-five percent of all respondents felt transracial adoption might be beneficial if no black home was available, while only 16 percent disagreed. Eighty-one percent preferred transracial adoption over keeping a child in a foster home or institution, whilst 14 percent did not. In looking at rationales, the study concluded: 'While the respondents were concerned about the child's possible loss of identification with the black community, the needs of the individual child were seen to be of prime importance' (Chavkin, 1981).

The underlying motivations for these policies seem quite clearly to include a complex mix, with white opposition to race mixing in the context of the family playing a part. There is no obvious answer to the question whether racial matching policies are likely to benefit or burden the black community, advance or impede black group interests. It is certainly questionable whether imposing on the black community an obligation to take care of 'its own', whilst providing limited resources for the job, does much to help that community.

What does seem clear is that current policies are harmful to the group of black children in need of homes. Affirmative action is not supposed to do concrete harm to one group of blacks in the interest of promoting what are at best hypothetical benefits to another. And adoption is not supposed to be about parent or community rights and interests, but rather about serving the best interests of children.

Adoption laws throughout this country provide that agencies are to make children's interests paramount in placement decisions. Arguments can be made that black children in general will benefit from efforts to strengthen the black community, and that racial matching policies represent one such effort. The problem is that as indicated above, racial matching policies seem contrary to the immediate and long-term interests of the specific black children waiting for homes.

Advocates for racial matching of course argue that growing up with same-race parents is a benefit of overriding importance to black children. But the claim that a black person, by virtue of his or her race, will necessarily be more capable than a white of parenting a black child is the kind of claim that courts have generally refused to allow as justification for race-conscious action. The near-absolute presumption under our anti-discrimination laws is that race is irrelevant to qualifications.

Moreover, the available evidence does not support the claim that same-race placement is beneficial to black children, much less that it outweighs the harm of delayed placement. Ultimately, the argument that racial matching policies are beneficial rather than harmful to the children affected rests on the unsupported assumption that black children will be significantly better off with 'their own kind'. This may or may not be true; empirical studies may not be capable of proving the proposition one way or another. But it is not the kind of assumption that has been permitted under United States anti-discrimination laws. More importantly, it is not an assumption that should be permitted in a situation where there is evidence that by insisting on a racial match we are doing serious injury to black children.

If racial matching policies are as inconsistent with the law of the land on race as I have argued they are, it is interesting that they have been allowed to exist. There seems to be an extraordinary level of agreement among policy-makers that whatever the law provides with respect to race in other contexts, it is appropriate to use race as a basis for decision-making in the context of the adoptive family. Courts have both failed to confront the issues involved in racial matching policies, and have shown significant sympathy for those policies.

The courts have generally agreed upon a legal doctrine that race cannot be used by agencies as the sole or automatically dispositive factor in placement decision-making, but can be used as a significant and even determinative factor. Some courts actually require that race be considered.

A major problem with the factual analysis in these adoption cases is that the courts tend to ignore or distort the systemic role race plays in agency decision-making. The cases portray a world in which the general practice is consistent with the courts' current legal doctrine that race shall not function in an absolute or automatic way in placement decisions. The courts act as if their role in these cases is to determine whether the agency decision in the case before them represents a transgression of the generally understood rules of the game – an aberration from an agreed upon norm of behaviour. They are either unaware, or unwilling to acknowledge, that adoption agencies throughout the country are operating under rules that regularly make race a central and determinative factor in placement decisions.

A major problem with the courts' legal doctrine in these adoption cases is that it is inconsistent with the way courts define the nature of unlawful discrimination in areas other than adoption. In other areas the anti-discrimination norm forbids decision-makers from giving race any role in their decision-making processes. If a party is able to show that race has played a part in arriving at the decision at issue, that decision is presumptively unlawful.

The judges have come up with little justification for treating the racial issue so differently in the adoption context. Some judges have relied on unsubstantiated claims that the evidence from the adoption world indicates that black children will necessarily risk serious identity and other problems if they are raised by whites. Some have relied on their own assumptions regarding such problems. Others have expressed what seems to be at the heart of much judicial thinking in this area – the sense that mixing the races in the context of the family is simply not 'natural'. In one leading case, the majority opinion states: 'It is a natural thing for children to be raised by parents of their same ethnic background'. The opinion speaks approvingly of traditional matching policies as designed to duplicate the 'natural biological environment' so that the child could develop a 'normal family relationship' (*Drummond v. Fulton County*, 563 F. 2d 1200, 12 (5th Cir. 1977) *en banc. cert. denied*, 432 U.S. 905 (1978)).

This sense that what is 'natural' and 'normal' in the intimate context of family are same-race relationships is at the heart of the law on transracial adoption. But in *Loving v. Virginia*, the Supreme Court rejected similar thinking in striking down Virginia's miscegenation statute. The trial court had reasoned as follows:

> Almighty God created the races white, black, yellow, malay and red, and he placed them on separate continents. And but for the interference with his arrangement there would be no cause for such marriages. The fact that he separated the races shows that he did not intend for the races to mix. (388 U.S. 1, 3 (1967); trial judge's unpublished opinion)

The Supreme Court reversed the trial court, holding racial classifications embodied in Virginia's 'Racial Integrity Act' unconstitutional, 'even assuming an even-handed state purpose to protect the 'integrity' of all races' (388 U.S., p. 12, n. 11).

Legislatures and executive policy-makers, like the courts, generally have, where they have not affirmatively intervened to mandate or permit the use of race as a criterion in adoption placement, taken a hands-off attitude towards adoption agency policies with respect to race.

One reason for the general tolerance of racial matching policies may be the fact that they have a direct impact on a relatively small and powerless group consisting of minority children without homes and the whites interested in parenting them. When white employees are denied seniority rights or job promotions in favour of minorities, this is experienced as a threat to significant economic interests by large portions of the population, and unions and other powerful organisations are galvanised into action to protect against the threat. The sight of older and disabled black children being held in foster care rather than placed with whites, or taken from whites to be placed with blacks, simply does not trigger the same kind of concern in the larger white community. Consequently, no major power organisations step forward to join ranks with white prospective parents to mount a campaign against the racial matching policies.

For the black and liberal white organisations that have traditionally focused on the welfare of children, racial matching policies pose complicated political issues since it is black adoption workers who have most vocally promoted the policies and who have condemned transracial adoption as a form of white racism.

Another reason for this general tolerance is presumably the existence of widely-held views that black children should be raised by black parents if this is at all possible. Professionals involved in adoption issues agree with near-unanimity on this proposition. Even those most active in criticising what they see as the excesses of current racial matching policies tend to concede that transracial adoption should be considered only if there is no viable inracial placement available. Almost no one advocates the elimination of any preference whatsoever for inrace placement – that is, the creation of the kind of race-blind regime typically considered the ideal to be achieved in other areas of social life.

The remaining issue is what to do about the discrepancy between our nation's general laws on racial discrimination and the adoption world's matching policies. It should be clear that the powerful preference for same-race placement embodied in many of today's policies violates guarantees against discrimination contained in Title VI of the 1964 Civil Rights Act and in the Constitution. The evidence that these policies are doing harm to the group of black children waiting for homes precludes any affirmative action justification. But it is not quite so clear how the law should view the issue of whether race should be entirely precluded from consideration in adoptive placement.

The issue cannot be seen as entirely determined by law; it presents a choice for those who make and interpret the law. Legislatures and courts are continually redefining the nature of the anti-discrimination norm and of permissible affirmative action. Current legal limitations on affirmative action programmes are far too restrictive, in my view, in their concern for the protection of white rights, and their demand for a close fit between the design of an affirmative action programme and a limited remedial goal.

Adoption puts the state, or state-licensed agencies, in the position of structuring the uniquely private relationship involved in a family. The Supreme Court cases dealing with state barriers to interracial marriage and with state use of race as a basis for deciding custody between biological parents deal with similar issues. These cases suggest strongly that the state should stay out of the business of promoting same-race families in the context of adoption. No exact legal analogue in Supreme Court jurisprudence exists, however, for the adoption issue. We need to think about what policies are appropriate in the adoption context. If policies embodying some limited preference for same-race placement seem the right ones, then it is our race law that needs to be changed, or adapted to accommodate them.

DIRECTIONS FOR THE FUTURE

Racial matching should not be seen as an issue on which black interests are pitted against white interests, with blacks on one side fighting for the rights of 'their children' supported by whites sympathetic to the black community, and opposed by white parents who want the children for their own benefit and by defenders of white privilege. There is no evidence of significant black support for current racial matching policies, and there is reason to think that if fully informed about the nature of these policies and their impact on black children, many blacks would oppose them. And it is clear that these policies are harmful to those blacks most affected – the children in need of homes.

White support and tolerance for racial matching policies should not be seen as necessarily benign. It may well be that liberal white guilt helps explain why white adoption workers joined ranks with the NABSW to close down transracial adoption. But something else is going on here as well. One would expect 'good liberals' to worry more about the apparent interests of the black children waiting in foster care in finding the best possible homes at the earliest possible time. If these white social workers were reserving for blacks jobs or other benefits prized by the white community, they would clearly meet a great deal of resistance. Given the impact these policies have on black children, it is hard to understand them as an expression of white community concern to advance the interests of black people. It would appear instead that the white community just does not care that much about the fate of black children who wait for homes. And the notion that the black community has a right to hold onto 'its own' is likely to strike a sympathetic chord among whites who would feel uncomfortable at the idea of a white child being raised in a black or biracial family.

The issues at the heart of current racial matching policies are the significance of racial difference and the role of racial separatism in dealing with difference. Historically, these policies represent the coming together of white segregationists with black nationalists and the merger of their racial separatist ideologies with 'biologism'.

Adoption professionals have idealised the biological family and structured the adoptive family in its image. They have argued that biological sameness helps make families work, and so have promoted the goal of matching adoptive parents with their biological look-alikes. Although adoption professionals surrendered various aspects of their matching philosophy as they struggled to keep up with the realities of the adoption world, they held onto the core idea that racial look-alikes should be placed together. Even at the high point of the transracial adoption movement, placement across racial lines was seen more as a regrettable but necessary last resort, than as a positive good.

The NABSW leadership's attack on transracial adoption met with relatively ready acceptance from white as well as black social workers, not just because of liberal white guilt, but because it fits with the traditional assumptions of their professional world. This adoption world is part of a larger social context in which there has always been a strong sense that racial differences matter deeply, and a related suspicion about crossing racial lines. Both black nationalists and white segregationists promote separatism, especially in the context of the family, as a way of promoting the power and cultural integrity of their own group. Even those blacks and whites generally committed to integration often see the family as the place to draw the line.

From a separatist perspective, current racial matching policies make a certain amount of sense, even if they do result in the denial of permanent adoptive homes to black children who could be placed. Those who believe in maintaining the separateness of the white community can take comfort from the fact that current policies provide a near absolute guarantee that white children will not be placed with black parents or with interracial couples. They might see as disturbing, as do the NABSW advocates, the evidence that the black children in these transracial adoptive families seem more likely than other black children to engage in interracial dating, and seem more open to the possibility of interracial marriage.

Those who believe in promoting a sense of black community can take comfort in the fact that most of the black children who do not find adoptive homes are growing up in the black community, whether in traditional foster homes or in relatives' homes. They can also take comfort from the fact that the current system has created added pressure for preservation or reunification of the black biological family. They can see as irrelevant or even as deeply disturbing the evidence as to the apparent wellbeing of transracial adoptees.

Thus, if one believes that black children should be an integral part of a functioning black community and should experience their black heritage and black culture as central to their being, then the evidence that black children are functioning as loving members of their white families and comfortable participants in their white social and educational communities would be problematic. The children's 'adjustment' to this white world might well, from this perspective, be read as evidence of pathology, rather than psychological health. One might be prepared to assume that transracial adoptees will pay a heavy price for living in a community in which they will never 'belong', whether or not they or their white parents are aware of their loss, and whether or not the studies are capable of measuring it. In any event, one might see some short term sacrifice of black children's interests as justifiable when weighed against the long-term interests of the larger black community. In this view, current policies might be seen as justified by virtue of the pressure they put on the white community to come up with the additional resources necessary to keep black children in their biological families or to place them with black families.

But one can recognise the importance of racial and cultural difference without subscribing to separatism. One can celebrate a child's racial identity without insisting that the child born with a particular racial make-up must live within a prescribed racial community. One can recognise that there are an endless variety of ways individual members of various racial groups choose to define their identities and to define themselves in relationship to racial and other groups. One can believe that people are fully capable of loving those who are not biological and racial likes, but are 'other', and that it is important that more learn to do so. One can see the elimination of racial hostilities as more important than the promotion of cultural difference.

From this perspective, which is one I share, transracial adoptive families constitute an interesting model of how we might better learn to live with one another in this society. These families can work only if there is appreciation of racial difference, and love that transcends such difference. And the evidence indicates that these families do work. Accordingly, I believe that current racial matching policies should be abandoned not simply because they violate the law but because they do serious injury to black children in the interest of promoting an inappropriate separatist agenda.

Assuming that the powerful matching policies of today were abandoned or outlawed, the question would remain as to what role, if any, race should play in the agency placement process. Most critics of today's policies focus their criticism on the degree to which race matching principles dominate the placement process, rather than on the fact that race is allowed to play any role at all. They tend to argue for a rule that would allow race to be used as a factor, but not an exclusive factor in decision-making, and for limits on the delay to which a child can be subjected whilst a same-race family is sought.

In my view, adoption agencies should be prohibited from exercising any significant preference for same-race families. No delays in placement – whether for six months or one month – should be tolerated in the interest of ensuring a racial match. Delay harms children because, at the very least, it will cause discontinuity and disruption. And any delay risks further delay.

Accordingly, any preference for same-race placement that involves delay or that otherwise threatens the interest of the children involved in receiving good homes should be viewed as unlawful racial discrimination, inconsistent not simply with traditional limits on affirmative action, but with ANY legiti-mate concept of affirmative action. The courts and administrators responsible for interpreting and enforcing the law should apply established legal principles to find any such preference in violation of the equal protection clause of the Constitution, Title VI of the 1964 Civil Rights Act, and other applicable anti-discrimination mandates.

The only real question, then, is whether agencies should be allowed to exercise a genuinely mild preference. A mild preference would mean that if an agency had qualified black and white families waiting to adopt, it could take race into account in deciding how to allocate the children waiting for homes. The agency could operate on the principle that all things being essentially equal, it would be better to assign black children to black parents and white children to white parents.

There are some valid arguments in support of a mild preference. There is some reason to think that, all things being equal, same-race placements could serve children's interests. There is, for example, reason to fear that white parents might harbour racial attitudes, on a conscious or subconscious level, which would interfere with their ability to appreciate and celebrate their black child's racial self. One has only to step into the world of adoption to realise how widespread and powerful are the feelings amongst prospective adopters that race matters as they think about what child they will want to adopt. Indeed, the adoption world is largely peopled by prospective white parents in search of white children. The urgency of their race-conscious quest seems to explain much about that world. But the picture is a complicated one.

There is tremendous variation among adoptive parents in their racial attitudes. And their attitudes are shaped and conditioned by messages they receive from adoption workers and the broader society, as well as by the adoption process. Many white adopters look to adopt black American or dark-skinned foreign children as their preferred option. Many others begin their adoption quest with the thought of a white child and later turn to transracial adoption after considering their options. For them transracial adoption may appear to be a 'second choice'. But the fact is that for a very large number of adoptive parents adoption itself is a second choice or 'last resort'. Many adoptive parents are infertile, and they turn to adoption only after discovering they cannot reproduce themselves biologically.

It is understandable in this context that in adoption their first instinct would be to look for a biological and racial look-alike. They are of course conditioned by current racial matching policies to think that they should do this. They are simultaneously conditioned by a variety of forces in our society to think of biological parenting as preferable to adoptive parenting. All adoptions require parents to transcend this kind of conditioning. The evidence indicates that adoptive parents are able to do so and that adoptive relationships work. The evidence similarly indicates that when whites arrive at the point of consciously choosing transracial parenthood and enter into parenting relationships with black children, the relationships work, and indeed, appear to work as well as same-race biological parenting relationships.

There is nonetheless some reason for concern that transracial adoption might add in a problematic way to the adopted child's sense of difference. It is difficult for children to be different from those they see as being in their group or world. All adopted children have to deal with the difference of having lost their biological parents. Many adoption professionals feel that this difference puts adoptees at risk of feeling that they do not really belong. One question is whether we want to add to the sense of difference by placing black adoptees with white parents in what are likely to be significantly white communities. We may believe that these children should feel they truly belong; research studies provide some evidence that they do. But it still seems likely that many children would find it more comfortable, all things being truly equal, to be raised by same-race parents.

A mild preference for same-race placement might also seem to serve the interests of black adults who want to parent, as well as the kind of black community interests discussed above. It would counter, at least to some degree, the tendency of transracial adoption to work only in one racial direction. This tendency has been, understandably, a piece of what critics of transracial adoption have found most offensive.

But there would be real dangers in a rule involving even a mild preference. On a symbolic level, it is problematic for the state to mandate or even tolerate a regime in which social agencies, rather than private individuals, decide what shall be the appropriate racial composition of families. It is similarly problematic for the state to decide what the appropriate racial identity for a child is and how it is best nurtured. The Supreme Court decided some time ago that the state should not be in the business of deciding whether interracial marriages are wise. Indeed, we would not want to live in a regime in which social agencies prevented such marriages, or prevented interracial couples from producing children.

Transracial adoption is, of course, different from interracial marriage in that it involves children, many of whom are unable to express their own desires with respect to the kind of family they would like. But it seems dangerous for the State or its agencies to assert that children should not or would not choose to ignore race if they could exercise choice in the formation of their families, and to conclude that it is presumptively in the child's best interest to have a same-race upbringing. Moreover, the existence of transracial adoptive families in which blacks and whites live in a state of mutual love and commitment, and struggle in this context to understand issues of racial and cultural difference seems a positive good to be celebrated. The state should not be in the position of discouraging the creation of such families.

On a pragmatic level, there is a real question as to whether it is possible to create a genuinely mild preference for same-race placement – a real danger that if any racial preference is allowed, enormous weight will in fact be given to race no matter what the formal rule of law. After all, agencies and courts commonly describe today's matching policies as if race functioned simply as one of many factors in decision-making, with nothing more than a mild preference for in-race placement at work. Current adoption law, as reflected in court rulings and the administrative guidelines interpreting Title VI, is that race should not be used in the absolute and determinative way that we know it systematically is used. Given the extraordinary level of commitment by adoption professionals to inrace placement and the amount of discretion they have traditionally enjoyed to make placement decisions, it may well be that the only practicable way to prevent race from playing the kind of determinative role that it plays today is to prohibit its use as a factor altogether.

On balance, then, it seems that even a mild preference is unwise as a matter of social policy. The generally applicable legal rule that race should not be allowed to play any role in social decision-making should be held to apply in the adoption area as well. Policy-makers should not treat such a preference as an appropriate form of affirmative action.

Black and white prospective parents should be free to adopt children without regard to any adoption agency worker's views as to which children are an appropriate race match. Agencies should use subsidies and other recruitment devices to reach out to prospective parents of all races to find homes for the children who cannot be placed without such recruitment. Agencies should revise traditional criteria for white as well as black prospective parents, with the goal of creating a pool of people interested in and capable of providing good homes for all the children in need.

A no-preference regime would remove adoption agencies from the business of promoting same-race placement. It would not mean that racial considerations must be ignored altogether in the agency process. Agencies could act in their educational and counselling capacity to advise prospective parents with respect to racial matters. They could encourage parents to explore their feelings with respect to race, and they could try to educate parents as to issues involved in raising a child of a different race. They could try to guide prospective parents in the direction of the children they seem most fit to raise. But neither agencies nor courts should, as some have suggested, use their decision-making powers to approve prospective parents as parentally fit, to match parents with a particular child, or to prescribe and enforce rules as to appropriate attitudes regarding a child's racial identity or the manner in which a child of another race should be raised. It is important for agencies to try to help parents think through what they should do to affirm their child's racial identity. But it is dangerous for the state to be in the business of mandating how people should think about their child's racial heritage, and for the state to establish requirements regarding who they should have as friends, where they should go to church, and where they should live.

Agencies could and should allow prospective parents and children old enough to express their views to decide what role race should play in the adoption process. In the adoption area the state is attempting to create a human relationship that is as intimate, as powerful, and as permanent as any that human beings know. It is as if the state were plunged by necessity into the business of arranging marriages. It is wrong for the state to presume that a racial match is central to the happiness of every coupled parent and child. But it is equally wrong for the state to insist on arranging parent-child couplings without regard to the racial feelings of the people involved.

CONCLUSION

Establishment of a regime in which there is no official preference for same-race placement seems the wise course and the direction in which we should move. But it is a proposal that will meet a good deal of resistance in many quarters. It should be possible, however, to achieve substantial agreement on the importance of moving promptly to eliminate the kinds of racial matching policies that exist today.

Both common sense and the available evidence from empirical studies indicate that racial matching policies are doing serious harm to black children. Accordingly, these policies violate the principle at the core of our nation's adoption laws, namely that the best interest of the child should govern the placement process. They also violate the anti-discrimination norm contained in the nation's various civil rights laws and in the equal protection clause of the Constitution.

The evidence from the empirical studies indicates uniformly that transracial adoptees do as well on measures of psychological and social adjustment as black children raised inracially in relatively similar socio-economic circumstances. The evidence also indicates that transracial adoptees develop comparably strong senses of black identity. They see themselves as black and they think well of blackness. The difference is that they feel more comfortable with the white community than blacks raised inracially. This evidence provides no basis for concluding that there are inherent costs in transracial placement from the children's viewpoint.

By contrast, the evidence from the empirical studies, together with professional opinion over the decades and our common sense, indicate that the placement delays of months and years that result from our current policies impose very serious costs on children. Children need permanency in their primary parenting relationships. They may be destroyed by delays when those delays involve, as they so often do, abuse or neglect in inadequate foster care or institutional situations. They are likely to be hurt by delays in even the best of foster care situations, whether they develop powerful bonds with parents they must then lose, or they live their early years without experiencing the kind of bonding that is generally thought crucial to healthy development.

Current policies also significantly increase the risk that minority children who are older and who suffer serious disabilities will never become part of a permanent family. Advocates of these policies claim that prospective white parents do not want these children anyway. But the last two decades have demonstrated that efforts to educate and recruit adults of all races are successful in changing attitudes and making people aware of the satisfactions involved in parenting children with special needs. Current policies mean that virtually no such education and recruitment is going on in the white community with respect to the waiting minority children. These are the children who wait and wait. They represent a significant piece of the foster care problem. It defies reason to claim that we would not open up many homes to these children if agencies were willing to look for such homes in the white community.

It is true, as advocates of current policies often say, that more could be done to find black families. More substantial resources should be devoted to recruitment. But it is extremely unlikely that our society will any time soon devote more than lip service and limited resources to putting blacks in a social and economic position where they are capable of providing good homes for all the waiting black children. It will always be far easier to get white society to agree on the goal of placing black children in black homes than to get an allocation of financial resources that will make that goal workable.

The danger in using black children as hostages to pry the money loose is that white society will not see these lives as warranting much in the way of ransom. Moreover, in a desperately overburdened and underfinanced welfare system, those who care about children should take children's many needs into account as they make decisions about allocating any new funds that might be available. Money is desperately needed to provide services that will enable biological families to function so that children are not unnecessarily removed from parents who could provide them with good parenting were it not for adverse circumstances. It is desperately needed to protect children from abuse and neglect. It is desperately needed to improve the adoption process so that children who should be permanently removed from their families are freed up for adoption and placed as promptly as possible with permanent adoptive families. Money is needed in these and other areas to help ensure some very basic protection for children that should take priority over the essentially adult agenda of promoting racial separation.

REFERENCES

Bartholet, E. (1991) 'Where do black children belong? The politics of race matching in adoption', *University of Pennsylvania Law Review* 139 (1163): 1207–26.

Bartholet, E. (1993) *Family Bonds: Adoption and the Politics of Parenting*. New York: Mathew Bonder Inc.

Chavkin, D. (1981) Memorandum from David Chavkin, Deputy Director for Program Development, US Department of Health and Human Services to Virginia Apodoca, Region X Director of the Office for Civil Rights, 19 January 1981.

Feigelman, W. and Silverman, A. (1983) *Chosen Children: New Patterns of Adoptive Relations*. New York: Praeger.

Howard, Royse, and Skerl (1977) 'Transracial adoption: the black community perspective', *Social Work* 22: 184–9.

McRoy, R. and Zurcher, L. (1983) *Transracial and Inracial Adoptees: The Adolescent Years*. Springfield, Ill. Thomas.

McRoy, R. et al. (1982) 'Self-esteem and racial identity in transracial and inracial adoptees', *Social Work* 27: 522–5.

NABSW (1986) 'Preserving black families: research and action beyond the rhetoric'. National Association of Black Social Workers, Inc.

NABSW Newsletter (1988) 'Jeff, President's Message'. National Association of Black Social Workers Newsletter, Spring, pp. 1–2.

Shireman, J. (1988) *Growing Up Adopted: An Examination of Major Issues*. Portland State University – Regional Research Institute for Human Resources.

Westat (1986) *Adoptive Services for Waiting Minority and Non-Minority Children H4-11, H4-14*. Rockville, MD: Westat, Inc., 15 April 1986.

Womack and Fulton, (1981) 'Transracial adoption and the black preschool child', *Journal of the American Academy of Child Psychiatry* : pp. 712–23.

IN THE BEST INTERESTS OF THE CHILD

JANE ALDRIDGE

Over the past 30 years it could be argued that the wheel has turned full circle: again there are ethnic minority children waiting indefinitely for permanent families because of their ethnicity. However, that is to overlook the fundamental changes in placement theory and practice that have occurred over the years which have led to so many children from minority ethnic backgrounds being successfully adopted into ethnically matching or trans-racial families.

Certainly, there can now be few people – professionally involved or otherwise – who would dissent from the view that a suitable ethnically matching family is the preferred placement for the child requiring a permanent substitute family. If children are to feel comfortable with their personal history and their ethnic background the most likely place in which this will be accomplished – if not in their family of birth – is in a suitable matching family which is at one with its ethnic heritage. Furthermore, in recognising the parenting skills of ethnic minority families, such placements reinforce our acknowledgement of them as a valued part of our society rather than – as may have sometimes been the case – seeing them as a marginalised group expected to be simply 'clients' of social services departments.

Similarly, few would dispute the claim that with adequate resources, effective training and appropriate strategies, it is possible to recruit more such families. Progress has been made in this area and it has frequently been made as a result of pressure from black people and others campaigning from the 'same-race only' perspective. Nevertheless, it is an enormous philosophical and logical leap to claim that because an ethnically matching family is the ideal choice for a child, it is the only possibility that the child has of growing up with an appropriate sense of her/his ethnic identity. One might as well ban all adoption and fostering on the basis that children are best raised in their family of birth.

Too often, and in too many adoption and fostering agencies, discussions on these issues have taken place in an intimidating and uninformed atmos-phere with emotion and political conviction taking priority over a rational appraisal of the best interests of the individual child. For the question remains as to how to proceed if a suitable ethnically matching family is not available when the child needs it or – a not infrequent consequence – if a child has bonded with a non-matching foster family in what was intended as a short-term placement but which has become long-term by default. It would be irresponsible to deny the existence of these difficulties, given the number of examples in media coverage and the results of the Chambers' survey of the 'Be My Parent' directory of 'hard-to-place' children (see Appendix 6).

For the sake of the children and families involved, it might seem reasonable to expect that placement plans would be discussed in an open atmosphere with due consideration to the requirements of the law, the individual needs and current situation of the child, that such discussions would be informed by past and current research and that the feasibility of finding the 'ideal' family would be taken into account. In resolving these problems a major hurdle that needs to be overcome is the conviction – endemic at least at practice level in many adoption and fostering departments and on some adoption panels – that transracial placements damage children and that this has been demonstrated by research. Many social workers are so convinced of this or are so overwhelmed by the orthodoxy of their departments that they or their colleagues would consider it a manifestation of racism to suggest a transracial placement for a child.

As a result social work practice in this area of adoption and fostering is now underpinned not by research and experience but by strongly held but ill-conceived beliefs. For in spite of all that is known about the attachment needs of the child and the importance of early placement it is still, in too many instances, thought necessary to keep a child waiting indefinitely for an ethnically matching family. Yet this is a strategy that frequently results in removing the child from a stable foster family and environment to which they have become deeply attached or moving them from one temporary situation to another with all the emotional and developmental damage that this entails and, in the case of older children, sometimes means that s/he grows up without a family of her/his own at all – the ultimate indictment of a supposedly caring service.

As Co-ordinator of Children First – a pressure group established in 1986 to maintain transracial adoption as a viable alternative for those children for whom a suitable ethnically matching placement cannot be found – I have encountered a large number of cases which demonstrate the effects of adhering to rigid same-race policies. The following are just a few examples.

CHILDREN REMOVED FROM FAMILIES

1. South London: A brother and sister, born to a white mother and an Afro-Caribbean father, were raised by their mother as a single parent. She died when the boy was twelve and the girl was ten and the children were placed

with white foster parents. After two-and-a-half years and against the wishes of the foster parents the children were moved to live with their elder sister. As predicted by the foster parents this broke down after a few weeks. The children were not returned to the foster parents but were placed in a residential home for 'preparation for placement in a black family'. The girl was subsequently placed with a black family; the boy maintained that he had always been raised by white parents and preferred a similar placement. Since this was not considered an option by the local authority agency concerned, he remained in the home and left aged 16 without a family.

2. West Midlands: A boy of mixed parentage aged nine was removed from white foster parents after four-and-a-half years. The foster parents had requested adoption but this had been blocked by the local authority. The foster parents initiated legal proceedings and the situation was featured in the local press. Subsequently they withdrew, feeling that the publicity and ensuing teasing at school were upsetting the child who had been severely abused before foster placement and, though much improved, still had behavioural difficulties. They felt a protracted legal wrangle which they could not be sure to win would cause him great damage. The child was placed with a black family for fostering with a view to adoption.

3. West Midlands: A girl of mixed parentage was placed with white foster parents at the age of three weeks. There was no contact with her Afro-Caribbean birth father and her white birth mother ceased visiting when she was five months old. Her foster parents repeatedly expressed a wish to adopt her but were informed that a black or mixed couple were being sought and were advised by the social worker 'not to rock the boat' or the child would be instantly removed. They were given the impression that if they cooperated quietly and the child remained with them long enough they would be allowed to apply to adopt her. The child was removed a few days before her second birthday.

4. Yorkshire: Three black children were removed after seven years with a white family by social workers arriving unannounced at school and removing the children, instantly severing all contact. The foster parents were told by their social worker of long standing that the disruption took place on the advice of their new social worker who felt the placement was damaging for the children because of its transracial nature. The question remains as to why the family were considered suitable for seven years and how such a traumatic removal for all concerned could be justified. After an emergency placement, the children are now fostered by a black family – the fourth family and fourth location in their lives. Repeated requests for access by the white foster parents have been rejected by the placement agency.

5. East London: Two boys of Afro-Caribbean origin were fostered by a white couple for five years. The younger child was removed at the age of 13 for fostering with a black family, the older boy remaining with the family as it was 'too late' to remove him. At the time the foster parents didn't challenge the

removal as they were told by the social worker involved that such placements cause irretrievable damage to the children and they felt guilty at having been the cause of this. They bitterly regret their naivety and now feel guilty at not having fought to keep the boy.

FAMILIES FORCED TO FIGHT FOR THEIR CHILDREN

1. West Midlands: A girl of Asian origin was placed at the age of six days with white foster parents for short-term fostering. Her foster parents requested to adopt the child but were told, when she was two-and-a-half and a matching adoptive family had not been found, that the plan was to move her to another foster placement whilst the search continued for a permanent matching family. The interim foster placement was to be with Asian parents of a different religion and culture from that of the child's family of birth with which her white foster parents had been working to establish a network of contacts. The foster parents had the child made a ward of court and the judge ruled in favour of the foster parents, giving them leave to apply to adopt.

This case was initially much publicised in the local press but became the subject of injunctions. The case was heard by Sir Stephen Brown, President of the Family Division of the High Court (i.e. the most senior judge dealing with these issues) who made the following statement at the end of the case:

> After a three-day hearing I have today given judgement in wardship proceedings concerning a child of Asian origin who from shortly after birth had lived with foster parents of a non-Asian origin in Birmingham. I have considered all the relevant factors involved, among others the child's attachment and bonding to her foster parents, the parental capabilities of the foster parents and the child's racial background. I have borne in mind throughout the paramount importance of the welfare of the child. I have made an order that the child continue as a ward of the court and that she should remain living with her foster parents and that they should have leave to commence adoption proceedings. (Brown, 1990)

2. North-west London: A boy of Afro-Caribbean/Asian origin was placed with white foster parents at the age of six months having already had six moves. After one month his foster mother reported developmental difficulties in the child but was advised by his social worker that these were probably due to pre-placement upsets. The foster mother continued to express serious concerns about his condition and at 14 months he was finally seen at the hospital. Tests confirmed the foster mother's suspicion of a genetic defect which would impede the child's mental development. When the foster parents sought to adopt the child they were told by the social worker that they had no chance because they would not be able to 'teach him his culture'.

Feeling that the child's condition and need for stability were not being sufficiently taken into account, nor was the fact that they lived in a mixed neighbourhood with friends from various ethnic groups, they appealed to the Director of Social Services after lobbying support from local councillors. They adopted the boy just before his third birthday.

3. East London: A child of Nigerian background with Down's Syndrome and other medical complications was placed with white foster parents at 11 days. After ten months the foster parents first requested adoption but were told that the plan was to place the child with a family of the same ethnic background. They continued to request to be considered for adoption. When the child was 22 months old his social work team decided to remove him for placement with an Afro-Caribbean single parent with a mentally handicapped teenage daughter but for fostering not adoption. The foster mother was particularly upset because a comprehensive paediatric assessment had not been carried out. Following intervention by the foster parents' solicitor the child has remained in his current placement.

4. Yorkshire: A girl born to a white mother and Pakistani Muslim father was placed at the age of seven days for fostering with a white couple who had already adopted two children, one of whom was of mixed parentage. Just before her first birthday the child was returned to her birth mother. During the four months of this rehabilitation attempt the mother and child had lived in four different locations with the child finally admitted to hospital with severe vomiting. The child was returned to her original foster family where she eventually began to settle again. They asked to be assessed to adopt her, and when the child was two were visited by a social worker whom they had not met before and who, after one visit lasting 15 minutes, recommended against adoption by the family on ethnic grounds. The foster parents appealed to the Director of Social Services who set up an inquiry and the family eventually adopted the child.

5. South London: Siblings now aged five and six, were born to an Afro-Caribbean mother and a white father one of whom has a mental problem with a hereditary factor . The older child was placed for fostering with a white couple before his first birthday and the second child was placed at birth. The plan had always been for adoption by a black or mixed couple but none could be found. The foster parents asked to be assessed as adopters when the children were two and three, and it was apparent that the placement agency's search for a matching family was unrealistic. The agency refused to consider the foster parents.

Two years on – and with no matching placement in sight – the agency eventually agreed to begin an assessment of the foster parents. This has proceeded extremely slowly and on their visits to the Social Services offices the fosterers are still confronted by photographs and written descriptions of 'their' children on the 'Family-finders' advertising board.

CHILDREN WHO HAVE WAITED TOO LONG
FOR A PERMANENT FAMILY

1. Central London: A boy born of an Afro-Caribbean/white couple was placed at three months with white foster parents for short-term placement whilst a permanent matching family was sought. Ten months later the child was freed for adoption, enabling the local authority agency to seek parents for a healthy, well-adjusted child aged 13 months with no legal complications. The foster mother who had had long experience with the agency as a short-term fosterer was anxious that this child – like all the others she had fostered prior to their adoption with other families – should be settled quickly with a new permanent family. Concerned that a matching family had not been found she asked the boy's social worker whether they could find a transracial placement. The authority's response was to advertise the child again as widely as possible, including within the ethnic minority press, specifying their requirement for black parents.

When nothing resulted from the search and as time went on the foster mother repeatedly asked why an alternative was not being considered – the child had become very much part of the family and was forming friendships in the local area. Just before his third birthday the child was placed with a couple of West African origins.

2. South London: A child was advertised for placement with 'a family with at least one black parent'. The girl, aged two, had been born to a white mother and an Asian/Afro-Caribbean father and placed into care at the age of two months by her birth mother who asked that she be placed for adoption. By the age of two the child had lived with three foster families. Eighteen months after the advertisement first appeared a white couple with an adopted child of Anglo/Afro-Caribbean origins asked the child's social worker if they could be considered as possible adopters for her. They were told there was no possibility of this because they were white and, therefore, unsuitable. Six months later this little girl (aged four) was still being advertised as needing 'at least one black parent'.

3. North London: A child was born to a white mother who was an inpatient at a mental hospital. It was decided that there was no possibility of her being able to care for the child. There were doubts about the child's paternity but it was believed that her father was also an inpatient at the hospital and it was thought that one of his parents might be Afro-Caribbean. The child was placed with white foster parents with a clear plan for early adoption in a black or mixed family. Unable to find a suitable family among its own bank of potential adopters or its own inter-agency contacts the agency advertised the child, then aged 18 months, as needing 'an adoptive family where at least one parent is black'. An enquiry from a white couple who already had an adopted child of Anglo/Afro-Caribbean mixed parentage was dismissed. At 22 months the child

was 'matched' with a family – a white mother and a father who is half white European, and half Hispanic/Latin American, raised in Barbados.

4. South-east London: A child born to a white mother and Afro-Caribbean father was received into care at the age of three weeks and lived in three different foster homes before reaching her second birthday. The child was advertised at the age of two for 'a family with at least one black parent'. The description of her, which was generally very positive included: 'She has coped quite well with the moves in her life but they have left her feeling a little angry and unsure about trusting people . . . she will need lots of love and affection to help her make another big adjustment in her young life.'

A white couple with three adopted children, one of Anglo/Afro-Caribbean parentage, phoned to enquire but were told the Adoption Panel would not consider them because they were white. They saw the child advertised again after two months and wrote to ask to be considered as there were clearly problems finding a 'matching' family. They received a letter saying they could not be considered. They noticed that the child was still being advertised another two months on. I have no further information about this child.

However, as demonstrated in this book in the chapters by Tizard and Phoenix, by Simon and by Bartholet, the research evidence supports transracial placement as a viable option to fulfil the placement needs of ethnic minority children. Studies show transracially adopted children to be doing well on all the normal criteria for assessing successful adoption. Early placement, the adoptive family's racial attitudes, lifestyle and determination to support the child's ethnic needs play an important role in terms of general development, the child's feeling of acceptance in the family and in helping the child towards positive self-affirmation and positive racial attitudes.

The longitudinal study by Simon and Altstein (1987) is of crucial significance, as its third part, 'Transracial Adoptees and their Families: a Study of Identity and Commitment', has followed the children through to early adulthood; moreover, it examines them alongside their other family members – their adoptive parents, their white adopted siblings and their white siblings born into the family – allowing many profound and fruitful comparisons to be drawn. The conclusions of this study unequivocally support the view that transracial adoption is a viable alternative for an ethnic minority child in need of a new family.

If same-race only practices are not based on knowledge derived from social research studies perhaps it could be assumed that the anecdotal evidence is overwhelming. Yet this is not the case. The two sources of anecdotal evidence usually referred to in Britain in support of the case against transracial placement are the 'Black and In Care' group's video and publications from the Post-Adoption Centre in London (see Black and In Care, 1985 and, for example, Howe, 1988).

The video certainly contains distressing testimonies about the experiences of black children in care, but even the briefest analysis of those taking part reveals that those featured in the film are not children who were transracially

transience of the care
es or a series of foster
ism or that their ethnic
nportance that we must
d learn from them. But
to keep the children in
in black foster homes
ss the need of the child
o, whatever their own
eeds as an integral part

g at the Post-Adoption
l workers as 'evidence'
ntre was set up in 1986
olved in an adoption. In
ild and Family Centre'
ings (1987) reveal that
of behaviour problems
nown to be transracial

e a high rate of identity
However, it is unclear
e family was in itself a
or not. Moreover, it is
more frequent users of
ore open attitudes and
ces to seek out and use

ore the problems of the
their personal experi-
rove our selection and
n mind the number of
positive nature and to
ent are busy getting on
of social work profes-

hich earlier transracial
en undertaken into the
in, it does appear that
considered a sufficient
ption assessment was
nly one absorbed into
ildren to be placed in
ith no ethnic minority

population. The general advice given to adopters regarding the child's ethnicity was to love the child and treat her/him in the same way as their birth children. With hindsight what is remarkable is that so many such adoptions seem to have turned out to be so successful for the families and particularly for the adopted children themselves.

Neither should we forget that the alternative for these children at the time was not an ethnically matching family of their own but a life in a residential home, staffed almost exclusively by white carers; the shortcomings of which have been painfully recorded by the National Children's Bureau in their publication *Who Cares? Young People in Care Speak Out* (Page and Clark, eds, 1977). So, if the research into transracial adoption is encouraging and if the anecdotal evidence is inconclusive one might expect the practice to have fallen from grace because it has become redundant; in other words that the children in question can now be placed speedily and appropriately in suitable ethnically matching homes. However, this is not the case.

In attempting to find out what is happening to ethnic minority children in the care system we can pose all sorts of questions: How many children from ethnic minority backgrounds are in care? Where are they placed? What is their ethnic background? What is the ethnic background of their carers? What is the ethnic background of their social workers? How many are in need of permanent substitute families? How many approved adopters from matching ethnic backgrounds are available? The list of questions can be lengthened but the answer is uniformly brief: we do not know.

Hilary Chambers' survey (Appendix 6) certainly indicates a disparity between the length of time that healthy ethnic minority pre-school children are waiting for a permanent family in comparison with their white counterparts and this must be a major cause for concern. However, it is impossible to develop a clear picture of what is happening to ethnic minority children as there are no national statistics of this sort collected and local authority and voluntary adoption agencies generally cannot or do not provide them.

As Rowe, Hundleby and Garnett point out in their study *Child Care Now: A Survey of Placement Patterns*: 'The current lack of information about black children in care is serious and startling. There are no national statistics and few local studies, even though concern was expressed 20 years ago about what already appeared to be disproportionately large numbers of black children in the London care system' (1989, p. 158). This study analyses information collected about all placement starts and all placement endings during a two-year period in six local authorities from April 1985 to March 1987, in order to draw up a picture of what is happening to children in care. It is a mine of fascinating and often surprising information. Concerning receptions into care and placement patterns for ethnic minority children the study yields useful information about the six authorities studied:

This study confirms that Afro-Caribbean, African and mixed parentage children are disproportionately represented in admissions to care while

Asian children are conspicuous by their absence. Contrary to expectations the black youngsters entering care in the project authorities were not predominantly adolescents but young children needing only temporary care. Few young Afro-Caribbean, African or Asian children come into long-term care but mixed parentage children do, and are very much more likely than other black children to be placed for adoption. (Rowe, Hundleby and Garnett, 1989, p. 180)

However, the scope of the project was unable to deal with the ethnic background of caregivers and social workers and the authors, aware of the need for more knowledge to inform current practice, affirm that in-depth research is urgently needed.

Firstly, then, in addressing the needs of these children more statistical information is required on both a local and a national basis and the Department of Health must take the responsibility for collating and publishing information drawn from local authority and independent agencies to provide comprehensive ethnic monitoring information on these children. Questions should be devised to highlight the ethnic background of children in care, the type of placement they are in, the ethnic background of their carers, the number awaiting permanent placement, the ethnic background of their eventual placement and the length of time awaiting a permanent family once the decision for such a placement has been made.

Secondly, the Department of Health should either carry out or fund the badly needed fourth follow-up of the British Adoption Project. The third part of the BAP study, which was the first project in this country to place a substantial number of ethnic minority children, the large majority with white families, was written up as *Adoption and Race* by Gill and Jackson in 1983, the children at that stage being in early adolescence. There is as yet no longitudinal study in this country that has followed a cohort of transracial adoptees through to adulthood – the implications of this in terms of the paucity of the current knowledge base on transracial adoption should be obvious to anybody seeking to establish an inflexible position on this issue.

Thirdly, for social workers and other professionals involved in adoption work and members of adoption panels there are legal and practice matters to be addressed. The Children Act 1989, which came into force in November 1991, places an obligation on a local authority, when making decisions about a child it is looking after or proposing to look after, to 'give due consideration' to a number of elements, including 'the child's religious persuasion, racial origin and cultural and linguistic background' (Part III Section 2 para. 5c). This clause has sometimes been misinterpreted to mean that the child must be placed with an ethnically matching family but that is clearly neither the meaning nor the intention. It is worth noting that the introduction to the Act stresses that 'the child's welfare shall be the court's paramount consideration' (Part I Section 1 para. 1) and that 'the court shall have regard to the general principle that any delay in determining the question is likely to prejudice the welfare of the child' (Part I Section 1 para. 2).

The Government White Paper *Adoption: The Future* presented by the Secretary of State for Health in November 1993 outlines changes to be made in adoption legislation. Sections 4.31 to 4.34 refer to issues of ethnicity and culture and make clear that whilst the law in the future will require these issues to be taken into account they must not be attributed with any greater significance than other relevant factors:

> The 1976 Act contains no reference to questions of ethnicity or culture though in recent years authorities and agencies have usually taken them into account. The Government believes it right to consider these factors alongside others in matching children and parents and will introduce a broad requirement to this effect in line with what is now in the Children Act.
>
> However, in some cases it is clear that those assessing parents may have given these factors an unjustifiably decisive influence and failed to make a balanced overall judgement of the parents' suitability. The Chief Social Services Inspector has emphasised that ethnicity and culture are amongst the issues to be considered but they should not necessarily be more influential than any other.
>
> There is no conclusive research which justifies isolating such questions from other matters needing assessment; or which supports the proposition that children adopted by people of a different ethnic group will necessarily encounter problems of identity or prejudice later in life.
>
> On these, as in all other matters, any preferences expressed by the birth parents or ascertainable from the child should be given weight alongside others in an assessment that covers all his characteristics, circumstances and needs. In assessing prospective parents, what should weigh most heavily is the judgement made of their capacity to help and support the child through all the challenges he or she will face in life and not just any risk of difficulty attributable to ethnic background. (Sections 4.31–4.34)

In the meantime, in seeking to improve practice in this area social work teams should follow the guidance notes 'Issues of Race and Culture in the Family Placement of Children', issued by the Chief Inspector of the Social Services Inspectorate at the Department of Health. This document (see Appendix 8) emphasises the need for social services departments and voluntary agencies to analyse and understand the needs of all the different ethnic racial and religious groups that make up the population of their areas so that they can provide the services that are required. The document asserts the desirability of providing ethnically matching families at the time of need:

> Such a family is most likely to be able to provide a child with continuity in life and care and an environment which the child will find familiar and

sympathetic and in which opportunities will naturally arise to share fully in the culture and way of life of the ethnic group to which he or she belongs.

Additional advantages of an ethnically matching placement are described as providing a more promising framework for further contact with the family of birth and a firmer sense of belonging to their ethnic group which will stand them in good stead when they encounter discrimination or prejudice in the outside world. However, the Inspectorate does not support the same-race only position. It draws attention to the importance of considering racial, cultural, religious and linguistic needs but emphasises that decisions must not focus on one particular factor but should consider and balance all relevant factors in each individual case: 'There may be circumstances in which placement with a family of different ethnic origin is the best choice for a particular child. In other cases such a placement may be the best available choice.'

The guidance draws attention to the need to provide an environment where the child can be encouraged to become familiar with his or her ethnic origins and cultural heritage and the need for careful planning and monitoring by practitioners is strongly emphasised. However the document clearly states that transracial foster placements should not be disrupted on the basis of an authority's policy on ethnic matching: 'Children should not be removed from placements which are otherwise satisfactory solely because the ethnic origin of the foster parents does not accord with the requirements of general policies.' Similarly, there is an unequivocal statement that children for whom a matching family is not available should not be kept waiting indefinitely for such a family to be found: 'A child must not be left indefinitely in an interim placement, or, even worse, a succession of interim placements, while a permanent placement is sought.' Rather, a plan should be drawn up for the child which has a specific time limit related to the needs and circumstances of the individual child and the plan should be reviewed and altered when the time limit expires.

Unfortunately no suggestions are included as to what would constitute reasonable time limits, and this is urgently needed. Whilst everyone involved in the adoption process would probably agree that it is a difficult area and the time limit must be an individual one for each child, it should be possible to establish a committee of paediatric psychiatrists and equivalent specialists to throw some light on this matter.

There are some authorities which have already introduced time limits but these are not always as helpful as they should be. One, for example, has a two-year time limit for finding an ethnically matching placement. This is considered an improvement on previous practice in this authority but whilst it may not be unreasonable for a ten-year-old Afro-Caribbean child brought up in his or her birth family and currently satisfactorily placed in an Afro-Caribbean foster family, it may be utterly unreasonable for a ten-year-old child of mixed parentage raised by his or her white birth mother and currently in a residential home or undergoing a succession of foster placements or for a

month-old Down's infant with a white mother and a father of mixed
tage.

In struggling with the question of time limits one possible route could be
to introduce a statutory responsibility for the adoption panel to consider every
three months the progress being made in finding parents for children it has
previously approved for adoption but who are still waiting for a family. This
would be a fairly minor technical adjustment but it would impose a responsibility on the panel – the only stage in the pre-court adoption process required
to include an independent input – to oversee the progress being made and to
suggest adjustments to the plan for the child where necessary. This would be
beneficial to all children whose cases come to the panel for consideration.

Fourthly, in all of this it is essential for discussions always to centre on the
needs of the individual child. A prerequisite for this must be an open
atmosphere for information to be presented and proper discussion to take
place. The child's ethnic needs will form a fundamental part but not the whole
of such a discussion. Matters concerning race are painful; misunderstandings
can and do arise; prejudices emerge and have to be dealt with. But if a
heightened racial awareness has been arrived at in many adoption and
fostering teams it is deeply ironic and profoundly sad for the children involved
if it is used to silence discussion or ignore viable options in considering a
child's future.

Finally, there must be general recognition of the fact that we must operate
within the parameters of a world that is far from ideal. Certainly, a society that
was genuinely one of equal opportunities would not be one in which so many
children needed to be found substitute families or where such a disproportionate number of them are from ethnic minority backgrounds. Certainly,
better training of social workers, more recruitment of social workers and
increasing the numbers of those from ethnic minority backgrounds would
help to bring forward a wider selection of potential adopters. These are all
important areas demanding attention.

But to be realistic, it is highly unlikely that those resources will become
available in the short term. And it is the children needing families now who
are most in need of our attention. It is not within the remit of adoption agencies
to decide whether contemporary society should be based on an ideology of
racial separatism or racial integration. It is clearly legitimate that they endeavour to predict the sort of children for whom they need to find families and
that they endeavour to build up a pool of approved adopters who will meet
the needs of these children. But even as this process continues to become
more efficient – a task of extreme difficulty considering the very complicated
children often involved – it is unlikely that it will ever be perfect.

At the end of the day the responsibility of those involved in the adoption
process is to make sure that the child is placed speedily with the most
appropriate family available – a process that demands open minds to ensure
an open door to the child's future.

REFERENCES

Black and In Care (1985) Video published by Black and In Care Steering Group. London.

Brown, Sir Stephen (1990) Press release, 29 March.

Gill, O. and Jackson, B. (1983) *Adoption and Race*. London: Batsford/BAAF.

Howe, D. (1988) 'Survey of initial referrals to the post-adoption centre', *Adoption and Fostering* 12(1).

Howe, D. and Hinings, D. (1987) 'Adopted children referred to a child and family centre', *Adoption and Fostering* 11(3).

Page, R. and Clark, G., eds (1977) *Who Cares? Young People in Care Speak Out*. London: National Children's Bureau.

Rowe, J., Hundleby, M. and Garnett, L. (1989) *Child Care Now: A Survey of Placement Patterns*. London: BAAF.

Simon, R. and Altstein, H. (1987) *Transracial Adoptees and their Families*. New York: Praeger.

APPENDIX 1

ASSOCIATION OF BLACK SOCIAL WORKERS AND ALLIED PROFESSIONALS: EXTRACT FROM 'BLACK CHILDREN IN CARE – EVIDENCE TO THE HOUSE OF COMMONS SOCIAL SERVICES COMMITTEE' (MARCH 1983)

TRANSRACIAL PLACEMENTS – A GOOD PRACTICE GUIDE

12(a). The essential ingredient of any substitute home for black children should be the ability of the placement in:

(1) Enhancing positive black identity.
(2) Providing the child with the techniques or 'survival skills' necessary for living in the racist society.
(3) Developing cultural and linguistic attributes necessary for functioning effectively in the black community.
(4) Equipping the child with a balanced bi-cultural experience thus enhancing the healthy integration of his personality.

12(b). It has been seen that children of mixed parentage, the so-called 'mixed race' children of lighter skin, with physical characteristics approximate to that of white adopters, are the first to be placed transracially. There is therefore a continuum based purely on colour. The lighter the skin the more powerful is the attraction, the darker the skin the more powerful the repulsion. Those who intend to adopt or foster black children should recognise that there are no 'mixed race' children as such. They are perceived and related to by society as black.

12(c). The concept 'mixed parentage' should be used instead of 'mixed race', since the former does not imply the race superior quotient as implied by the latter. If there is a need to ascertain the race of the parents of the child/children, then this can be done by individualising the parents. We should be constantly aware that when the majority of prospective adopters and some social workers use the term 'mixed race' they do not mean the child of Indian and African parents nor Chinese and a person of African descent.

They generally mean a 'white' person and any other person who is not white. It is this which is repugnant to the black community, because it is reinforcing the very attitude that we are struggling against in our multi-racial society.

12(d). The concept 'mixed race' should not be used by administrators or social workers. Its use should be discouraged among prospective applicants. The term is derogatory and racist. It is a conscious and hypocritical way of denying the reality of the child's blackness and the ways in which society generally perceives black people. This is indeed fortunate but in a society where race and colour has been made into such an issue children of mixed parentage are seen and want to be seen as black, except in instances where reality and self-image have not merged. ' . . . It may be that those parents do not consider colour to be important, but such a blind attitude towards the role of group differences in the Society is unwise. It is possible that parents do convey to their children that they themselves do not judge and relate to people on the basis of their skin colour, but they should also tell the child that many people in the society do. Failure to do this will obviously leave the child unprepared to understand and deal with the first time he or she is called 'nigger' or some other racial slur . . . ' (Lander, Joyce (1977) *Mixed Families*). The majority of transracial adopters find it difficult to refer to the child as black or moreover they feel that telling the child about its ethnic origin is potentially dangerous.

They should be helped to recognise that racism is a reality in society and that although they cannot protect the child from it, they can prepare the child to deal with it when it is encountered. Consequently helping the child to develop a positive racial identity and pride in being black is an essential component of good parenting in a transracial setting. It is crucial to good self-concept and for the healthy integration of the child's personality.

12(e). White families who are currently fostering or who have adopted a black child should be given race awareness training. These training sessions could be conducted along the lines of pre-adoptive and foster-care classes. The outline presented in relation to transracial placements is done in note form with focal areas which should be useful for topic-focus training of transracial adopters.

THE ISSUES OF IDENTITY WITHIN THE FAMILY

12(f). (1) The geographical location of the prospective family must be considered carefully, since it is important for the child to see black people:
(i) to reduce the feeling of isolation
(ii) to mirror the blackness of the child
(iii) to provide black role models
(iv) to protect the child from racial abuse.

(2) The family should be sensitive to the prevailing race relations climate and be cognisant of the possible effect of this on the child's identity formation.

(3) The family should have clear concepts of what a multi-racial society is, or should be, and should be willing and able to provide the child with a balanced view of the different races.

(4) The family must be prepared to have black friends to demonstrate to the child that blacks and whites do have common interests and can interact harmoniously.

(5) The family must be prepared to develop contact with the black community in order that the child does not feel that he/she is being cast off

from his/her roots which often creates the condition whereby negative images emerge.

(6) The family must be willing and able to carry the child's past into the present and sustain it into the future, thus linking the child with its ancestral past in a positive way.

(7) The family must be able to accept the child as a black child in a positive way and not dismiss the child's colour as insignificant because society generally sees the child's colour as significant.

(8) The family must be prepared to find ways and means of linking the black child with other black children.

(9) The family must demonstrate that they have the capacity to 'work through' their conscious or unconscious feelings of threat from blacks if they are thinking of the ultimate interest of the black child.

(10) The family must be prepared to foster an awareness of the child's religious background.

LIFESTYLE OF THE FAMILY

12(g). (1) Reality for the child is defined and controlled by the family. Consequently the neighbourhood they live in, the interests they have, the life-style of their friends and colleagues will necessarily determine what is reality for the child. These issues must be confronted.

(2) The attitude of the extended family and friends towards blacks and to a black child being part of their family must be ascertained.

(3) The family must be able to demonstrate their willingness and ability to differentiate between different lifestyles, race and colour, without inferring the inferiority of one and the superiority of the other.

(4) The motivation for wanting a black child should be carefully examined. Is it ideological, is it guilt, is it to fight a political battle, or to make a political statement? Is it religious or is it out of pity? Is it concern for over-population? Is it to resolve curiosity about blacks or is it an experiment? Is it the second best or is it in line with current fashion?

(5) Every effort should be made to discover whether the family have the ability to put themselves in hypothetical situations and conceptualise and deal with the difficulties that are likely to arise with the black child, particularly during adolescence – what is the prevailing attitude in the family towards the black child dating the neighbour's daughter, etc? Can they deal with what may appear to be sexual threat and the reality of mixed marriages?

(6) There are no institutionalised support systems particularly in relation to adoption. Can the family, friends, and local community help the black adolescent to overcome these difficulties?

(7) Can grandparents accept that they may have black grandchildren which will change the context of their family?

IDENTIFICATION WITH WHITE ADOPTERS AND THE BLACK
COMMUNITY

12(h). (1) Can the family provide the environment for bridging the gap in
the interest of the child's personality?

(2) Can the family accept what may not be the attractive child (race and
colour) that they initially wanted?

(3) Can the family help or allow the child to develop a black personality
without feeling that a wedge is being driven between the family and the child;
does the family expect the child to be a white person in a black skin?

(4) Can the child or children of the prospective family accept and relate
meaningfully to the black child?

12(i). (1) The attitudes of neighbours and parents to black children mixing
with their own children should be ascertained.

(2) What opportunities exist for relationships at the boyfriend/girlfriend
level?

(3) What opportunities exist for socialising at the bicultural level?

(4) What is the attitude of friends, neighbours and the community to mixed
marriages?

ADAPTATION OF THE FAMILY AND CHILD TO EXISTING AND FUTURE
CONDITIONS

12(j). (1) Can the family deal with conflicts about colour within and outside
the family? Is the family aware of the stresses and strains that will be brought
about for the child and family if the child should experience rejection on the
basis of its colour; can they deal with that type of problem?

(2) Can the family provide the child with the skills that the black person
learns in the black community – the skills to cope with racism; can the family
provide the cultural and linguistic skills necessary for the child to relate to and
be accepted by black people?

(3) Can the family accept the fact that all people in the UK are not white;
and those who are not white are by definition black?

(4) Does the family realise that they may be ostracised by friends and
relatives – that they may become isolated in that they may be regarded as
having 'sold out'?

THE SCHOOL ENVIRONMENT

12(k). (1) Is the school multi-racial? If not –

(2) What is the prevailing attitude of teachers towards blacks generally?

(3) What expectations do teachers have of black children?

(4) What concept does the school have of a multi-racial society?

(5) What is the attitude of the pupils in the school towards blacks?

(6) What is the attitude of families towards black children attending the same school that their own children attend?

FURTHER CONSIDERATIONS

13(a). Transracial placements as an aspect of current childcare policy is in essence a microcosm of the oppression of black people in this society. The evidence for this statement is located in the following:

(1) Black people historically have always been forced in one way or another to serve white people.

(2) There is a shortage of healthy white babies available for adoption and so black children are being used to satisfy the needs of white families.

(3) The most valuable resources of any ethnic group are its children. Nevertheless, black children are being taken from black families by the process of the law and placed in white families.

(4) There is a one way trafficking of black children from black families to white families.

(5) No white children are taken from white families and placed with black families.

COMMENT

14(a). It is argued that transracial placements are a healthy activity because it enhances integration, but this is rationalisation after subjugation. This concept of integration is totally immoral. It operates in the interest of the 'strong' and not the 'weak'. Integration is seen as white domination. The current policy and practice is directed towards the progressive fragmentation and destruction of black families. The black community cannot possibly maintain any dignity in this country if success is defined in white terms only and black children are taken away from their parents to be reared exclusively by another race.

This policy and practice begs questions as to the type of service we are providing for black children and the type of society we are creating. Transracial placements pose the most dangerous threat to the harmonious society to which we aspire. It calls into question the basic philosophy of the social services. When it is looked at closely, social services is actually perpetuating the very racist ideology that our liberal democracy abhors. It is, in essence, 'internal colonialism' and a new form of slave trade, but this time only black children are used.

Measures should be taken to make this practice unnecessary and thereby terminating this dangerous aspect of current childcare policy.

APPENDIX 2

FOUNDING STATEMENT OF 'CHILDREN FIRST IN TRANSRACIAL FOSTERING AND ADOPTION – WHERE WE STAND' (1986)

CHILDREN FIRST is a group of black and white social workers, parents who have adopted fostered children from minority ethnic backgrounds and young black adults who have grown up in white families.

We believe that once the decision has been taken to find a permanent substitute family for a child in care then the needs and rights of that child must take precedence over the needs and rights of the adoptive, foster or natural parents.

Every child has a right to be placed as quickly as possible with a suitable family because all children need to grow up with at least one permanent caring parental figure. A loving family is a better environment for a child than even the best set of short-term foster parents or the most satisfactory of children's home.

When considering a permanent placement the child's race, religion, culture, age, parental background, medical and emotional history all need to be taken into account. However, a permanent family needs to be found as quickly as possible to avoid the child being disturbed by repeated moves or becoming institutionalised.

We welcome the efforts being made by many local authorities to recruit more social workers and potential families from minority ethnic groups; nevertheless suitable families of comparable ethnic background cannot always be found. In such cases placement with a family from a different ethnic background is a viable alternative.

Such families should be carefully identified, properly prepared and well-supported. When, looking for such families it is the responsibility of adoption workers to select families who will bring up their children with a sense of pride in, and awareness of, their ethnic origins.

There are numerous examples of transracial placements which have produced happy, well-adjusted and racially-aware adults. We therefore are fundamentally opposed to any policy which either implicitly or explicitly results in the implementation of bans on transracial placement.

APPENDIX 3

BRITISH AGENCIES FOR ADOPTION AND FOSTERING: EXTRACT FROM 'PRACTICE NOTE 13, THE PLACEMENT NEEDS OF BLACK CHILDREN' (1987)

BAAF POLICY

BAAF believes that all children need families in which to grow and thrive. There are many thousands of black children in this country, children who come from minority ethnic groups, principally from African, Caribbean, Indian, Pakistani and Bangladeshi backgrounds. For the vast majority of black children – as with all children – the best place for them is within their own family. It follows that agencies should provide appropriate services which will enable these families to stay together or to be reunited quickly.

In the small number of cases where children cannot be brought up within their family of origin, we believe that a substitute family should be sought urgently. We further believe that the placement of choice for a black child is always a black family. Agency policy and practice should therefore be geared to ensuring that an adequate number of black staff and of black substitute families is recruited to meet the needs of the black children in their care.

It makes sense to aim for placements which will most easily enable black children to accept and be proud of themselves as black people as well as enabling them to mix in the society which constitutes Britain today. Every transracial placement is not bound to fail any more than every same race placement is bound to succeed. However, a same-race placement carries with it the better chance of all-round success for a black child including the development of a positive identity.

It does not follow that policies and practices geared to achieve same-race placements will result in black children languishing in residential care indefinitely. There is plenty of evidence, from many agencies which have used specific recruitment techniques, that black families can be recruited. In fact black adolescents in some agencies are found substitute families quicker than white adolescents. The 'Soul Kids' project (1975–76) was the first recruitment campaign targeted specifically at black people. Social workers learned a lot about ways in which to recruit black families from this project, including the need for more black workers who could contribute their own valuable experience of being black in Britain and were thus sensitive to the needs and fears of black families and also to their strengths.

Although in the immediate future some transracial placements may have to be made, it is essential to recognise that there will inevitably be 'gaps' in what they can offer a black child – gaps which the black community will need help to fill. There are guidelines available for social workers who, as a last resort, are assessing white families for black children (ABSWAP, 3). It should be stressed that white transracial substitute parents must have additional qualities over and above those needed for nurturing a white child. As already stated, a good black family can provide good nurturing and also provide black positive role models and the knowledge, experience and coping strategies for dealing with racism. It is therefore particularly important in transracial placements that there are black people in the child's immediate vicinity to act as positive black role models, and that the child goes to a multi-racial school, lives in a multi-racial neighbourhood and that he or she and the substitute parents have black friends. Transracial placements should never happen on an ad hoc basis but should only be used as part of a plan for the child when efforts to find a black family, sensitive to the needs of black children in Britain, have failed. It is worth waiting, if need be, to find a black family who will be capable of meeting all the black child's needs. White substitute families, in the decreasing number of transracial placements made, will need help and support. Agencies who have been innovative in meeting the needs of black children have also accumulated experience in this area.

IMPLICATIONS FOR PRACTICE

Who is the black child?

Britain today is a multi-racial society with people from many different cultural and ethnic backgrounds. Social workers in different parts of the country will, of course, work with different minority ethnic groups but nationally the groups encountered will include:- Afro-Caribbean, Asian (e.g., Indian, Pakistani, Indonesian), Chinese, African, Arab. This practice note is about working with and for children where at least one parent is from one of these groups.

These groups differ culturally and, ideally, children should be placed in a home which has a similar culture to that of their birth family. The term 'black' is used for all these groups because all of them will have similar experiences of belonging to minority ethnic groups in this country and being easily recognisable as such. Although some individual members of the groups may not define themselves as black and their views should be recognised, they all experience racism, colonialisation and neo-colonialisation. Used in this way 'black' is therefore more a political than a cultural term.

Some of the questions we are regularly asked are:-

1(a). 'Are children of mixed parentage really black?'

Children of mixed parentage who have a white and a black parent are no different to other black children. Almost invariably they will be identified as black by society. They too need to feel proud of their black heritage and it is this that is hard to achieve in Britain today.

Such children, with parents from different races, should feel good about having one white and one black parent. Society makes sure that they will feel good about being white. It follows that the children are best placed in homes which will redress the balance and make sure that they are proud of being black too. They need a positive black role model in the home with the skills required to help the children accept and become proud of their blackness. This policy does not deny the right of the children to accept their white parent heritage. We aim for them to be proud of both their parents and their parents' heritage.

(b). 'But what happens when these children placed with black families face racism in society? Surely they will then over-identify with their black parent and dislike and be ashamed of their white parent?'

In our experience black people, wherever they have grown up, rarely think of white people as inferior. They may not like them or respect them but they rarely think them inferior. Such attitudes are the result of colonialisation. So we do not believe that the identity or self-image of these children will be threatened by being placed in a black family.

In assessing any substitute family, agencies should ensure that children are placed in homes where they are helped to accept the various cultures/races that make up Britain. This should be the same for any child irrespective of race and background.

(c). 'But the child may look white?'

If this is the case, and it is rarely so, it does not change the fact that the child should be proud of both the parents and of their different races and cultures. If the child denies a black parent and attempts to 'pass for' white, this can cause psychological problems in the child's future. The child is a black child and should be treated by the agency as such.

2. 'This black child has been living with white people all his or her life. Isn't thirteen old suddenly to get used to living with black people?'

It is important that the child gets to know people who look like him or her and is allowed the chance to make a realistic choice of friends, marriage partner, etc. later in life.

Those social workers who know little about the different cultures that black people operate in tend to rely too heavily on cultural stereotypes. There will, in a case like this, be a black family sensitive to the needs of a black child, who can provide a home not too dissimilar to the one the child has grown up in. Careful assessment, as always, is important.

3. 'But some black children actually say they will not go to a black home?'

Social workers sometimes say that their black adolescents refuse to live with black people. This is a sad example of the internalisation of the negative messages that society gives to children about being black. The reverse, white children who insist on going to live with a black family, is never reported (and it is likely that any such insistence would lead to concern about that child's identity development).

It is important that such black children are not allowed to continue with the unrealistic belief that black people are somehow different and less worthy. The child is black and it is all too easy for children to believe that although they are black, they are somehow 'different'. The child must learn that like the white population, black people vary – some are good, some are bad, some are clever, some are not.

We do not, however, suggest that such a child is immediately placed with a black family without proper preparation. To do so would be to set the placement up to fail. Nor do we suggest that the child should be placed immediately in a white family. To do so would be colluding with the child's identity confusion. A bridging plan has to be made and the child given help to come to terms with a black identity. The plan and intervention will depend on the individual children, their ages and their expectations. Special provision should be made, in some situations a 'specialist' bridging family may be the right placement while in others a residential placement in a unit with appropriately trained and experienced staff will be preferred. Such children should only remain in residential care where this is part of a positive plan.

4. 'A mother says she does not want her black baby to go to a black home.'

The social worker should, of course, try to find out why the mother is saying this. It could be that she has internalised the attitudes towards black people caused by racism or it could be something much simpler. Parents may have different views about the most important characteristics of a new family and therefore about what would be best for their child.

Sometimes their expectations of the placement and their wishes for the child may be unrealistic and social workers will need to explore this with them sympathetically. Ultimately, however, the duty of the agency is to find the home that best meets the needs of the baby.

5(a). 'We cannot find an Indian family for this Indian child – shall we place transracially with a white family?'

Ideally black children should go to families of the same race and culture. This is not always possible as at any given moment a particular family may be unavailable. There will, however, be other black families who may be suitable, perhaps an Asian family from another part of the continent with a different culture (but one more similar than the white culture), or perhaps a couple with partners of two races one of them Asian.

If, after exploring all possible avenues, you cannot find a family with at least one parent of a reasonably similar background to the child, you may have to place that child transracially. You would then be looking for a family with an understanding and appreciation of other cultures and the additional skills mentioned earlier (see ABSWAP guidelines). You should assess which of the families available most nearly meets the child's needs and has best access to the resources that will be needed to fill the gaps left because they do not share the child's culture and ethnicity. This may be a white family (assessed according to the ABSWAP or similar guidelines) or a black family of a different culture to the child. For each child, an individual decision must be made but you should bear in mind that all black families, whatever their ethnicity, share the common experience of racism. They are likely, therefore, to be better able than white families to combat the subtle messages of racism as well as coping with the more blatant examples and can provide the child with a positive role model as 'good' black parents.

(b). 'But if we place transracially in a black family the child will need to get used to the white majority culture, the culture of his/her substitute family and also get to know his/her own culture – surely this is confusing?'

There are black people living in a range of lifestyles who can be sensitive to the needs of black children. We are suggesting not that the child be placed in a black family where it would be difficult to get to know his/her culture, but that a suitable black family be found.

The ideal is to have a cultural/racial and religious match but, where this is impossible, the basic need is for the family to be capable of counteracting the stereotypes of black people presented through racism. A black family of any culture, provided they are assessed as suitable substitute parents, may therefore have more to offer a particular child than a white family.

In Conclusion

We aim for a society in which all cultures and races are respected and accepted for what they are. Britain today is not yet such a society. Good child care practice is embedded in the society in which it operates and until Britain becomes a truly multi-racial society there can be little place for transracial placements. It is essential for black children to be placed with families who can help them deal with the experience of being black in a racist society and can counteract the negative stereotypes of black people presented to children as a result of racism. Black families can provide this added dimension to the nurturing which all parents – black or white – need to provide. They therefore have the best chance of successfully caring for black children unable to live with their own families. In order to achieve the goal of finding sufficient numbers of black foster and adoptive parents, agencies will need to ensure that good training is available to all its staff and that adequate numbers of black staff and consultants are recruited. Agencies will also need to review their recruitment and preparation procedures to ensure that they are appropriate not just for white European families but for all the ethnic and cultural groups in the community.

APPENDIX 4

BRITISH ASSOCIATION OF SOCIAL WORKERS: 'PRACTICE GUIDE FOR SOCIAL WORKERS ON THE PLACEMENT OF BLACK CHILDREN IN CARE' (1988)

INTRODUCTION

Britain today is a multi-racial society with people from many different cultural and ethnic backgrounds. Social workers in different parts of the country will, of course, work with different minority ethnic groups but nationally the groups encountered will include: Afro-Caribbean, Asian (e.g., Indian, Pakistani, Indonesian), Chinese, African, Arab.

These practice notes are about working with and for children where at least one parent is from one of these groups. The term 'black' is used for all these groups because all of them have similar experiences of belonging to ethnic minority groups in this country and being easily recognisable as such. Although some individual members of the groups may not define themselves as black and their views should be recognised, they all experience racism, colonisation and neo-colonisation. Used in this way 'black' is more a political than a cultural term. (BAAF Practice Note No 13).

These guidelines are an acceptance of the existence of a black British identity and the need to make this cultural identity available to children in care.

PREAMBLE

1. Every child has a cultural identity – which should be fully acknowledged and thoroughly assessed when plans are made by departments for that child and his/her family.
2. The presence of racism both institutional and personal is acknowledged within British society.
3. Cultural identity is taken to embrace all aspects of the child's religious, racial and ethnic identities.
4. These rights apply to every child, regardless of their care status.

PREVENTION

1. In recognising that a black child's needs are best met by his/her own family and community, it is the duty of every local authority and voluntary agency to take positive action to prevent a black child being removed from his/her family and community and to provide all necessary resources for that action.

2. In order for a black child to develop a positive black identity and the skills to enable him or her to combat the effects of racism (s)he must grow up in an environment where it is thoroughly understood exactly what the child will have to face and where the child is enabled to develop that positive identity and the necessary skills.

3. In making thorough assessments of a child's needs, especially the need for substitute care on any basis, it is vital to recognise and plan for the child's cultural needs.

In Short-term Care

Duties upon placement

1. A child has a right to a culturally matched placement. The first priority for authorities and agencies is to attempt to secure such a placement, having taken into account the child's own wishes and feelings, appropriate to his/her age and understanding and to find an appropriate solution, bearing in mind the individual situation of each child.

Authorities and agencies should consult with a black child's family when considering a child's placement needs.

If it does not prove possible within appropriate time scales to place the child in such a placement, then the next least detrimental alternative needs to be taken. In planning and providing this alternative, proper account must be taken of the compensatory resources necessary in such a placement.

(a). The development of effective equal opportunities policies within authorities and agencies.

(b). The training, as a priority of existing field, residential and domiciliary staff and foster parents.

(c). Active recruitment of black staff and foster parents.

(d). Localised programmes to enable the child to keep in meaningful contact with his or her community and culture of origin.

(e). The recruitment and preparation and support of intermediary figures, such as social aunts and uncles.

(f). Access to religious observance as appropriate to the individual child's needs and wishes and those of their families.

(g). Provision within authorities and agencies of a facility to provide all staff and substitute carers with advice and guidance on cultural issues.

(h). The development of a proactive review system to pay particular attention to the needs of black children.

(i). Opportunities for black children for peer support.

(j). Formalised consultation processes with local black communities aimed at supporting the child and his/her substitute carers.

2. Every child in care has a right to a comprehensive plan for his/her stay in care.

3. This plan should involve him/her as appropriate to his/her age and

understanding, and should be aimed at a stable and long term placement, either with the family of origin, or with an alternative one.

4. Where it is consistent with his/her best interests, plans should aim at reuniting the child with his/her family at the earliest opportunity.

DUTIES IN CARE

In review processes, including statutory reviews, specific attention should be given to the objects stated in the preamble, and a record kept of how those needs are being addressed.

DUTIES IN PERMANENT CARE

1. No child should be placed in a permanent transcultural family placement. Permanence is taken here to mean adoption, long term foster care, or any other family based solution.

2. In acknowledging this, authorities and agencies must therefore make the acquisition and development of a full range of appropriate resources an equal priority:-
- recruitment, preparation and support of black families to offer varieties of permanent substitute care.
- the use of all recognised existing networks to actively seek black families, both in this country and where services are sufficiently developed, in the family's country of origin.
- the use of the ethnic minority media and other range of contacts, agencies and authorities can create and have access to.

DUTIES IN RESIDENTIAL CARE

1. As in short term care, authorities and agencies should actively recruit, train and support black staff for work in children's homes. Black staff provide essential role models and culturally sensitive care for black children and young people.

AFTER CARE

1. Some young black people will not have benefitted from a permanent black family experience. In providing post-residential and community alternatives, authorities and agencies must have regard to all the issues in the preamble in planning for the needs of black young people.

APPENDIX 5

NATIONAL FOSTER CARE ASSOCIATION POLICY STATEMENT: '1, CULTURAL AND RACIAL IDENTITY' (SEPTEMBER 1989)

NFCA believes that:

> The cultural, racial and religious identities of children and young people, their parents and foster carers must be respected in the development of the foster care service and in the making and support of individual placements. (*Article 2 of NFCA's Foster Care Charter*)

All children need love, care and security to enable them to develop into well-rounded balanced individuals. Most children will have these needs fulfilled by their own families, and will grow up secure in their own identity, and with a pride which is associated with a sense of self-worth as part of a loving family. It is vital that children and young people who are received into care also develop their own worth and pride as well as respect for their own families, and are given role models which reinforce the positive qualities of their own families and culture.

Britain is a multicultural society and children coming into care reflect this society. It is essential that fostering agencies ensure that those people who provide substitute care also mirror our multicultural society so that children can be placed with carers who share their racial, cultural and religious experience. Agencies must accept as a priority the need to recruit a wide multicultural force of foster carers to ensure that appropriate 'matching' can take place. This must be within the context of a commitment to anti-racist policy and practice.

Unless positive efforts are made by agencies to recruit carers from all racial and ethnic minority groups the myth that they cannot be found will be perpetuated. Carers from ethnic minority communities can be recruited. They do need, however, to be convinced that agencies want them. Half-hearted attempts to recruit will fail. NFCA will make positive efforts to support black and other ethnic minority carers and offer a service which meets their needs.

Although Britain is a multicultural society, the diversity of that society and the richness it brings is not yet valued by the majority of the population. Black* and other ethnic minority children are faced with both personal and

---

* We use the term 'black' in this document in a political sense to include all people who are oppressed by racism and discriminated against because of their skin colour, or their cultural or ethnic background.

institutional racism. This will gradually diminish their self-esteem unless they are able to experience their own culture in a positive way. Such children need to be placed with carers of the same race and culture who can provide positive role models not only for the children, but also for the parents, helping to achieve a return home with the least trauma for the child.

The majority of children who come into care will eventually return home. Research shows that even those who spend many years away from their families re-establish contact in late adolescence or adulthood. To enable them to move back into the family successfully requires skill and patience on the carer's part and must include a positive reinforcement of the child's and parents' worth.

NFCA believes that the placement of choice for all children and young people should be with carers who share the child's race, culture and religion. However, to deny recognition and support to those already in existing transracial placements is unhelpful and damaging. Many transracial place-ments have been made in the past. These children and their carers need the support of the black community, and especially black social workers, to ensure that the children have access to their own heritage, and are helped to develop their own identity which will give them pride in themselves and their own culture.

Many white carers, whilst recognising that the black children they care for need to know black people and be accepted within the black community, feel threatened by workers who state that black children need black homes. They are frightened that the children in their care will be turned against them, or will see the care that they have provided as second best. Denying a child's colour, being 'colour-blind', is not in the child's long-term interests. It is one way in which white carers have attempted to protect themselves and the children they care for from the reality of racism. But denial makes things worse for the child, who cannot share with their white carers the offensive and damaging racist behaviour they may experience.

Becoming familiar with black people, learning about black history and achievements, and knowing the music and language of their own culture will help the children to begin to build up an inner store of self-worth of their blackness. This will help them to combat the damage done by racism. The child or young person needs direct contact with black people who are positive about their own black identity and needs positive black role models to counteract the negative images so often presented by the media. Agencies must provide the necessary help and training for these carers and children.

The well-being of the child or young person must be the first consideration in a placement and the child or young person's racial, cultural and religious background are vital factors in selecting a carer.

New transracial placements should be made only if workers can clearly demonstrate that the efforts they have made to find carers who match the child's race, culture and religion have been unsuccessful. Clear planning when

they are received into care is essential for all children. The care plan for
children in transracial placements must include those tasks which need to be
undertaken to meet the child's identity needs. The plan should also identify
who is responsible for carrying out those tasks. Specific time limits must be
set which are relevant to the age of the child or young person.

Carers who agree to care for children of a different race, culture and religion
must also accept their responsibility to meet the child's racial, cultural and
religious needs and the fostering agency must state how it will help carers to
provide this. So far as is practicable such carers must be able to demonstrate
a commitment to anti-racism, and links with a community which is similar in
race, culture and religion to the child who is to be placed.

APPENDIX 6

HILARY CHAMBERS: 'CUTTING THROUGH THE DOGMA' (SURVEY OF BLACK CHILDREN AWAITING PLACEMENT IN THE PAGES OF 'BE MY PARENT', *SOCIAL WORK TODAY*) (5 OCTOBER 1989)

Many adoption panels currently find themselves wrestling with the same difficult dilemma. Many of the children they want to place are black. Most panels now recognise that same-race placement is an important objective. At the same time, those working in the field of adoption know too that long delays and uncertainty in the placement process can be harmful to any child.

The two objectives, speedy placement and same-race placement, often pull in different directions. How does a panel set about striking a balance?

This dilemma is of a kind familiar to professional social workers. They are well used to facing not just one problem but several problems at once where the actions which would solve problem A make it that much more difficult to solve problem B. What evidence would help a particular adoption panel to strike the balance least harmful to a particular child?

Whatever else this list covered it would have to include data on the lengths of time children were currently having to wait before placement, and reports on the actual childhood experiences of adults who had been adopted in the past.

Evidence of this kind is not available on any comprehensive basis. However, there now is some information on waiting times for a limited sample of children in the adoption system.

Many adoption agencies in the UK now make use of a photo-listing service 'Be My Parent' (BMP) which started in 1980. An agency uses the service when it has been unable to find prospective adopters for a particular child through its own direct methods of recruitment. The book contains loose-leaf photos and biographies of the children for whom families are being sought.

Some 450 copies are held up and down the country – and continually updated – in social services departments, with the 100 or so area co-ordinators of the organisation Parent to Parent Information on Adoption Services (PPIAS), other individuals who are members of larger black ethnic minority groups and in some public libraries. The BMP service focused initially on family-finding for handicapped and older children.

In the early 1980s there appeared to be a surplus of potential adopters for healthy pre-schoolers of whatever ethnic origin, and at that time the agencies saw no need to refer these children to BMP. The fact that most of the potential adopters then coming to the agencies were white was not seen as a major problem.

But by the mid-80s many adoption agencies had come to recognise how seriously they had underestimated the extent of racial prejudice and harassment in UK society and how important it was to equip black adopted children to cope with racism.

Most of the agencies were still poorly equipped, by training or experience, to find and recruit adopters from the black communities. Many embarked on serious programmes to change their ways, with recruitment of black social workers and panel members. The BMP service began to be used as one of the devices for widening their net for finding black adopters. As well as featuring older and handicapped children it began, for the first time, to include healthy, uncomplicated black children of pre-school age in its pages; with the proviso that only black adopters or racially mixed couples would be considered by the placing agency.

From March 1987 to July 1989 the number of these children for whom substitute families were sought through the pages of BMP rose three-fold. The corresponding population of healthy white pre-schoolers did not feature at all (except for a few members of larger sibling groups) since the agencies could still identify families for these children without the help of BMP, usually in a matter of weeks.

It is encouraging to see that 112 black healthy pre-schoolers found families in the period between March 1987 and July 1989, but it is far from good news to find that 24 of them had to wait more than a year (see Table 1). If we add to this number the children still waiting for placement for more than 12 months in BMP, the number rises to 39, 12 of whom were under two years old when they first appeared in the book.

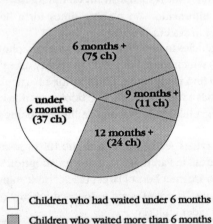

☐ Children who had waited under 6 months

▨ Children who waited more than 6 months

Table 1 Length of time spent in waiting for parents by 112 black, healthy children under 5, during the period from March 1987 to July 1989

Table 2 shows the waiting-times experienced by a sample of this group of children. It covers only the 'easy-to-place' children, that is pre-schoolers with no serious problems of ill-health or handicap. The table refers to the children in this category who were featured in BMP in the month of March 1988. That month was chosen as being sufficiently far back for most of the children then featured to have had families found for them by the time of writing, that is July 1989.

A very similar picture results if any of the neighbouring months is taken for the sample. March 1988's BMP featured 49 healthy black under-fives. Fifteen months later, by July 1989, 38 of these had been placed with prospective adopters. The remaining 11 were still waiting for placement.

The table shows the number of children in each age group (one-year-olds, two-year-olds, etc.) waiting for different lengths of time. Thus, in section B, one child who was less than one-year-old when first featured had still not found a family by July 1989. At that point her total waiting time had been in the range 19–24 months. Out of the total of 49 children, only 24 were placed within one year of being first featured in BMP. Six children who were under two when first featured waited for more than a year.

In some respects the children featured in BMP form a relatively privileged sample from the larger population of healthy black pre-schoolers in need of new permanent families. They appear in the book because their social workers have put exceptional time and effort into the search for parents, and have won their authorities' support for paying travel costs and inter-agency fees. If these children are waiting so long, what is happening to other children?

As adoption panels compile their own versions of Table 2, they will begin to develop their own pragmatic guidelines. Same-race placement is now firmly on the agenda, and few agencies would now quarrel with a policy that accepted the consequence that waiting times may have to be longer than they were in the past. But it is hard to accept the waiting times shown in the columns of Table 2. At the very least, good practice would seem to require the following for each child:

at the outset, a clear decision about the upper limit to the wait for same-race placement

a requirement that during this period, a systematic search for same-race placement should be undertaken *and monitored*

careful and explicit support for the limited number of transracial placements which will occasionally have to be made.

American experience can provide some pointers. As long ago as 1977 Joyce Ladner, a black American sociologist, published a study of 136 transracially adopted children: *Mixed Families* (Doubleday Anchor Books). Having started by being 'sceptical about whether the adoptions could work out well', after completing the study – and despite her doubts about the suitability of some of the families – she concluded that black children 'who are reared in the

A: Children featured at 3.88 and placed by 7.89

		Wait between first listing and placement, in months					
		0–6	7–12	13–18	19–24	25–30	
Child's	Under 1 yr.	3	1	1	–	–	
age	1-yr-olds	2	4	1	1	1	
when	2-yr-olds	–	4	1	1	1	
first	3-yr-olds	1	4	2	1	–	
featured	4-yr-olds	1	4	2	1	1	
		7	17	7	4	3	Total: 38

B: Children featured at 3.88 and not yet placed by 7.89

		Elapsed time since first listing, in months			
		13–18	19–24	25–30	
Child's	Under 1 yr.	–	1	–	
age	1-yr-olds	1	–	–	
when	2-yr-olds	–	3	2	
first	3-yr-olds	–	1	1	
featured	4-yr-olds	–	–	2	
		1	5	5	Total: 11

Table 2 Waiting times for the 49 healthy black pre-school children listed
in *Be My Parent* at March 1988

special setting of multi-cultural families do not acquire the ambivalence towards their own race' that has been reported among all other groups of young black children.

She further concluded that 'there are many whites who are capable of rearing emotionally healthy black children'. That was said 12 years ago. Since then, a number of the state and civic authorities in the US have removed their blanket bans on transracial adoption.

EVIDENCE

Some of the evidence which adoption panels will find most useful, as they formulate new guidelines, comes from the experiences reported by black adults who were themselves reared by white adoptive parents. Case by case there is a wealth of evidence both of happy and unhappy experience to better inform good practice. Two quotations demonstrate some lines that this kind of evidence can open up.

Michael Tubbs, a young black journalist adopted at age thirteen by white parents, writes about 'the predicament of real children now caught in the crossfire from the firmly entrenched camps'. His conclusions is that 'however caring an institution may be, and however efficient its system of pastoral support, it can never substitute adequately for the love of a parent . . . a child's race, religion and cultural heritage are an important part of its identity and need to be considered along with age, medical history and any other individual characteristics. In an ideal world these could all be noted and used to find the perfect parents without delay but, of course, the reality is very different. Transracial placements are a desirable alternative provided the potential families are identified carefully, properly prepared and well supported' (*Social Services Insight*, 19 July 1986).

Rebecca Buckfield is a student, and one of a family of ten. She writes: 'I share in that almost legendary instant rapport with other blacks, yet having been brought up by whites it is perfectly ordinary and easy for me to have great friends that are white. I cross the race boundaries uninhibitedly. It frightens me to think that if I were a child requiring a placement at the present time, expressed or implied current adoption agency attitudes would mean that I would not have been placed for adoption with my present parents' (PPIAS Newsletter, no. 51, Summer 1989).

When you meet competent young adults like these, the dogma that they must be less sure of their identities than the rest of us and that they must be unusually ill-equipped to combat racism, seems patently absurd. Before the dogma gets set in concrete, there is some professional obligation to understand these counter-examples.

Can good practice find ways of fighting on two fronts at once: combating racism, and defending the essential need of a child to have a family?

The author is a member of PPIAS.

APPENDIX 7

COMMISSION FOR RACIAL EQUALITY: EXTRACT FROM 'ADOPTING A BETTER POLICY: ADOPTING AND FOSTERING OF ETHNIC MINORITY CHILDREN – THE RACE DIMENSION' (1990)

RECOMMENDATIONS

1. The findings of the Commission's 1988 survey into the practices and policies of social services departments confirmed that departments have not been taking appropriate steps actively to recruit ethnic minority adoptive parents and foster carers. The Commission recommends that this should now be given high priority, so that the ethnic minority children in their care can be placed in an environment most suited to their needs.

2. Mainstream funding and resources should be allocated by central and local government to develop and maintain recruitment and support programmes for ethnic minority adoptive and foster carers.

3. Social services departments must recognise the importance of committing themselves to race equality policies that take account of children in care, and which are fully implemented and regularly reviewed.

4. To measure the effectiveness of their equal opportunity policies, departments should record and monitor the ethnic origins of all children in their care, as well as those of existing and prospective adoptive and foster carers.

5. Social services departments and adoption agencies should be aware that their decisions to take children into care may be influenced by cultural misunderstandings. They must therefore ensure that staff receive appropriate training, and that staff involved with the welfare of children, at all levels, reflect the ethnic composition of the community they serve.

6. When a family is considered for a possible transracial placement the department or agency should be fully satisfied that the family has the necessary skills to meet and to further the child's best interests. Families who foster or adopt a child of a different racial group must be fully supported by the department or agency and given appropriate training and counselling.

7. It is essential that the cultural and linguistic needs of ethnic minority children in care are fully met. This will include employing ethnic minority staff who are part of the decision-making process as well as having day to day involvement in the lives of resident children.

8. Ethnic minority communities should be involved in all consultation processes, both for the sake of the children in care as well as for the organisation itself.

APPENDIX 8

THE DEPARTMENT OF HEALTH: DOCUMENT C1(90)2 'ISSUES OF RACE AND CULTURE IN THE FAMILY PLACEMENT OF CHILDREN' – LETTER TO DIRECTORS OF SOCIAL SERVICES FROM CHIEF INSPECTOR, SOCIAL SERVICES INSPECTORATE (29 JANUARY 1990)

INTRODUCTION

1. This letter sets out the principles which should inform the practice of social services departments in the family placement of children. It enlarges on passages of special relevance in the Handbook of Guidance on the Boarding-Out of Children and points out where a similar approach is called for in adoption work and decisions. The letter must be read, however, in the context of all the guidance contained in the Handbook, since it applies to all children who are fostered, whatever their ethnic origin.

2. Directors are asked to make the content of this letter known to all managers and practitioners who are providing services for children and families; and to ensure that all such managers and practitioners are familiar with the Handbook of Guidance on the Boarding-Out of children.

3. Copies of this letter go to Heads of approved adoption societies and voluntary child care agencies to assist them in the adoption and family placement work of their agencies.

PROVIDING CHILD CARE SERVICES IN A MULTI-RACIAL SOCIETY

4. Social Services must address and seek to meet the needs of children and families from all groups in the community. Society is made up of people of many different ethnic and racial origins and of different religious affiliations. The provision of services which will reach all members of the community calls for the development within social services departments of awareness, sensitivity and understanding of the different cultures of groups in the local community; and an understanding of the effects of racial discrimination on these groups. Necessary experience and expertise should be provided for in staffing of services and through relationships with other professions and services and with the community. In some areas the local community may include too great a variety of ethnic groups to be reflected fully in the composition of staff. In others, departments may be called on only rarely to provide a service for a child or family from a minority ethnic group. In both these circumstances, departments will need to identify sources of advice and help so that the necessary experience, expertise and resources are available when needed. These principles apply to services to help children to remain

within their own families as well as to services for children in care and their families, so that children are not admitted to care through lack of appropriate and effective social work support for the family. This is especially important in the light of indicators that children from certain minority ethnic groups are over-represented among children in care.

5. Where placements are needed or likely to be needed for children from minority ethnic groups or for children of particular religious affiliation, sustained efforts may be needed to recruit a sufficient number and range of foster parents and prospective adopters from those groups and of that religion. Such efforts are essential if all children who need substitute families are to have the opportunity of placement with families which share their ethnic origin and religion. The development and planning of fostering and adoption services should aim to ensure that the resources of the service, including the arrangements for the recruitment, assessment, approval, preparation and support of a pool of foster parents, are responsive to the demands on the service. This calls for forward planning to identify the range and estimated numbers of foster homes which are likely to be required. Publicity and recruitment campaigns, resource networks and exchange arrangements must aim to reach all groups in the community and to increase awareness and understanding generally of the needs of children. Appropriate assessment and training must be available for all foster parents.

6. In assessing a child's needs social workers should strive for a real understanding of the child's cultural background and religion and guard against simplistic assumptions of similarity between different ethnic groups. Clients have a right to expect the understanding, knowledge and sensitivity which are essential if their interests are to be served. Assessment must identify, and advertisements explain, a child's ethnic origins, religion and family experience in such a way as to provide as helpful a guide as possible to the child's needs. Care is needed so that the terms 'black' and 'black family' are not used in isolation in such a way as to obscure characteristics and needs which are of particular importance to groups and to individuals. An insufficiently precise message may not reach people of the particular group at which it is aimed; and other prospective carers who could have much to offer a child of a different ethnic origin or of mixed ethnic origin, by virtue of particular knowledge, language, understanding and family or neighbourhood links, may be discouraged from coming forward or be rejected out of hand. A white family which has adopted or is fostering a child of minority ethnic origin or mixed ethnic origin should not be told that placement of another such child cannot be considered solely on the grounds of general policy. Each case must be considered on its merits, having regard to the needs of children requiring placement. A family with some members of minority ethnic origin may be well placed to meet the needs of a child or another child of similar ethnic origin.

The Legal Framework

7. Directors should ensure that practitioners and their managers observe the framework of statutory requirements, regulations and Department of Health guidance within which their departments operate: In particular, the requirement in child care and adoption legislation to promote and safeguard the welfare of each child through childhood, taking into account the child's wishes and feelings, having regard to his age and understanding. The Boarding-Out of Children (Foster Placement) Regulations 1988 require agencies to be satisfied that a child's needs arising from his racial origin and cultural background are met in a foster placement, so far as practicable; and to ensure that a child is placed with a foster parent who is of the same religion, or if that is not practicable, with a foster parent who undertakes that the child will be brought up in that religion. While there are currently no corresponding specific statutory requirements in relation to adoption, it is of equal or greater importance that the same considerations should be applied. When the Children Act 1989 comes into force, agencies will be required, in all decisions in respect of a child they are looking after, to have regard to the child's religious persuasion, cultural and linguistic background and racial origin; and to the wishes and feelings of parents and other adults who have played a significant part in the child's life as well as to the wishes and feelings of the child. Local authorities will be required, in making arrangements for day care and fostering services, to have regard to the racial groups to which children needing the services belong. These requirements will formalise in relation to child care an approach which should already be an indispensable element in both child care and adoption practice.

8. All factors relevant to the welfare of the individual child must be taken into account in assessing the child's needs and making decisions about the child's welfare. None of the separate factors involved should be abstracted and converted into a general pre-condition which overrides the others or causes any of them to be less than fully considered. The only general policy that is acceptable in making decisions about placing children in adoptive or foster homes is that all relevant factors should be considered. Different factors will obviously vary in importance in relation to different children or in relation to the same child at different times. It will be right in those circumstances to weigh different factors differently. But it is not right to define any factor as of such general significance or primacy that it overrides or qualifies the duty to consider all factors bearing on the welfare of the child as an individual. Such a rule applied in respect of a decision affecting an individual child could expose the authority (or adoption agency) to judicial challenge.

Placement Decisions

9. Within this framework, a child's ethnic origin, cultural background and religion are important factors; it may be taken as a guiding principle of good

practice that, other things being equal and in the great majority of cases, placement with a family of similar ethnic origin and religion is most likely to meet a child's needs as fully as possible and to safeguard his or her welfare most effectively. Such a family is most likely to be able to provide a child with continuity in life and care and an environment which the child will find familiar and sympathetic and in which opportunities will naturally arise to share fully in the culture and way of life of the ethnic group to which he or she belongs. Where the aim of a foster placement is to re-unite the child with his or her own family, contact and work with the family will in most cases be more comfortable for all and carry a greater chance of success if the foster parents are of similar ethnic origin. Families of similar ethnic origin are also usually best placed to prepare children for life as members of an ethnic minority group in a multi-racial society, where they may meet with racial prejudice and discrimination, and to help then with their development towards independent living and adult life.

10.   Guiding principles are valuable only insofar as they are applied with proper consideration for the circumstances of the individual case. There may be circumstances in which placement with a family of different ethnic origin is the best choice for a particular child. In other cases such a placement may be the best available choice. For example, a child may have formed strong links with prospective foster parents or adopters or be related to them. Siblings or step siblings who are not all of the same ethnic origin may need placement together. A child may prefer and need to remain close to school, friends and family even though foster parents of the same ethnic origin cannot be found in the locality. A child with special needs may require carers with particular qualities or abilities, so that choice is limited. The importance of religion as an element of culture should never be overlooked: to some children and families it may be the dominant factor, so that the religion of foster parents or adopters may in some cases be more important than their ethnic origin.

11.   All children should be encouraged and helped to understand, enjoy and take a pride in their ethnic origins and cultural heritage. This principle applies to all children for whom services are provided and to all children in care in any placement. Special care is needed where placement with a family of different ethnic origin is being considered, for whatever reason, including of course white children placed with families of minority ethnic origin. What is the extent of the family's understanding and experience of the child's culture? Do they live near or among people of similar origin and background to the child? Are there relatives or friends and neighbours of the child's ethnic origin who can help and advise the foster parents or adopters and take on the responsibility of a significant role in the child's life? Will the child have the opportunity of going to school and enjoying friendships with children and young people who share his or her culture? Practitioners must satisfy themselves that all a child's needs will be addressed, in such a way that the child

will not feel cut off from his or her origins or culture and his or her choices in later life will be preserved.

12. For a child whose parents are of different ethnic group, placement in a family which reflects as nearly as possible the child's ethnic origins is likely to be the best choice in most cases. But choice will be influenced by the child's previous family experience and, as with all placement decisions, by the child's wishes and feelings. In discussing and exploring these with a child, practitioners should be ready to help the child with any confusion or misunderstandings about people of different ethnic groups which may have arisen through previous family or placement experience. Children of mixed ethnic origin should be helped to understand and take a pride in both or all elements in their cultural heritage and to feel comfortable about their origins. Foster parents and adopters must be able to provide this, with the help and support of others where necessary. This applies equally whether a child is placed with a minority ethnic family or with a white family or a family including members of differing ethnic origins.

13. The choice of the most suitable placement for any child presents a difficult task in assessing and reconciling a child's needs. Requirements in respect of a child's welfare must be met within practical limitations of choice which mean that the ideal placement may not be available. Optimum choices for each child are more likely to be available within a fostering service run on the lines set out in the Handbook of Guidance and summarised in respect of fostering and adoption services in this letter.

THE IMPORTANCE OF PLANNING, MONITORING AND REVIEWS

14. Planning is of vital importance. Planned admission to care will allow more opportunity for the child's needs to be carefully assessed and a plan developed before placement. Hasty, emergency placements should be avoided as far as possible. Clear agreements with foster parents on the aim of a placement can serve to avoid the frustration arising from mistaken, confused or disappointed expectations, but only if the agreement is honoured by the agency. Careful reviews of each child, following the requirements of the Boarding-Out of Children (Foster Placement) Regulations, should consider whether the placement continues to be appropriate and whether the child's needs, including needs arising from racial origin, cultural background and religious persuasion are being met in the placement. Otherwise, steps must be taken to remedy any deficiencies identified in the review and to make any necessary changes. Children should not be removed from placements which are otherwise satisfactory solely because the ethnic origin of the foster parents does not accord with the requirements of general policies. Such a decision should be made only after assessment of the needs of the child and review of the placement in each case. Monitoring, planning and decision making should not, of course, be restricted to statutory reviews. Short term and interim

placements, in particular, must be kept under continuous and careful scrutiny to ensure that they are being properly used. A child must not be left indefinitely in an interim placement, or, even worse, a succession of interim placements, while a permanent placement is sought. The plan for the child must include limits of time, which will vary with individual children and their circumstances, with which progress towards objectives is reviewed and the plan revised where necessary.

W. B. Utting
Chief Inspector
Social Services Inspectorate

APPENDIX 9

BRITISH AGENCIES FOR ADOPTION AND FOSTERING: PRACTICE NOTE 26 (CHILDREN ACT 1989), CHILDREN AND THEIR HERITAGE: THE IMPORTANCE OF CULTURE, RACE, RELIGION AND LANGUAGE IN FAMILY PLACEMENT 1991

BACKGROUND

During the 1980s, understanding grew of the importance to children of their culture, race, religion and language,* particularly for children separated from their parents, whether short-term or throughout their childhood. The decade ended with two major and welcome developments: the Chief Inspector of the Social Services Inspectorate issued a letter in January 1990 (C.I(90)2) to all directors of social services highlighting issues of race and culture in the family placement of children, and the first recognition of the issue in primary legislation appeared in the Children Act 1989. This requires that:

> Before making any decision with respect to a child whom they are looking after, or proposing to look after . . . a local authority shall give due consideration . . . to the child's religious persuasion, racial origin and cultural and linguistic background. (Children Act 1989, Section 22)

The aim of this practice note is to highlight areas where special efforts may be needed to ensure that this requirement is observed and to offer suggestions for good practice in placing children in foster or adoptive families, giving due regard to their heritage. Many of the areas covered are, of course, equally relevant where residential placement is being considered.

As the decade progressed, a number of child care agencies began to address the issues around the importance to children of their heritage. In BAAF, a Black** Perspectives Advisory Committee was established and, with its help, the Black Issues Project was set up. Through their activities and through collaboration with other relevant organisations such as the Commission for Racial Equality and the Race Equality Unit, BAAF worked steadily during the 1980s to improve understanding the needs of children and to encourage better

---

* For brevity, described as 'heritage' hereafter, except where an individual element of the four needs to be highlighted.

** 'Black' is used in this context to refer to groups who, as a result of their ethnicity, are visibly different and who are exposed to racism as a result. It thus includes a considerable range of 'heritages' and its use is not intended to obscure the need to take individual heritage into account for each child and family.

placement practice through publications, seminars, workshops and direct work with children and families.

CHILD CARE SERVICES IN A MULTI-RACIAL SOCIETY

It is no accident that BAAF's focus, like that of others interested in child care services in a multi-racial society, has concentrated on the needs of black children and those from other minority ethnic groups. Heritage is important to all children, whatever their race, religion, culture or language may be, and good practice should acknowledge this. However, it is significantly harder to provide adequately for minority groups, particularly in a country where racism is a continuing and substantial problem. Statistics alone will ensure that, for example, there will be more people available as foster families from the majority ethnic group than from any one of the minority groups (more, too, in almost all cases than the total available from all the minority groups combined). When other factors which may affect recruitment are combined with this statistical fact (such as housing problems, employment prospects, and the overt effects of racism), it inevitably requires greater effort to recruit adequate numbers of families who can meet the needs of children from minority ethnic groups for continuity of care.

> A child's need for continuity in life and care should be a constant factor in choice of placement. In most cases this suggests a need for placement with a family of the same race, religion and culture in a neighbourhood within reach of family, school or day nursery, church, friends and leisure activities. (The Children Act Guidance and Regulations, vol. 3, *Family Placements*, para. 4.4, HMSO, 1991)

Efforts have, therefore, generally concentrated on achieving better practice for children from black communities and other minority ethnic groups and this paper also reflect that emphasis. This is not to deny the importance of heritage to all children, as already stated – in BAAF's view it should be taken into account in assessing *each* individual child's needs and making appropriate plans. However, the principles involved will be the same whatever the child's heritage and any agency which demonstrates good practice in relation to their children from minority groups can be reasonably certain that they are offering a good quality of service to all the children in their area who may need to be looked after away from their families.

It is important, too, that agencies examine their practice to ensure that they are not, unintentionally, deterring certain sections of the community from offering their services as foster carers or adopters, or setting up systems which make it more difficult for some groups to be accepted as carers than others.

> Social services must address and seek to meet the needs of children and families from all groups in the community. Society is made up of people of many different ethnic and racial origins and of different religious affiliations.

The provision of services which will reach all members of the community calls for the development within social services departments of awareness, sensitivity and understanding of the different cultures of groups in the local community; and an understanding of the effects of racial discrimination on these groups.

These principles apply to services to help children remain within their own families as well as to services for children in care and their families, so that children are not admitted to care through lack of appropriate and effective social work support for the family. This is especially important in the light of indicators that children from certain minority ethnic groups are over-represented among children in care. (Letter from Chief Inspector of Social Services Inspectorate to directors of social services CI(90)2, January 1990)

To ensure that an agency has an appropriate mix of substitute carers available, special efforts are likely to be needed. Many agencies already have experience of campaigns to recruit families from different communities within their area and we need to build on those successes (see *Recruiting Black Families*, BAAF Practice Note 18, 1990).

BASIC PRINCIPLES

BAAF's view is developing continually as we learn from our own experience and that of our members. However, the fundamentals remain unchanged. In all BAAF's activities, we operate from two over-riding guiding principles: first, that every child needs a family in which to grow and thrive – ideally their original family but where this is not possible a substitute one; and second, that each child is an individual with both the moral and legal right to have a plan made for his or her future which takes into account that individual's specific needs and circumstances.

We believe that culture, race, language and religion are important aspects in making plans for children and we welcome the encouragement to good practice in this area given by the relevant sections in the Children Act and the associated Guidance and Regulations. While it is undoubtedly true that love knows no racial boundaries – capable adoptive and foster parents, irrespective of their ethnicity, provide loving and caring environments for children in their care, and there are many examples of transracial placement where the child has received excellent care – our concern is for the wider needs of black children and those from other minority ethnic groups, which often only become significant as they grow older and start to separate from their families.

Families who share a child's heritage can offer an added dimension, over and above a loving environment, covering such things as continuity of experience, contact with a relevant community, understanding of and pride in the child's particular inheritance and, for children from minority ethnic groups, skills and support in dealing with racism.

For children who are looked after by a statutory or voluntary agency temporarily, the value to them and their families of a familiar environment should not be under-estimated both in coping with the trauma of separation and in aiding the process of reuniting the family. Somewhat different considerations may apply where a child is already living or is to be placed with familiar adults, such as extended family members. Some or all of the child's needs for continuity will be met; the agency's task will be to identify any gaps in relation to the child's heritage and work with the carers to fill them. However, where children have to be placed with strangers, the agency will seek to ensure – in discussion with the parents – that all the child's needs can be met in the placement. Whatever the child's heritage, a family which shares it will be best placed to meet those needs arising from the child's race, religion, language and culture. For black children and those from other minority groups where the impact of racism is a factor, the carers will have the added task of helping the child overcome the negative effects of racism and develop a positive sense of themselves and their heritage. In order to meet this particular need for those children whose heritage places them in a minority ethnic group, the best placement option will be with a family who, in addition to meeting the child's other identified needs, shares the child's heritage.

PLANNING

Good planning is the foundation of good practice – few people would quarrel with this statement, but making good planning a reality is not always easy. The Children Act gives added impetus to planning, both of resources:

> Every local authority shall, in making any arrangements
> (a) for the provision of day care . . . or
> (b) . . . to encourage persons to act as local authority foster parents, have regard to the different racial groups to which children within their area who are in need belong. (Children Act 1989, Schedule 2, 11)

and in making individual arrangements, for example, through the Placement of Children with Parents etc Regulations 1991.

The Guidance includes many helpful pointers (e.g., at paras 2.40 and 2.57 in vol. 3). In particular, it declares that:

> The plan should . . . contain . . . [as one of the] key elements: the child's identified needs . . . arising from race, culture, religion and language, special educational or health needs. (vol. 3, para. 2.62)

Planning to meet the needs of children arising from their heritage requires more than a knowledge of the composition of the local community although this is, of course, essential. Information will be needed on the way the groups within the community function – for example, who are seen as leaders and may therefore be useful in gauging need and identifying resources within the group. Many agencies already make good use of their 'own' resources – their staff and foster carers, for example – but more could be done, particularly in seeing the minority communities as a source of strength and resources rather than as mainly one of needs and problems. Agencies also have to be realistic – some local authorities contain such a diverse range of ethnic group that they are unlikely to be able to meet every need that may arise from within their own resources. Ensuring that each agency has a foster home waiting to cover every possible eventuality at all times may not be feasible. Even where it possible to recruit the number and range of families needed to achieve this, it would mean some foster carers caring rarely if ever for a child – a poor use of resources and a very difficult prospect for the foster carers. Agencies can, however, collaborate to ensure that a sufficient pool is available. As the Children Act Guidance suggests:

> Local authorities will need to identify sources of advice and help so that the necessary experience, expertise and resources are available when needed. (vol. 3, para. 2.57)

An essential component of good planning is well-planned training. Everyone involved in child placement services should have an opportunity to learn about different heritages, to appreciate the importance of those heritages to children and the role they have to play in developing and maintaining good practice in this as in other aspects of child placement. Many people have absorbed the ethos of the 'colour-blind' approach which was so prevalent in the 1970s and into the '80s. This was a valiant, if over-simplified, attempt to deal with the evils of racism, which equated the concept 'we are all equal' with 'we are all the same'. People can best be helped to develop their thinking and to recognise and celebrate the importance, validity and persistence of different heritages, if the good intentions of the 'colour-blind' approach are acknowledged along with its real flaws. Provisions in the Act, such as s18(3) (which gives local authorities the power to provide families such as training and guidance to people working in daycare settings including childminding), can and should be used to develop a policy on training and support with the aim of enduring that those providing services to children who are being or may be looked after by the local authority are properly prepared for the task.

PREVENTION

It is now widely acknowledged (see *Patterns and Outcomes in Child Placement*, HMSO, 1991) that disproportionate numbers of children from the black and minority ethnic communities are looked after by local authorities. The Children Act, with its heavy emphases on prevention, partnership, planning and parental responsibility, provides an opportunity to look afresh at the practice implications of these findings. Partnership should be extended to include partnership between different local community groups and the local authority, so that together they can explore the extent to which the 'traditional' preventive services fail to meet the needs of particular groups. It can be hard, when a particular service has been developed at great cost (of energy as well as money) and with great staff commitment, to hear the message that it will not meet the needs of a sizeable minority of the local community. Not to do so, however, is to fail in the general duty (Children Act s17) to safeguard and promote the welfare of children in need. Assessment of need should:

> take account of the particular needs of the child . . . in relation to . . . religious persuasion, racial origin, cultural and linguistic background, [and] the degree (if any) to which these needs are being met by existing services. (Children Act 1989 Guidance and Regulations, vol. 2 *Family Support, Day Care and Educational Provision for Young Children*, para. 2.8, HMSO, 1991)

Agencies can be helped in this difficult task by forming positive relationships with their local communities and establishing a climate of mutual trust, so that problems can be raised and discussed with confidence on both sides. The Children Act envisages services for children in need being provided *on behalf of* and not just *by* local authorities and sees promotion of the upbringing of children in need by their own families as a central task. In achieving this, it may often be better to enable and empower minority groups to provide appropriate services themselves, than to seek to provide them from within local authority resources. As the Guidance recognises:

> Necessary experience and expertise should be provided for in staffing of services [but] In some areas, the local community may include too great a variety of ethnic groups to be reflected fully in composition of staff. (vol. 2, para. 2.9)

In such circumstances, while neighbouring authorities and other agencies may be able to offer some help, the best source of knowledge and resources is likely to be within the minority community itself.

PARTNERSHIP

One of the key principles of the Children Act is that caring agencies should work in partnership with parents. This will be a significant factor whether the issue is enabling children to continue living with their parents or providing the best possible placement for children who have to live away from their families. In planning for placement, the child's needs in relation to their heritage will be one of the topics to be discussed with parents. Many will be well aware of the importance of heritage and may be able to open up new avenues to explore in providing for this aspect of their child's needs. Such families will also be in a good position to help the agency reach decisions about how to proceed where it is not possible to make a placement with a family which shares fully the child's heritage. They will have ideas about which facets of the child's heritage should be given priority and have a role to play in filling any gaps as a result of the placement. Other families may need help in understanding why heritage is considered so important that it is recognised in law. Social workers should be ready to discuss with them the different ways in which heritage is significant to children who are living apart from their families and how different aspects may be highlighted at different times for the child.

Partnership is also about continuing to work together after placement. Clearly families – not just parents – have a major role to play in maintaining continuity and meeting the child's needs related to heritage through their contacts with the child. It is important that agencies avoid using restrictive definitions of family and instead recognise the range of kinship networks that may apply. In addition, parental involvement in planning and review (and thus considering whether the placement is meeting and will continue to meet the child's needs) will help the agency to monitor the impact of the placement on the child's heritage. It should be possible in most cases to work with parents to identify any problems early and take steps to improve the position where necessary.

SHORT-TERM PLACEMENT

Achieving a high standard of practice in short-term placement is very much dependent on good planning (including good training, information and monitoring services). Many short-term placements are provided at relatively little notice and it will be too late, at that stage, to start efforts to recruit appropriate foster carers. Much of the concern which has arisen in recent years about the placement of black and minority ethnic group children in longer-term or permanent families has been exacerbated by the initial or interim 'in care' placement being transracial and/or transcultural.

BAAF does not advocate the removal of children from well-established and otherwise satisfactory long-term placements solely in order to achieve a same-race placement. Indeed, members not infrequently seek our help with transracial placements where difficulties have arisen as the child approaches adolescence and becomes more aware of issues such as racism. The first priority, in such otherwise suitable placements, is to work with the agency on ways of 'filling the gaps' – perhaps by creating appropriate community involvement – in order to sustain and enhance the existing placement.

However, too many short-term placements still seem to be made on the basis that 'this is all that is available right now, we can sort it out later'. Unfortunately, not only do such placements often last much longer than originally planned but they can seriously exacerbate problems for the child and the birth family. Since the aim is to work in partnership with the parents and provide the child with accommodation as part of a supportive system to enable the family to function adequately, it is more likely to succeed if the foster carers and the birth family share a common heritage, including common expectations of parent-child relationships and behaviour. For the child too, the inevitable trauma of going to live with strangers – however careful the preparation has been – will be greater if he or she also has to get used to a completely different pattern of family life, with perhaps a mismatch of linguistic backgrounds involving different names for common objects. Equally, a lack of shared religion can bring different expectations about religious observance which cause a child confusion and distress, even where the carer is trying to meet the child's religious needs. Children who are returning home will also have to face this 'culture shock' in reverse, as they move out of the now familiar foster carers' 'culture' and back into their own.

There will always be some children for whom it is impossible to achieve a complete 'match' of heritage where speedy short-term placement is needed, even when good inter-agency co-operation is the norm. In these cases, an individual assessment of the losses and gains to a child of mismatch or match in the various aspects of heritage will need to be made. Much will depend on the level and type of continuing involvement with the child's original family and community. For example, the impact of their religion on a child's daily life may be of such fundamental importance that some other aspects of heritage will be given lower priority in order to preserve this. In other circumstances, where the child's belief system is such that religious observance can be maintained through school and friends and relations, it may be that shared religion could take a lower priority than, for example, shared ethnicity.

For black children and those from other minority ethnic groups, the impact of racism – both in its obvious manifestations and on the development of a positive sense of identity – must be borne in mind. Where it is not possible to find a suitable family which shares totally the child's heritage, a black or minority ethnic group family which shares part of the child's heritage and can meet their other identified needs will usually be best placed also to meet those needs which arise from racism.

LONG-TERM PLACEMENT

The circumstances – and therefore the needs – of children in long-term placement tend to be rather different from those of children in short-term placements. Aspects such as continuity do not lose their importance, but attention also has to be given to maintaining the child's welfare throughout their childhood and to preparing them for adult life. In addition, a significant proportion of children lose contact with their families as time passes and they remain separated from them. Both legislation and good practice require that efforts are made to maintain family links but this is unlikely to be universally achievable. Lack of contact with the family puts additional responsibilities on carers to enable children to remain in touch with their heritage, to have a pride and knowledge of it and to equip them to participate fully as adults in their original community should they wish to do so.

These tasks are most easily accomplished by substitute families who fully share the child's heritage. However, it should not be assumed that they therefore do not need training and support to undertake the tasks. There can be particular problems for families who take on the care of a child who has had an interim placement in a setting where his or her heritage was not shared (particularly if it was also not valued). If the child is confused or has lost touch with aspects of their heritage, the carers are likely to need support in the delicate task of sorting out the confusions and losses.

Because long-term placements are not usually made in an emergency, it should be possible to find carers who share the child's heritage in the vast majority of cases. While it is important not to lose sight of the child's timescales, it is also important to weigh up for each child the relative merits of quick but not entirely satisfactory placement against waiting to achieve a more satisfactory link. Drift is never acceptable but planned delay while purposeful action is taken to locate a suitable family can often be the right decision. No-one would advocate a system where a child needing placement is simply linked with the nearest available family; time given to finding an appropriate level of consonance between family and child is time well spent. Equally no-one would advocate waiting for ever for that elusive 'perfect' family to come along. Proper planning, purposeful activity and regular review are all necessary components of good practice in this area.

For the minority of children where it is not possible to find families who exactly share their heritage within a timescale appropriate to them, an individual assessment will need to be made to determine the 'next best' option. Training for all foster carers and prospective adopters should include exploring their own heritage and its importance to them, as a springboard for developing an understanding of the importance to children of their heritage. They will also need to learn about the impact of racism and strategies to counter it. Assessment should, of course, include consideration of the applicant(s)' ability to meet a child's needs arising from their cultural, religious and linguistic background and racial origins (see Association of Black Social Workers and Allied Professionals, *Evidence to the House of Commons: Black Children in Care*, 1983). Only carers who demonstrate considerable ability in these areas should be considered where a child is to be placed in a family which does not share their heritage. The agency will also need to plan, from the start of such a placement, ways of filling (or helping the carers to fill) the gaps – in knowledge, experience, contacts and so on – which are likely to become increasingly evident as the child grows older and begins to move out from the immediate family circle. Continuing contact with relatives and family friends must be built on wherever possible; if such links prove tenuous, consideration can be given to using the 'independent visitor' provisions of the Children Act. As the Guidance suggests:

> Where it has not proved possible to make a placement which entirely reflects the child's race and culture, the independent visitor could be a link with the child's racial and cultural background. (vol. 3, para. 7.15)

MAKING THE EFFORT

Finally – is it really necessary to go to such lengths in relation to a child's heritage? Is it really true that young people leaving care

> from ethnic minorities may need help – preferably from someone with the same background – to enable them to take a pride in their racial, cultural, linguistic and religious background (vol. 3, para. 9.53)?

Much of the research on those who have been transracially and/or transculturally placed is American and has centred on children within their families rather than on their views as adults. There is relatively little British research and almost nothing reflecting the attitudes and experiences of, for example, young black and minority ethnic group adults who have grown up in white families. There is an urgent need for such research to be undertaken. However, we do have a growing amount of feedback from young adults who were transracially placed, mainly as a result of the development in post-adoption services in recent years (see *A Glimpse through the Looking Glass – A Summary of Personal Experiences and Reflections of a Group of Transracially Adopted Adults*, Post-Adoption Centre, 1990). The message they seem to be giving is complex. As one would expect, there are extreme points of view – from those who feel completely satisfied to those who belive their experience to have been a total disaster. From the majority, though, we hear of a great deal of mutual love and respect between adoptive parents and their children which persists into adulthood. From those same adopted adults we also hear of their real sense of discomfort and dissonance, of 'something missing', sometimes expressed as a feeling that as adults they belong in neither the white nor the black community. There is also often a feeling of loss of part of themselves, of lacking knowledge, experience and understanding which would normally be acquired as an unnoticed part of growing up but can be an extremely difficult gap to fill in adulthood. We have a responsibility to listen to what these young people are telling us and to take the appropriate steps to improve our practice and make placements which give children the best possible chance of making a successful transition into adulthood.

APPENDIX 10

EXTRACT FROM *ADOPTION: THE FUTURE* – GOVERNMENT WHITE PAPER ON ADOPTION, CM 2288 (NOVEMBER 1993)

4.31. The 1976 Act contains no reference to questions of ethnicity or culture though in recent years authorities and agencies have usually taken them into account. The Government believes it right to consider these factors alongside others in matching children and parents and will introduce a broad requirement to this effect in line with what is now in the Children Act.

4.32. However, in some cases it is clear that those assessing parents may have given these factors an unjustifiably decisive influence and failed to make a balanced overall judgement of the parents' suitability. The Chief Social Services Inspector has emphasised that ethnicity and culture are amongst the issues to be considered but they should not necessarily be more influential than any other.

4.33. There is no conclusive research which justifies isolating such questions from other matters needing assessment; or which supports the proposition that children adopted by people of a different ethnic group will necessarily encounter problems of identity or prejudice later in life.

4.34. On these, as in all other matters, any preferences expressed by the birth parents or ascertainable from the child should be given weight alongside others in an assessment that covers all his characteristics, circumstances and needs. In assessing the prospective parents, what should weigh most heavily is the judgement made of their capacity to help and support the child through all the challenges he or she will face in life and not just any risk of difficulty attributable to ethnic background. The Government will reinforce this approach in guidance.

INDEX